LOSE YOURSELF

Published by OT Press
First Printing, 2024

PRAISE FOR LOSE YOURSELF

2024 Best Baseball Fiction Book, The Twin Bill baseball literary magazine

2024 The BookFest Award Winner, Inspirational Fiction

2024 Readers' Favorite Honorable Mention, Sports Fiction

Lose Yourself is a riveting and passionately written sports tale which effectively emphasizes the power and allure of baseball. Wetzel's accessible novel keenly illustrates how baseball can profoundly affect the lives of everyone it touches, both on and off the field. Wetzel's text is effervescent, vividly telling Brett Austen's story with wit and panache. He confidently builds tension and drama with a scrupulous attention to detail that really brings the "in-game" scenes to life. Written with verve and style, *Lose Yourself* effectively covers all bases: life, love and sports. Wetzel brilliantly captures the magic of sport as well as offering up an often touching and sentimental study of family dynamics. A candid and vibrant sports drama.
   - The BookLife Prize

A kaleidoscopic look at the power and beauty of the sport both on and off the field, Lose Yourself is ample proof that baseball is life. Written with a keen eye for humanity, and wrapped around a story of high stakes, Vince Wetzel's latest novel is a powerful contemplation on choices we make and how we keep score. Baseball fans will gobble this up.
   - Mark Stevens, author of The Fireballer

With Lose Yourself, Vince Wetzel has skillfully crafted six engrossing stories about life, love and baseball. And really, what else is there?
  - Rich Ehisen, The Open Mic Podcast

While Brett Austen may be the focal point, the All-Star's quest for .400 touches the lives of everyone from sideline reporters and ushers to lemonade hawkers and fans. Wetzel's second novel weaves their stories as the tension builds over nine innings on the final dramatic day of the season.
  - James Bailey, author of The Greatest Show on Dirt

Lose Yourself features six interconnected stories centered around a thrilling chase for .400, and Vince Wetzel manages to go 6-for-6. is a baseball book that is so much more than a baseball book, beautifully showing the impact the game has on our lives.
  - Scott Bolohan, thetwinbill.com

Wetzel's writing sizzles like a fastball in the afternoon sun. In Lose Yourself, he offers a riveting glimpse into the psyche of all-star slugger Brett Austen and his pursuit of baseball history. Equally fascinating are the interwoven stories of a half-dozen characters outside of the spotlight who, like Austen, have life-altering choices to make while consumed with their own personal dreams and demons. It all culminates in the last of the season where on the fateful day there is much more at stake than the final score. Couldn't put this book down!
  - J.C. Wesslen, author of Ace on the Hill

Six stories wrapped around one baseball game? Only Wetzel's vivid storytelling can do something like that! Weaving everything (and every character) together beautifully, I could not turn the pages fast enough to find out what was next. Sports knowledge is not required - everyone will love this!
  - Tobin Walsh, The Good Bad Dad

To my parents,

Whose unquestioned support allowed me
to take leaps toward new endeavors.

LOSE YOURSELF

VINCE WETZEL

OT Press

Prologue

July 27, 2013
Stockton, California

Though he'd never say it out loud to anyone, the twelve-year-old boy next to him was his favorite grandchild.

It wasn't that he disliked his three other grandkids. They were all a joy, and he loved them dearly. Still, only one shared his passion for baseball. While he watched his other grandchildren play hide-and-seek or pretend on summer afternoons, this boy learned the game perched on his grandfather's lap watching TV. He read infield alignments before *See Spot Run*, learned long division through batting average calculation, and knew the league-MVP candidates better than the presidents.

Their special bond was why he had no problem with picking up the boy from his son's house in Sacramento for an impulsive forty-five-minute drive to watch a low-minor-league game in Stockton. He wanted to make a lasting memory. But he should have remembered the unrelenting Stockton heat in the middle of summer.

He pulled off his damp green Oakland A's cap and wiped the sweat from his forehead.

The heat didn't affect the boy. He took another bite of his hot dog, one so big the grandfather thought he might choke. The boy leaned forward and admired the field in front of him, unfazed by the temperature or possible suffocation by beef parts. He was there for the game and enjoying their seats, just a few rows behind the Stockton dugout.

"So, you think some of these guys are going to make the majors?" the boy asked, keeping his eyes forward.

"I'm sure of it. Maybe even the guy who signed our tickets. What was his name?"

"Brett Austen," the boy read on the back of the tickets. The stubs were still sitting on his knee, the black ink still fresh and pungent from being signed before the game. "I wish it was a ball, though."

"This is better. Look, he personalized it with a note, and it's his first game as a pro. We need to hold onto these. They may become valuable."

"That means he'd have to become legendary. Do you think he'll go that far, Grandpa?"

"Well, this is his first game at the lowest levels of the minor leagues." The grandfather put his hand on the boy's shoulder. "He's got a long way to go. But who knows? Each player starts somewhere."

Although a high draft selection with a lucrative signing bonus, Austen was starting his professional-baseball career in Stockton, home to Oakland's lowest-affiliated minor-league team. Austen needed to be promoted at least three levels just to make the big club. Even then, the odds were against him for making a major impact on the game. At this point, the grandfather wasn't interested in Austen's career. He was just happy to be here with his grandson and felt lucky to see San Jose pitcher Clint Shakely, an actual major leaguer recovering from an injury and making a minor-league start before returning to the big club in San Francisco.

"Pretty neat we get to see a big leaguer here too," the grandfather said.

"But he's a Giant. I hate the Giants." The boy smiled.

"I've taught you well," the grandfather joked, laughing and wrapping his large arm around the boy's awkward shoulders to bring him close. He knew this would be one of the last times outward affection would be welcomed by the boy. He pointed to the on-deck circle and Austen, the lanky eighteen-year-old. "Looks like we'll get to see how close that rookie is to the majors. See? He's on deck."

Austen, who they learned had just graduated from high school but hadn't needed to shave in a week, stood in the circle and swung the bat back and forth. He was lean and would need to add muscle to his frame if he was going to make it to the Show. Austen focused on Shakely as he finished his warm-up tosses.

A man rushed down from behind them and claimed an empty seat in the front row, right next to the on-deck circle. There was no shortage of available seats for an evening minor-league game on a random Tuesday in July, and no usher prevented this breach of protocol. The man started talking to Austen, who nodded but otherwise kept his eyes on Shakely. Shakely was in major-league form, and the Ports leadoff hitter was overmatched, striking out on a devastating curveball that dropped right before the plate.

"Wow," the grandfather said. "The rookie's got his work cut out for him."

"Now batting," the PA announcer boomed, "in his professional debut, number five, Brett Austen."

A singular guitar riff with a deep bass line came over the loudspeakers as Austen walked to the plate. The man who was talking to the player in the on-deck circle stood up and clapped.

"C'mon, Brett," he said. "C'mon, son. Get this guy. Show 'em how we hit in Central Texas. You got this."

With about three hundred fans in the stadium, the man's voice carried. At first, Shakely was surprised the man had broken his concentration. But when he looked over at the man, a beer in one hand and many more in his system, Shakely was amused. He smiled and shook his head and went into his windup and whipped the pitch past Austen.

"Steerike," the umpire called.

"That guy isn't doing the rookie any favors," the grandfather observed.

The boy nodded.

"C'mon, Brett. You seen better. This is your competition in the bigs. Show 'em what he's got to deal with, son."

Austen kept focused on Shakely, but Shakely owned the mound. He commanded this space, and no heckles from the stands, certainly not some rookie straight out of high school, were going to knock him off his stride. Shakely looked to the catcher for the sign and went into his windup. Shakely's left hand whipped across his body for a wicked slider that fooled the young rookie into flailing at the pitch.

"Steerike two," the umpire called.

"That looked ugly," the boy said.

"Really ugly," the grandfather said.

"Goddammit, Brett," the man yelled. The last few sips of his beer sloshed out of the cup as he threw his arms down. "He's making you look silly. Jesus Christ, boy, we've given too much to this game for you to look that goddamn stupid. Get your head out of your damn ass, and show this asshole what you can do."

"Yikes, who's that guy?" the boy asked.

"Yeah," the grandfather said. "It's gotta be his dad or something. That's not how you talk to anyone, let alone your own kid. At any level."

"He's making a fool out of us, son. This time, you show him who's boss."

The man's tantrum finally drew attention from one of the teenage ushers, the standard blue Ports Guest Services polo hanging off his scrawny shoulders. The teen had neither the confidence nor the life experience to distract Austen's father. Instead, the man waved off the usher, stood up, and placed his hands on the railing separating the seats from the field.

Shakely looked at the man and shook his head before returning his focus to the catcher. Shakely's amusement of the man's schtick was over.

Another usher, this one the same age as the grandfather, joined his younger colleague and tried talking to the man. Their efforts were fruitless. The man kept looking at Shakely and Austen.

"I've got a ticket. I'm just watching my boy," the man said. He pulled his Texas A&M cap down and pushed the air in front of him to clear some space. "I've had a couple drinks, so what? You guys sell 'em. I buy 'em. I drink 'em. That's how it works."

The man turned back around in time to watch Shakely throw another curveball that hit the dirt before crossing the plate. Austen still swung. The umpire pumped his fist. Shakely looked at the drunk man, smiled, and tipped his cap in a wicked taunt.

Incensed, the man focused back on the rookie.

"You're such a fucking loser, boy. I'm embarrassed to be your daddy. Goddamn disgrace."

The ushers began to push him back up the steps. The man, defeated, didn't protest.

"You don't have to take me anywhere. I'm outta here. I can't stand watching these losers."

After striking out, Austen turned, his eyes following the man stumbling up the steps. He was defeated and dragged his bat back to the dugout.

"Well, this won't do," the grandfather said, and he stood up and began to cheer Austen. The boy joined him. Soon, the other fans in the small stadium did too. Austen looked around, first surprised by the attention, then heartened by it. He smiled, though his eyes wanted to cry. He tipped his helmet to the fans and went back into the dugout.

After the fans returned to their seats, the boy turned to his grandfather.

"Why did we do that, Grandpa?"

"Sometimes, at your lowest moments, you just need an unexpected sign of support to show that you matter. Sometimes, when you lose yourself in your own expectations, you need a reminder to lose yourself in the moment instead."

THE LINEUP

Nine Years Later

CHAPTER 1

Brett Austen
Right Fielder, Oakland A's

Hit or no hit, the best thing about tomorrow? No more egg sandwiches.

Brett Austen flipped the eggs one more time, his strong, hairy forearms maneuvering the spatula almost as well as he swung a bat. After ninety-seven straight mornings of supporting this superstition, Brett knew when the eggs were just right, the cooked side of runny, and he laid them on the slices of English muffin, ham, and cheddar cheese.

Back in June, it took him a couple weeks to realize his hot streak was tied to his breakfast routine. From then on, he didn't deviate. At home, he made the sandwich. On the road, he instructed hotel room service to have the breakfast request at his door at 8:30 a.m. Even when he had an overnight guest, he made one for her too. But after more than three months of having the same breakfast every day, he was craving tomorrow's crispy Belgian waffle with blueberries, strawberries, and powdered sugar. As far as today, well, he wanted to get this breakfast down.

With the sandwich in one hand, black coffee in the other, and the newspaper displayed on the iPad in front of him, Brett plopped down on his couch and turned on the TV.

"It's the final day of the baseball season, and the nation's eyes turn to Oakland where A's outfielder Brett Austen is attempting to cap a season that hasn't been seen in more than eighty years," the morning host said. "Not since Ted Williams in 1941 has a baseball player had a .400 batting average for an entire season."

Brett's season flashed across the screen through a preproduced package highlighting his accomplishments, along with interviews with his manager, Frank Garza, some of his teammates, and clips of the postgame press conference the previous night. Brett wasn't surprised. The .400 average captivated the nation, and his image was everywhere. For the last month, each mention of him on TV included a perfect ten-to-twenty second highlight reel of him hitting the ball, some for home runs, some for doubles into the gap, and some to win a game. Brett shook his head. Nobody appreciated this accomplishment more than him, but unlike the casual fan, each hit was its own story—the hard work, the context, the battle between pitcher and hitter.

"Let's bring in Dana Peck with the Baseball Broadcast Network, who will be in the ballpark today to see if Brett Austen can make history," the host said.

The screen split, and Dana Peck joined the morning show via video conferencing from her hotel room, AirPods in her ears.

"Dana, thank you for joining us," the morning host said from the studios in New York. "So, what's the mood in the clubhouse? Is Brett Austen going to do it? Will he finish the season above .400?"

"Well, he's at .40033 today, and he could take the day off and preserve his place in history," Peck said. "Sources tell me that the league would like for him to sit and play it safe. Manager Frank Garza told me last night that if Austen wanted to take the day off, he could. Though, Garza expects Austen will play."

"Damn straight," Brett said at the TV, a piece of dried yolk spittling out of his mouth.

"However, if he doesn't get a hit in that first at bat, then his average drops to .39966," Peck continued. "Then, he'll need to get a hit in one of his next two at bats to be exactly at .400. People around here are a little worried that he's gambled with history by playing today but still expects him to get the hit."

"Is .400 the only thing at stake, Dana?"

"No. With a win, the Mariners will secure home field for the Wild Card Series beginning on Tuesday. They would rather play in front of their rabid fans. As for the A's, their season never got started. Injuries to pitching and their second-best player, JT Berman, derailed any chances early, and they never recovered. No, Brett Austen is the only hope for anything remarkable for the A's in this season finale."

"The other uncertainty is Austen's contract after this year," the host said. "Could this be his final game in an A's uniform?"

"Yes. Back during spring training, the A's and Austen discussed a contract extension, but talks broke off when Austen said he didn't want the distraction during the season. Of course, now the will-he-stay story is almost as big as hitting .400. Austen's also the leading MVP candidate, which, for a team with a losing record, brings more value to the franchise. The question is whether the A's want to completely rebuild or commit big money to a player who has perhaps three or four years of prime production ahead of him.”

“Bullshit,” Brett said under his breath and shook his head. When the season started, he knew the club wouldn’t extend the contract. They were looking to rebuild. But with .400 looming, the PR pressure on the club was intense, and Brett was unsure if he wanted to stay. He wanted a ring and to contribute to a championship. Still, he’d miss his Alameda house overlooking the Bay and the intensity and the loyalty of the A’s fan base.

“So, this could be a celebration or a severely disappointing game today,” the host said.

“It should be a sellout crowd, all wondering not only if history will be made, but if it’s the last game for their star.”

“Big stakes, indeed. Thank you, Dana, for joining us today. Up next, new apps that can help relieve the stress of the holidays.”

Brett scanned his phone as he finished the final bites of his sandwich. Most of the local and sports news echoed what he had just seen on TV. What were the chances he’d hit .400? Should he just sit out the day and guarantee his historic average? Some posts even said he was being selfish for taking the field that day. All this attention, and it only affected him. Since mid-June, when his average peaked at .418, the gaggle of reporters grew with new faces every day from different media outlets. Their questions started focusing more on the average than just the key hits and highlights of the game. He had to recall each pitch of each at bat and supply analysis. His statistics and the expectation for a hit became more important than the game and the team. There were more national interviews and nonsports media interested in how he swung the bat.

He shook his head. They just didn't know. A ballplayer worth anything didn't sit tight and back into an achievement. An athlete always went for it, confident he would achieve. That mindset, pounded into him from the first time he had picked up a bat, brought him to this moment, and he wasn't stopping now. Besides, he knew if he sat, he'd always think of himself as a fraud.

Brett's phone buzzed. It was his agent, Sal Grant.

"Brett, this is it," Sal said. "Are you ready for today?"

"Just another game, Sal."

"BBN has got Dana Peck all over the morning shows pumping up the game today. You hitting .400 is a big deal. The level of expectation and anticipation is unreal. And if you make it happen, you guarantee yourself a huge payday. I mean, you could sit it out, and it's done."

"Shit, the league talk to you too? They got to Garza last night, trying to convince me to take myself out of the ballgame. Garza even told me he'd take the heat if I decided to sit. They seem to forget this is *my* average. This is *my* accomplishment, not theirs. They shouldn't be negotiating this with me. All this backroom smoke-and-mirrors bullshit."

"I did get a call, and it does make a little sense. In two years, no one will remember you sat with an average of .40033. They'll just write you into the Hall of Fame."

Brett was sick of justifying his decision. He did it last night at the postgame press conference and would again today during the pregame press conference and his one-on-one sit-down with Dana Peck.

"We went over this. I'm not backing into this. I want to do it right. I want no unofficial asterisk, like 'Brett Austen hit .400, but he chickened out and didn't play to protect it.' No, I don't shrink from challenges. I exploit them. I've thought about it. I want it this way."

"Okay, but don't say that when you have your pregame sit-down with Dana today," Sal said. His tone was serious.

"I know. Talk about the fans and how they're coming out and I don't want to disappoint them." Brett didn't hide his sarcasm. "It's not my first time. I know how to play the game now."

"I'm just saying, Dana knows how to play people, and you have to be as on top of your media game as your hitting game."

Brett understood he was a commodity to be fed to the media beast. It brought the money which paid his salary. The fans ate it up because he also looked the part of the everyman; well, if every man worked every day to will his body to perform at the highest level. He just wasn't a superhuman giant, and that made him relatable to every weekender who ever played a lick of baseball.

"She just caught me off guard."

"You were distracted by her figure."

"Same thing."

Dana Peck had the looks and brains ballplayers wanted to make a prize, someone to bed and perhaps marry if she was agreeable. Brett regretted making that assumption. At their first interview as a rookie six years ago, she was one of countless tall, thin, and pretty ESPN reporters, and he had the machismo and confidence to believe that the world was made to serve him. Brett made flirty eyes, complimented her clothes, and shared how good she looked on camera. He even asked if she was staying in Oakland after the game. Maybe meet for a drink or two? But instead of volleying back, she laid into questions about the clubhouse atmosphere, his contract, his beef with red-ass veteran and clubhouse leader Kendall Jameson. When it got around to her asking an innocuous question about his father, Brett lost it. Brett was so unprepared and naïve, his interview was a tutorial for what not to do in media classes. He and Sal had worked overtime just to rehabilitate what he had lost in those five minutes. Because of Dana Peck, he would always be skeptical of interviews and not misjudge someone's beauty for affability again.

"She's going to lead with the average, so continue to talk about the egg sandwiches, seeing the ball well, and the help of your manager, the coaching staff, your teammates, and all the way down to clubhouse staff," Sal said. "And if she brings up the contract stuff, just unload the bullshit about how it's out of your hands. You're just focused on this game and this season, and you'll see what happens when the time comes to negotiate."

"I got it," Brett said. "All right, I need to clear my head. See ya at the park."

Brett ended the call and looked out the huge window of his rented waterfront house in Alameda. The seagulls and other waterfowl rode the offshore breezes. Behind them, the gray, foggy skies obscured the San Francisco skyline enough to give the city a ghost-like quality. For the past five years, this house had been his in-season home, a stark contrast to Bryan, Texas, where he grew up and where he spent the offseason to get away from baseball and recharge. While he wasn't happy about missing the playoffs again, in two days, he'd be back home, and in three, at his favorite fishing hole with nothing more than a pole, a cooler filled with Shiner Bock, and Pat Greene playing on his Bluetooth speaker.

For most of the season, the hitting gods were on his side. It was more than just the breakfast sandwiches that started around the same time as his tear. Every swing he had ever taken, from T-ball to the majors, was culminating in this moment. The ball had never been clearer as it left the pitcher's hand and came toward him. Everything slowed down. He picked up the rotation of the ball's red stitching, revealing the pitch coming his way. The decision to swing came effortlessly in that microsecond, and the eyes fed information to the brain, which delegated the effort to the legs, the hips, the arms, and most of all, the hands. Every time Brett swung the bat, he connected with the ball, and the hitting gods moved the ball to the empty spots in the field.

Brett also knew everything could turn at any moment. The demons came for any ballplayer, regardless of talent. The season was so long, it was just a matter of time. Most people called it a slump, but most people didn't play professional baseball. The demons peeked their heads out and made a ball find a mitt or shatter a bat when you saw the ball clearly or have a gust of wind kill the ball in flight or take it foul. Then, they climbed inside the brain and attacked the psyche, cultivating seeds of doubt, destroying confidence, and questioning the skill so that suddenly, the player has gone 5-for-40, and a slump is born. For most of the year, and much of his career, he had appeased the gods and suppressed his demon.

But Brett's demon was always there, just under the surface, ready to set up shop in his head if given the chance. He prepped hard and used every still moment to tell the demon he wasn't coming for him on these at bats, not on this day. And he was sure the goddamn egg sandwiches were some kind of voodoo. Just one more day, and it would be all done. This was the pinnacle of his career. No matter how well he played for the rest of his career, he'd never have a season like this again. And his legacy would always be tied to this season and what he did today.

This was his destiny. Since he first held a ball in Texas, he was groomed to be one of the best hitters in the game. His father was a very flawed man, but he pushed Brett past all points of sanity to develop into a big-league ballplayer. Every time he came to the plate, he went to war. He obsessed over pitchers. He read scouting reports, watched film, and read the pitcher in the moment. Each pitch meant something new. Each throw a salvo coming across his bough.

He was at this one defining moment. He was going to create history and fulfill the destiny laid out for him. This was his chance. Get this hit, and nobody, not even the demon, could ever take the moment away from him. Today, he had to meet the expectations.

CHAPTER 2

Dana Peck

Sideline Sports Reporter, Baseball Broadcast Network

Dana ended her third television interview of the morning. The Baseball Broadcast Network had her video conferencing every Sunday-morning news show pumping up the national game of the week and the big story of the moment, Brett Austen.

Just as she did every time she was on TV, she pulled up the recording of her on her laptop to critique herself. Every moment in the spotlight was a moment to improve, and if she was going to break through in her dream job as a play-by-play baseball announcer, she couldn't pass any opportunity to improve.

She pushed *Play*. Even before she spoke, she shook her head at the image of herself on the screen.

"Ugh. Looks like I need to go get my hair colored again," she murmured, typing the note. Though a natural dirty blonde, Dana dyed her hair to dark auburn, because she was told the color added credibility.

Before she went further, her agent's name came up on her phone. She paused the video. Her eyes were half-closed, and her mouth was open. She cringed and quickly toggled to a better image on her screen.

"How did I do?" Dana asked as soon as she hit answer.

"It was great, though I missed part of your rounds. You won't believe the intel I just got," Jen Small said.

"You mean you didn't see me with George Stephanopoulos?"

Dana loved immediate feedback, particularly if she learned something from it. But when Jen shared why she didn't watch, Dana's mood changed.

"You're kidding me, right?"

"Nope. Charley Sasser is announcing his retirement after the game today, and the Royals may have an opening. Now, we have a long time until next season, but it's never too early to put your name in the mix."

Sasser's departure was certainly a loss to Kansas City. For more than three decades, he was the lead play-by-play TV announcer for the Royals. He wasn't Vin Scully or Jack Buck or Harry Caray, legends that were forged over the radio waves in postwar America, but he was that next generation of baseball play-by-play announcers who came into regional homes through cable boxes every night. If you were a Royals fan, then you knew and loved him.

With Sasser moving on to a life of travel trailers and KOA campgrounds, Jen explained how the Royals would promote Ted Wilson from the radio team to TV, leaving a radio spot for the hundreds of aspiring announcers hoping to break into one of the most exclusive jobs. There were countless play-by-play callers from the minor leagues who would be sending in their tapes, along with anyone who had experience.

"So, what happens now? How can I put my name in?"

"My source says the Royals want to explore bringing a woman into the broadcast booth," Jen said. "My guess is that the talent will be a hybrid hosting local TV pre- and postgame show and be the primary radio backup."

"That sounds like a foot in the door. Next steps?"

"I can reach out to Stan Love, the Royals' director of broadcast operations and in charge of the baseball talent. He's one of the first voices in the conversation but certainly not the last. My little source also says that Stan is going to be in Los Angeles tomorrow, just like you. I can see if I can arrange a casual coffee meet-and-greet, if you want."

"As long as it's not drinks," Dana said. After ten years of meetings with sleazeballs, Dana maintained a no-meeting-after-five rule to which she strictly adhered. She couldn't count the number of smarmy men who had used their positions to try and coerce her into some compromised position. Usually, it was under the auspices of getting together "for drinks." Oh, it started innocent and professional. But after some liquid courage, the smiles coming at her turned more leering—a glance at her legs, a sly wink and grin. Soon after came the innuendo and subtle proposition. When that was rebuffed, the request was more blatant, prompting an abrupt departure. It set a tone. Too many meetings with assholes had tainted her belief in goodwill.

"Of course," Jen said. "Stan is one of the good ones and won't be trying to get in your pants, like the guy in Minnesota. Plus, he's already seen your tapes."

"How?"

"I would be a shitty agent if I hadn't sent him your tapes even before ol' Charlie bought his Winnebago. From what I hear, Stan likes what you did in Lancaster and Savannah and ESPN and even the simulated games you've done on your own. Plus, you have a great look, and you know as well as I do, you've got to use every asset you've got to get that foot in the door, then you go for it."

Dana sighed. "I know, I've just worked so hard on making my calls flawless, sometimes I wish I also didn't have to spend as much time working on those assets."

"Darling, you're perfect, and you're going to get there. When you hired me years ago, you were adamant that this was your dream, and we plotted this course for you to achieve it. You've endured being the weather and traffic girl. You've driven day and night just to fill in for some Single A radio bullshit. You've stayed after hours to dub your own calls to pretaped games. No job has been below you, whether Division III baseball or cornhole or axe throwing. Heck, I remember you sharing how you'd call play-by-play to the video games your boyfriend and his frat brothers played in the dorms. You've put in the work and sacrificed a normal life of love, vacations, and holidays with family. Didn't you even tell me you waited until after your shift on SportsCenter to go see your mom when she'd suffered a heart attack?"

"It was minor. Plus, it was after the NFC Championship game. Everybody was going to watch that night."

"My point is, I admire what you're doing. You're meeting your own high expectations."

"You sure? This is the first time we're looking at an opportunity that may pay me less."

"Of course. I've seen this glass-ceiling thing firsthand, and if you can help pave the path for more women in this field, then we all benefit in the long run. But, if you want to go back to SportsCenter, I'll happily oblige."

"Let's not go there yet," Dana said. "It's just a coffee, and we don't even have that yet."

"Exactly. And you've got this huge game with national attention. Do you think he's going to do it?"

"Who? Austen? I think he can get the hit. He's seeing the ball so well. In the production meeting this morning, we agreed that if he gets four plate appearances, he'll get a hit. Plus, Seattle has Kenny Roberts starting today, and Austen's hit him well in the past."

"That would be something," Jen said. "How was the production meeting? Is that fat ass Palmetto going to let you shine? He'd better cut to you during the interview and not let it be Austen's talking head."

"I was assertive in how I should be used," Dana said. "Asking good questions, not just cutaways of me looking good on camera. I'm also going to get a couple live shots in the stands and an on-field interview with Austen if he gets the hit. I'm not missing this chance, particularly with Kansas City in play."

"Any exposure is good exposure. Be the pro you are, look good like you always do, and you'll make an impression."

"Yep, gotta look pretty," Dana said with more than a hint of sarcasm. "Well, speaking of which, I need to finish getting ready for today. God, men have it so easy. I wish I could just get in the shower, get out, comb my hair, get dressed, and be done with it."

Dana thanked Jen and promised to call after the game. She looked at the time. Too late to critique her morning-show appearances. She'd just have to do that tonight. She looked in the mirror. Fucking double standard. It was 9:00 a.m., and she already had an early production meeting and had been to the hotel fitness center for ninety minutes of sweating and toning. Then her shower included shaving and hydrating her skin, so each pore was open and smooth, followed by twenty minutes of working her hair to the wavy style of the day, before finally primping her eyebrows, gluing on fake eyelashes, applying eyeshadow, foundation, and contouring. And that was just for this Zoom interview. Once at the stadium. she'd reapply for her "camera look," which meant another layer of image applied over her true self before she got in front of the cameras for the day's interviews. While men just woke up and stepped onto an equal playing field, she had to work hard just to get invited. She appreciated all the hard work and dedication to be where she was. Still, she sometimes thought it would be easier to have a penis.

Dana took one last look in the mirror before heading downstairs to join her producer, Kent Clarkson, and drive to the stadium together. Dana had worked with Clarkson for almost a year at the Baseball Broadcast Network. She liked him. He was professional, but she learned early he didn't find referencing his name and Superman amusing.

The night before, he had supplied her with a brief on all things Brett Austen, everything you'd expect prior to an interview with a ballplayer, including his stats, tough at bats, strengths, weaknesses, and where he liked the ball. Clarkson also included childhood influences in the game, background, and anything that would draw out some good sound bites to be used again and again during the pregame, in-game, and postgame analysis. Over a couple glasses of wine and room service, she internalized those notes so much, she felt she'd covered the A's all season.

"Great notes," Dana said when she met Clarkson in the beige marbled lobby. "I can't believe the A's are still going through the motions on this contract. They're really willing to let him walk?"

"Yeah, he's getting too expensive," Clarkson said. "Austen even gave a hometown discount, but they wouldn't budge off their number."

"Well, he's going to get paid. The question is whether the fans will resent him for it."

"Get a hit today, and I think they'll understand. Don't get a hit, and they'll think he was chasing a payday or a championship."

"So that's the difference between .400 and .398? It's .002, and we're making such a big deal out of today."

"In 1946, it's not too big a deal. Williams did it in '41, and after the war, they're just excited. Now, it's been over eighty years. That .002 is huge in the history of the game."

The hired black car the network had sent met them out front. They loaded their bags in the back and headed the eight miles from downtown to the stadium. Dana checked her phone. There was a text from her mom to call her. She had no time for a check-in conversation where her mom would talk about everything happening in Bloomington, Illinois. She didn't care about the new restaurant opening near the old State Farm headquarters or how her old classmate was now a professor at Illinois

State. At least not today. She'd call her tonight from her hotel in Los Angeles.

She also had four texts from "Brian." She rolled her eyes. She reminded herself that drinking, scrolling Tinder, and feeling lonely in a hotel room didn't mix. So now she had four messages from this character she'd had over last night for an hour. First one, thanking her. Second one, wondering if she was sticking around today. Third one, hoping she'd contact him later. And fourth one, a picture of his penis. She groaned. Delete.

"So, how are you going to play the interview with Austen?" Clarkson asked. "Maybe that .400 versus .398 question is worth something."

"You're right." Dana nodded. As she went through her daily physical routine, she thought through the tone of the interview. "We can lead into that and with his obsession with hitting. I just know the higher-ups want it positive and bland. No controversy. They don't want to tarnish the golden boy."

"No matter what, he's going to give a bland answer to both. He's not doing anything different. He's playing for the fans and for his teammates, blah, blah, blah," Clarkson said.

"Well, I should take partial blame for those vanilla answers. I mean, he totally went off on me his rookie season when I asked him about his dad and how it felt when he died while Brett was in the minors. He totally went apeshit."

"Didn't he call you a hot-ass bitch?"

"And he was never going to see my ass to find out. He deserved it. He came in trying to seduce me and thinking I was some bimbo off the street. I wasn't going to back down. I'm sorry, he dug his own grave and put me up to the ESPN anchor desk. No, today is going to be light stuff. We'll lead in easy, get him comfortable, talk about why .400 is important, then get him to talk about his contract, what the A's offered, his disappointment, and his plans for next season."

"I get ya now," Clarkson said. "You gotta play nice so the Royals see you play ball?"

Dana looked at him. How did he know so quickly?

"What? I wouldn't be a good producer if I didn't know these things. I really hope you get the job. I'll miss you, but this is a great opportunity. You deserve this as much as anyone."

CHAPTER 3

Fred Stephenson
Usher, Lower Cross Aisle, Section 104

"I don't care what you do with it," Fred Stephenson said. He was frustrated. Sitting on the stool and still wearing the white T-shirt and striped pajama pants he had slept in the night before, he watched his son, John, and his daughter-in-law, Carla, uproot the utensils from their three-decade home and place them in temporary cardboard containers. It was moving day, and Fred didn't like it.

"Dad, you shouldn't talk to Carla like that," John said. John's hands were on his hips, and Fred was reminded of that exact pose when John was a petulant child asking for ice cream before dinner. John was even standing in the same spot on the checkerboard tile and wearing the same wardrobe of shorts and a T-shirt featuring a comic-book character. "She's just asking if you want this pour-over cup since you're more Folgers than Starbucks."

Fred sighed and ran his black hands across his white beard and down his face, still waking up from a fitful night of sleep without his Marjorie. John and Carla let themselves into the house at 7:00 a.m. with three Starbucks coffees and fancy pastries. He heard his Marjorie in his head chastising him: *I still can't believe you're still looking like you just got out of bed.*

"I know. I'm sorry, Carla. It's just something that Marjorie cared about," Fred said. He crossed and rested his arms on the belly shelf he had been trying to get rid of for twenty-five years. "This was our home. I fully understand why I'm leaving, but I don't have to enjoy it."

Carla went to him and put her thin arm around him. He reached up and grabbed her hand. It was only 157 days since Marjorie had died, 145 days since her service, and thirty days since he had signed the papers to sell the house. He was still unsure if it was the right decision, but when the buyer offered more than two hundred thousand dollars above his inflated asking price, he had to take it. Or that's what John had said. Fred was now debt free, paying off the accumulated medical debt with plenty of money left over to enjoy retirement.

"It's okay, Pop," Carla said. "I know this has all been tough. But you'll love it in Sacramento. You'll get to see the twins every day and sit back and enjoy life."

Fred wasn't sure about Sacramento, but he was looking forward to seeing his grandkids, Donovan and Walker, every day. Fred was moving into John and Carla's guesthouse, a feature that sold them on the property when they'd bought it a couple years ago. At the time, it was so Fred and Marjorie had their own space when they visited. But now, the back bungalow was his new home while he transitioned to being a widower. It was all moving so quickly.

"I just can't believe you're still working today," John said. He and Carla had moved on to the pantry, pulling out years-old packages of Pasta Roni and crackers and discarding them into trash bags. Fred rarely made food for himself these days. He either picked up something at the ballpark or pulled off the plastic film and placed his meal in the microwave.

"It's the final game of the season," Fred said. "I've only missed a handful of games in twenty years, and I'm not going to miss this one and the chance to see something historic."

"But we're moving you tomorrow," John said.

"Which means I can work today," Fred said. He used to take this defiant tone when he laid down the law for John as a child. "I have the best seat in the house, and I'm not going to let it pass, today of all days."

Fred had spent nearly 1600 games over the last twenty-two years helping Oakland fans get to their seats and then keeping his eyes and ears open to make sure they had a safe and pleasant experience. He had held his spot on the right-field line for ten of those years and had watched Brett Austen grow from a lanky rookie to a full-on superstar. Over the years, he'd built a relationship with Austen, even if it was peripheral. Austen knew Fred's name, and in his first couple seasons on the club would engage Fred in conversation. As the demands grew, Austen closed off but still acknowledged him. It made this season extra special as Austen pushed past any expectations and got hit after hit. To Fred, Austen finishing the season at .400 would be like when John had stepped across the stage to accept his diploma at the University of California. So, Fred wasn't going to miss today for anything. He had missed enough games this season because of Marjorie's illness and had arranged the funeral around the team's road trip so it wouldn't conflict.

"Plus, I get to say goodbye to all my friends at the park," Fred said. He wanted to say final farewells to his ballpark family, from his fellow ushers to the hawkers to the front-office people to the fans in his section. This year had been tough, and everyone at the stadium had shown grace and empathy. It would be another tough goodbye. "I wish you would have brought the boys. I could have got you tickets."

John shook his head. "Dad, we have to get you out of here tomorrow, and you spent the last month not packing much at all. We need to get this done. It was best for Donovan and Walker to stay with Carla's folks today. They'll see you tomorrow."

John spread a strip of packing tape on top of another box. In spite of growing up an A's fan, John's passion for the game didn't survive adolescence. Fred understood that not everyone had to love baseball like he did, but he was always a little disappointed that he hadn't instilled within his only son the same passion for the game.

"You've been there a long time," Carla said. "I'm sure you're going to miss it."

"More than you know. Being an usher was unexpected, and it all started with Marjorie just wanting me out of the house."

Fred took a deep breath, smiled, and recalled the unlikely circumstances that led to his second career as an usher for the A's. They were right here in this kitchen a little more than twenty-two years before.

"I can't handle you being in this house all the time," Marjorie said. Fred had just spilled coffee grounds all over the kitchen counter and floor. "You're going to tear this house down if you don't find something else to do."

"Hey, I'm just a couple weeks into my retirement, and you're already sick of me?" Fred said. "We haven't even stopped talking about Y2K yet."

"I'm just saying that you're going to drive us both crazy unless you find something to do."

Fred and Marjorie had had an idyllic marriage and raised their son in a stable home, an oddity in their San Leandro neighborhood. Through thirty years as a postal carrier, Fred had had the same routine every day. Get up early, start the coffee, read the paper, pour a second cup into a small thermos, say goodbye to Marjorie and John, work a full shift, come home, help John with his homework or take him to sports practice, go to bed, and do the same thing the following day. When he learned he had earned a full government pension after thirty years, he decided to retire at the end of 1999 to start 2000 fresh. But as he looked to his wife, he was only fifty-four. She was right. He still had a lot of living, and a new chapter didn't mean full retirement. But he had no idea what that meant.

The opportunity came just two weeks later. Hanging out with some old-timers over a cup of coffee and a donut wasn't the healthiest way to get out of the house, but it was something to do. Like clockwork, every Tuesday morning, Charles, one of the regulars and a part-time, low-scale bookie, would settle his accounts at the donut shop with Derek, a twenty-three-year-old ball of energy. Derek always came in with varying vendor uniforms, depending on which team was in town that day.

"Hey, is it fun to sell food at the games?" Fred had asked Derek once. "I mean, do you get to watch?"

"No, guy, I'm straight commission, and I gotta be hustling to make the dough, okay," Derek said in a tinny voice that could cut through a crowd. "Most of the time, I'm watching the concrete steps and the stands more than what's going on in the game. The ushers, though, they have the life."

"Oh yeah?" Fred asked.

"For sure, guy. They get to watch a whole lot more. They make sure those who have tickets go to the right seats. They watch out for drunk fans or call security when things look like they're getting out of hand. The worst is Raider games."

"Yeah, I bet," Fred said. "What about baseball?"

"They're among the easiest. You know, they're hiring. Might be a good opportunity for a young man like yourself."

Fred called and got the job. In his first years he monitored different sections in the second deck. Because he had to scan the crowd throughout the game, he didn't get to see as much of the game as he'd hoped. But he got out of the house eighty days of the year with new stories, coworkers, and experiences to bring home to Marjorie, who was happy Fred was doing something again.

"I'm going to miss the A's games," Fred said, his mind returning to the present, John and Carla wrapping glasses in newspaper and placing them in another box.

"Are they planning anything for you?" Carla asked. "I mean, you've been there forever."

"Nah. I've asked them not to make a big deal out of it. Besides, they've got too much other stuff going on with Austen and everything that goes with the final game. I'm fine with that, though."

They should make a big deal out of it. You've been there more than twenty years, the voice of Marjorie chided.

"Well, I still think they should give you a shoutout during the game or something," Carla said.

See, Carla agrees with me.

Fred stood and went to the kitchen and placed his hand on Carla's shoulder and gave it a squeeze. Fred was so happy John had found her. He and Marjorie knew it from the first time they'd met her shortly after John had graduated college. John was a programmer, and Carla was in a law firm that contracted with his company. From that moment at the Italian restaurant, when he and Marjorie had watched their son purely enamored with this beautiful, smart young woman, and that love returned, they knew it was a good match.

Sure enough, John proposed the next year, followed by a wedding eight months later. A year after that came Donovan and Walker.

As Fred watched John and Carla continue to place the Pyrex dishes into boxes, he moved toward the hall and to his room. He needed to get ready for work. As he turned back to the kitchen, with John and Carla pulling out the frying pans, he over-layed memories of John in his childhood running elaborate Hot Wheels tracks across the kitchen and later his grandkids playing with remote-control cars and a Christmas tree with stockings pegged to the wall.

Fred turned away. He felt the overwhelming anxiety of his adult life slipping away. Life without Marjorie was not what he had expected. His chest constricted, his throat got tight, and he felt his eyes burn, but facing John and Carla like that was unbearable, so he did what any man would do—he rushed to his room, slammed the door, and held onto the dresser for dear life, trying to breathe. This was the last day of the life he had known for almost fifty years.

Fred felt tightness in his chest, and if he hadn't felt the same sensations over the course of the last few weeks since he had put the house on the market, he might think it was time to contact 9-1-1. But he knew what this was, and he felt Marjorie's arm caressing his.

Now breathe, Frederick. Breathe. It's okay. There's just a lot of stuff going on right now. But you've got this, sweetheart.

"Yes," Fred whispered. He pulled his hand over his face and blinked his eyes hard. Even though he'd said goodbye to his bride almost six months ago, she was still there, reassuring him.

Fred took a couple deep breaths and went to his closet to pull out his green usher uniform with black undersleeves. He also had comfortable black slacks and his Skechers Max Ultra Comfort shoes, footwear he'd discovered just three years ago and was sure had postponed his retirement by a season. As he stared at himself in the mirror, he whispered, "I can do this, Marjorie. I can do this."

Of course, you can. I wouldn't have married you if I didn't think you could hack it.

When he finally pulled on a hat and sunglasses, he felt ready. Time to put on a confident and defiant face. He strutted out of his room and back into the kitchen.

"Looking good for your final day," Carla said.

"Still don't know why you have to work today," John said under his breath. He had moved onto the countertops and placed the decorative cookie jars, sugar bowls, and spice racks into their own bin. Watching John just discard the things Marjorie took care in buying for her kitchen angered Fred.

"If I wasn't here today, I wouldn't be able to move on, and that's what you want, don't you? For me to move on and move to Sacramento?"

"We've been over this, Dad. This was an offer you couldn't refuse."

"I know that, *son*," Fred said, raising his voice. How dare John patronize him in his own house, even if it was for one more day. "But it doesn't mean I can't savor every little bit of time I have left, and if that means going to see Brett Austen trying to achieve history, then that's what the hell I'm going to do."

"Dad—"

Fred put up his hand, and Carla gave John a look to let it go.

"Thanks for helping pack," Fred said. He opened the door and stepped into the hallway, then peeked his head back in. "Be sure to watch the game today. Should be a good one."

Fred closed the door a little harder than he should and re-focused his purpose for one more day. He had a destination. He was going to work, maybe for the last time ever. What would he do now? Go to the park and feed pigeons? Play chess with the other retirees? Hang out with John and Carla and the grand-kids? Donovan and Walker were more bearable than his son, but singular devotion to them wasn't an option. No, he would need to find a new reason to get out of the guesthouse. He was looking forward to joining Marjorie but not quite yet. He liked living. Fred boarded BART at the San Leandro station headed toward the Coliseum. He realized that this would be his last BART ride to the game. Much had changed in the neighborhood since he had first started taking BART. Well, going way back, when the A's first moved to Oakland, it was ten years before BART even opened. Even when he was working at the post office, he took the Bay Area's subway to A's games, Raider games, Warriors games, even sometimes heading up to Berkeley or across the Bay to San Francisco.

How many times did we ride BART together? Always holding hands.

Fred looked out the window toward the Bay. It was another beautiful early fall day, the temperature currently at fifty-five degrees with the high forecasted for twenty degrees higher. When he'd moved to Sacramento, he could expected triple-digit temperatures all summer. At least the guesthouse did have its own AC unit.

"So, you work the game?" a young woman sitting across the car said. She was pretty dolled up for a baseball game, wearing a fitted V-neck A's T-shirt that showed more of her cleavage than he thought was proper, with torn jeans. Her eyelashes were fake, and he still didn't understand what made the excessive eyeliner attractive.

"Yes," Fred said. "Going to be a good one."

"Yeah, I'm meeting my boyfriend and his friends there," she said.

"Be sure to get in early, just in case Austen gets his hit," Fred said.

"Oh, yeah," she said with a blank face. For all of the information at her well-manicured fingertips, she didn't know Austen was on the brink of history.

"Now just don't let your boyfriend and his buddies drink too much." Fred turned semiserious. "You won't have fun, and I don't want any trouble on my last day."

"Really, your last day? That's cool. How long have you been doing it?"

"This will be the end of my twenty-second year."

"Oh my God, you started when I was born."

Fred smiled, put his hand to his head, lowered it, and shook.

"Oh, yeah, you don't want to be reminded of that."

"Oh, I'm reminded every day, believe me."

The now three-quarters full BART train pulled into the Coliseum Embarcadero Station. A's fans dressed in green and gold poured onto the platform. Fred let the young woman go in front of him, then tipped his cap and went his own way toward the stadium. As he got older, he always wanted to sit down with every new young person he met and share what he'd learned from fifty-five years of working with two organizations—thirty-three years with the post office and twenty-two with the A's—and share all of life's meaning. Over the last few years, as he watched his wife wither away, he began to understand that wisdom was wasted on the old. All of what he had learned was useless now. His body was deteriorating, and his mind wasn't as sharp as it once was. Unfortunately, the folks he came across who needed some of that wisdom, really use it for good, were too consumed with trying to figure it out on their own. And they certainly weren't open to hearing it from some old usher. He watched the woman walk ahead and waited to see if she looked back, if maybe she wanted to hear some sage advice. She never did. Instead, she looked for answers on her small screen, looking up enough to make sure she didn't run into anything. Soon she was just part of the crowd, and he was again just an usher going to work.

CHAPTER 4

Will Jenson
High School Sophomore

Will's Instagram scroll stopped the moment her picture flashed on his screen.

"Off to watch the A's!" the caption read across a photo of Amanda Wright in a bright-yellow A's throwback jersey tied in a knot showing off her hips and stomach, her dark, straight hair framing her brown skin. Her puckered lips were a cross between a kiss and a duck face. It was almost too much for his fifteen-year-old hormones to take.

Oh God. She's going to be at the game too, Will thought.

Will had had a crush on Amanda ever since Ms. Givens's kindergarten class. They had grown up together, been in the same classes, even went to each other's birthday parties, but middle school had a way of disrupting the social classes and budding crushes. While she rose to another stratosphere of popularity, he kept to a small circle of friends. But here was his chance. She was going to be at the same game. Maybe they could hang out or something. He shook off that thought. She was way out of his league.

"Will, hurry up," his mother called from the kitchen. "You're the one who begged Paul to leave early to see the players."

Will looked past the autographed Brett Austen baseball and bobblehead in his bookcase and back to the mirror again. He was dressed fine for a game with his stepdad—*future* stepdad—but if he was going to meet Amanda, well, was this enough game to impress her? He had on his Brett Austen, number-five, green-and-gold T-shirt and a black zip-up hoodie. It was okay for him, but he had yet to fill out his clothes like the jocks and other guys in Amanda's circle. The bucket hat had to go, but he didn't comb his long, curly hair, and it was poofed hella crazy after taking a shower last night. He pulled his kelly-green A's hat from the top shelf in his closet and pushed it down on his head. He exhaled, nearly defeated. Who was he kidding? Unless he suddenly added inches to his biceps and chest, this was his best impression.

"Will." His mom's voice rose. "You better not be playing video games with your friends."

True, he liked hanging out in his room, either playing *Madden* or *FIFA* or *NBA2K* or *MLB: The Show* on his PS5 or scrolling Instagram, YouTube, or TikTok on his phone. Mostly, he wanted to avoid the awkwardness that came with being in the same room with his mom and future stepdad, Paul.

It didn't used to be this way. Paul had been like an uncle to Will. He was one of his dad's best friends, and when Will's dad died in a car wreck seven years ago, Paul had stepped in. He played catch and took him camping. He was the guy Will had trusted to talk about the stuff that was too awkward to share with his mom. And Paul always pulled off great seats at sporting events. Well, that was a no-brainer. Paul was a local celebrity. He used to be on ESPN and now was the local sports guy on KARC. Tickets to sporting events were never a problem.

But for the last few months, it had been weird. Ever since Paul and his mom sat Will down and told him their plans, the air felt thick with cringe. Paul's attention had been focused on his mom, and his mom was ready and willing to push the memories of his dad aside. Before, Paul was one of Will's dad's best friends, but now? The two of them together? Gross.

Will shook off that thought. His mom was happy, and that made him happy. One of the first things she told Will was that she still loved his dad, but Paul had shown her she could love again. They had been a comfort for each other in grief, and eventually that comfort developed into something neither of them could have predicted. Yet, being at the game with the two of them made him anxious. But if he was able to hang out with Amanda?

Before he thought, he typed a comment on her story: "Cool. I'm going too. Maybe I'll catch you there."

His throat closed, and his stomach did a flip. *Oh crap.* Commenting was an Insta-sin. Nobody—well, except adults— commented on posts like that. Now he felt lame. But what else should he do? Sliding into the DMs was a slimy move. He looked at his response again. It was fine, casual. He was just saying he'd be there too, and maybe they'd see each other. Of course, he wanted to see her. He would look all around for her while at the game, but he wasn't going to say that.

A notification came up. She wrote a DM? She slid into *his* DMs?

Amanda: *Where r u sitting? Will be there w/ parents. stupid little brother.*

Will resisted the urge to write back with all his might. He had to play this cool. This was a chance of a lifetime. A chance to hang with the hottest girl in school without all those other guys trying to hang off her.

For the first time since Will had started high school, he felt a little strut in his step. He wasn't an athlete. He wasn't into any clubs. He just liked playing video games with his friends. So he was practically invisible, keeping to the side in the hallway and walking around all the people who mattered. But his strut was short-lived. He walked into the kitchen only to see his mom's head buried into Paul's chest, her eyes closed. She was smiling. Weird.

She also wasn't ready for the game.

"Mom, why aren't *you* ready?"

"I'm not going," she said, breaking the embrace with Paul and crossing the kitchen to Will. "I think it's better for you to go with Paul. It will give you some time to hang out together."

She turned to Paul and smiled. She smiled a lot more with Paul. When Will's dad had died, Will watched his mom withdraw into herself wearing his dad's clothes and sitting on the back patio with a glass of wine. Even though he was still young, Will realized that the presence of Paul had helped his mom through their crisis.

"Right, bud," Paul said. "We haven't done anything together since the engagement."

Paul said "bud" a lot more now. He'd never said that before. Was that some kind of dad thing he'd read in a book?

"I won't be much fun anyway." She was reading an article on her laptop. She turned back to Paul, who preferred to scroll on his phone. "Do you think it's going to happen?"

Paul went into his analysis of Austen's swing, his presence at the plate, and his preferred pitches. Will's mom looked at Paul with admiration, which made this pairing even more odd. Paul knew sports, knew the games, knew the people in the games and they knew him. His mom was more into politics and worked in the California capitol for a state senator.

If Will had half the genetics of his future stepdad, he'd have no problems hanging out with Amanda. Paul's hair was wavy and full. His teeth were white and cut out of ivory. Everything he wore fit exactly as the designers had intended. Even if he wasn't on national TV, Paul would be noticed the moment he walked into the room. People were sucked in, and Will was left on the sidelines, invisible as always. When he was younger, that was fine. Paul took him to sporting events and the press box and sometimes even the locker room. After nearly seven years, the shine had rubbed off. Now, he just saw the attention sucked toward Paul, constantly stopping so that Paul could sign autographs, take selfies, or talk about his time at ESPN. And if Will had to hear another reference to Paul's "Catch of the Day" catchphrase, he was sure he'd vanish from existence.

"All right, .400 history awaits," Paul said, picking up his mitt and raising it in the air.

Will shook his head and rolled his eyes. If he did meet up with Amanda, would he look more like a small-time loser if he had his own mitt in tow? He couldn't risk it.

"I'm not bringing my mitt today," Will said.

"Why not?"

"We never come close to a foul ball anyway. It's lame."

Paul looked at Will like his body was possessed by some football-loving knucklehead. He shook his head, then continued toward the garage. "Suit yourself."

Will half ate, half wrapped up his ham-and-cheese bagel, and they poured themselves into Paul's Ford Mustang. The engine rumbled to life when Paul pushed the ignition. Will felt the energy pulsate through the engine and created a rush of excitement and adrenaline that caused him to smile.

Paul sped out of the Pocket neighborhood, where they lived in Sacramento, up I-5 and then onto I-80 for the ninety-minute drive to the Bay Area. They pushed past Davis, Dixon, and into Vacaville, mostly silent. Will didn't know what to say to Paul. They hadn't been able to shake this awkwardness between them. Instead, they just listened to sports talk radio and some host droning on about the NFL, including a bad take about the Las Vegas Raiders not playing well on the East Coast. To Paul, bad on-air content was worse than awkward babble with a teen boy about to become a stepson.

He turned down the radio. "So, when do you think Austen gets his hit today?"

Regardless of how their relationship was changing, sports, particularly baseball, were the lifeline to avoidance. Stats, situations, players, and history were a distraction.

A smile appeared on Will's face. "I think he gets it in the second at bat. He'll chase Roberts out."

"Do you think Austen is gone after the season?" Will asked. "I hope he stays."

"Austen is too pricey now to stay in Oakland. Take in today and watch every moment. It could be the last time you see Austen or another performance like this ever again."

Will was torn. Paul was right. This was a game not to miss. Yet, there was Amanda and an opportunity to spend time with her. Was there a way to do both? Watch the game and hang out with her? He scrolled through his phone and looked at her Instagram pic again. He smiled.

"What are you smiling about?" Paul asked.

"Just something on Instagram. A friend is going to be at the game."

"Oh yeah?"

"It's a girl I've known forever."

Paul's eyes went wide, and the dimples in his cheeks deepened. "Oh really? Tell me more."

Will was hesitant to tell him about Amanda and the crush he's had for so long. This was the exact conversation that confused Will. Paul was the perfect person to ask advice on women. He had charm and game for days, and his advice would be great in this situation. Paul was the big brother he didn't have. But now, talking about this to his stepdad? Was he going to share this with his mom? Did he share other stuff with her too? What was he expected to share and not share now, and would it be held against him?

"Just don't tell my mom, okay? She'll make it a big deal, and I don't even know if anything's going to happen."

"I can't keep something big from her, but if it's casual, I'll make sure she doesn't make it big, sound good?"

"I guess. Okay, so there's this girl I've known forever, and she's really cool, like out of my league, but she's going to be at the game today. She posted on Instagram and wondered if I'd wanna hang out. So, you know."

Paul smiled, then laughed. "You dog. Is that why you didn't want to bring your mitt?"

"Shut up."

"No, this is good. You smell good too, by the way. So, what's your play?"

"What?"

"Are you meeting her somewhere?"

Will's eyes went wide. His heart started beating, and he pulled out his phone and opened Instagram. He still hadn't responded to Amanda's DM.

"Damn," Will said. "Before we left, Amanda sent me a DM to say she wanted to hang out at the game, but I didn't send anything back."

Paul sighed. "Oh boy."

Will stared at the screen.

"Omigod, what do I say? It's been an hour! What's she going to think now? I friggin' blew it already! Why did I even think I had a chance with her?"

Will was spinning out and on the brink of tears. She was used to being with guys, seniors, who probably already had sex and knew the world. He had nothing. He was just a fifteen-year-old virgin loser.

"C'mon, Will, all is not lost. Who knows? Maybe she didn't even notice."

"Great, she forgot I existed. Thanks."

"That's not what I meant. Let's just start with the message back to her, okay? Just apologize for not getting back to her and feel free to blame me. I took away your phone, and you just got it back."

"That'll work? Lying?"

"Good point." Paul took a beat. "Okay, give me your phone."

"What? You're driving."

"Just give it. Give it now."

Will handed it over. Paul took it and then handed it right back. "Now you can say I took your phone, and it's not lying."

Will smiled. Okay, that was a smooth move. He started typing. "Now what?"

"Just say you're heading over now and to have her DM when she gets to the game."

Will typed as instructed and hit sent. "Okay, sent."

Paul nodded. "So, who's this girl going with?"

"Her family."

Paul stroked his chin, and his eyes focused on the road. "Do you know what kind of parents she has?"

"What do you mean?"

"Tell me about her mom and dad."

"Well, her dad's a cop, and her mom teaches at our school. I took her English class last year. You've probably seen them around. It's the Wrights. Amanda Wright."

"Oh, that's Wright." Paul stuck out his tongue. None of his friends believed him when Will said Paul was so corny. "Okay, bad one. So, how did you do in Mrs. Wright's class? You were an exemplary student, right?" He smiled again.

Will looked out the window. He didn't want to encourage Paul.

"I got an A, and yes, I was pretty good in class. Why?"

"Well, if she's as 'cool' as you say, then your only chance is to go in as the good, safe kid. She knows you and knows you're a nice kid. But you've got to show off your maturity and respect to her dad. And you sure as hell have to call her Ms. Wright and call him sir or Mr. Wright. Just don't call him Mr. Wrong."

Will swore he was going to jump out of the car.

"Okay, that was the last one, promise. So, they're big fans?"

"Huge."

"Then that's how you get the dad on your side. Win him over with your knowledge. Now, here's the tricky part with her. Wait, What's her name again?"

"Amanda."

"Amanda. Right. Wright! Oh, I remember your mom talking about her at your promotion. Okay, so she's probably got all these dangerous guys and jocks trying to take her as some kind of prize, and I'd say she's tired of them trying to impress her with their coolness or physical prowess. And she knows you. She's known you forever. So, you don't talk about you. You ask about her. Almost exclusively. You may chime in a couple things about some shared experiences, but you're mostly asking about her. Follow up about how she felt about whatever it is. What's in her future? All that. She'll be appreciative that you're interested in her."

"And that's going to get her to go out with me?"

"Oh, I didn't say that, bud," Paul said with a laugh. "That's going to get her to enjoy her time with you today. For one, she may be all about that rebel-asshole guy right now. Or someone who pisses her parents off. But, without anyone else around, this will help you have a good afternoon with her. After that, it depends on her and what she wants. To be honest, you may end up in the friend zone, but she may be even cooler to you in school, or in ten years, you might fall in love."

"That does a lot of good," Will said, disappointed.

"What I'm saying is, don't create an unrealistic expectation. Come at it with appreciation for what happens in the moment. Look, I get it. This time is tough. At your age, I was the guy you would have hated. It was effortless. I had my choice, but you know what? I didn't care about them, and they didn't really care about me. All I wanted was... well, that's a conversation for another day. It was never anything more than surface attraction. And looking back, yeah, it was fun, but it took me a long time to move beyond that. Meanwhile, your dad was just friends with your mom in high school. In fact, he dated this one girl who was clingy and we all hated. She was a piece of work. But anyway, it wasn't until years later that your mom and dad fell in love. And your mom's really the only meaningful relationship I've ever had, if you want me to be totally honest with you. So, yeah, I was one of those guys, but I'd trade places with the man your dad was and who you're becoming in a heartbeat."

Will felt a turn in his stomach. It wasn't the bagel either. Paul had steered the conversation to his dad, his mom, Paul, and this weird love triangle. Was this the type of comparison he would have to worry about whenever he talked to Paul or his mom?

Will looked over at Paul, who felt it too. The vein in Paul's neck pulsated. His teeth grinded, clenching his defined jawline.

They were both in the awkward place. All these years later, and they both dearly missed the man Paul knew as Jim and Will knew as Dad.

"Let's see if the A's pregame show is on," Paul said and turned up the radio.

CHAPTER 5

Derek Nguyen
Lemonade Hawker

Derek had a Sunday routine, particularly in the fall, when the 49ers, A's, or Giants provided plenty of work. He'd pull on a uniform, put on his most comfortable and durable Nikes, and be ready for another day of hawking beer, pretzels, ice cream, churros, hot dogs, or popcorn, though he liked lemonade the best, particularly for day games.

Sundays were also Derek's big betting days, and Club Maui became a part of this routine. Just like every NFL Sunday, he navigated though his Fruitvale neighborhood and under the BART station, past the drugged-out zombies, unintended mobile homes, makeshift campsites, and not-so-distant realities of living on the edge and approached the white mission-style building with red tile. His watch showed 9:04 a.m., just in time to make his picks, have breakfast, watch some of the pregame shows, then meet up with Owen, his bookie, who owned the place. He opened the door. The smells of days-old sweat and spilled liquor wafted past him.

"Hey D, coffee?" E asked when Derek closed the door behind him, shutting out the morning sunlight. Derek thought the E stood for Eliot, but he wasn't sure. E liked to shorten everyone to their first initial. And when there was a group of Scotts, Steves, Susans, Simones, etc., E would just add a "dog," "daddy," 'baby," or "sizzle." Derek thought everyone had a thing, and if this was it, then he wasn't going to complain. After all, E had a much better chance at getting one letter right than a whole name.

"Yeah, guy," Derek said, his voice loud and nasal, effective for hawking lemonade. "Also, my usual, okay?" Derek usually ordered a three-egg, sausage, spinach, tomato, and onion omelet, which came with potatoes and toast. It didn't matter what Derek ate on Sundays. He climbed enough steps for six gym memberships.

E pulled out a clean mug and poured some bad coffee. Since the Club Maui opened at nine, at least it was fresh, unlike some cups of sludge he'd had around noon sometimes. Derek sidled up to the bar, his pick sheet in one hand, a newspaper in the other. He was old school and still carried a flip phone. At Club Maui, he watched for any last-minute injuries before heading to the back to see Owen, his bookie.

Today needed to be extra big. Sundays in the fall had so much action to bet; baseball, football, even soccer and a little hockey. His plan was to lay down a three-game NFL parlay for the early games, another for the afternoon games, plus a couple props. He'd put down four thousand dollars today with the chance to score at least fifteen thousand if everything went his way. Of course, that was if Owen would let him bet. Derek was down eight large to Owen, and he may not let him float much longer.

E set down the coffee while Derek eyed his lines. Derek took a pull of the black tar.

"Whatcha got?" E asked.

"I'm going to lay fifteen hundred for Bucs, Rams, and Jets early and another fifteen for Bears, Cards, and Dolphins in the late games, maybe a prop bet. How you like that, E?"

"Jesus, at least three *K*? Aren't you against it with Owen already? And what the hell do you have against our local teams?" E asked. "You've got the Niners and the Raiders losing."

"Owen knows I'm good for it. And don't give me that bullshit. The Raiders are in Vegas now, okay?"

"Yeah, I thought you'd be there too."

Derek would be in Sin City, if not for his eight-year-old daughter, Jasmine. She lived with her mother down the track in San Lorenzo, which meant Derek was staying put in the East Bay. She was also why Derek needed the quick cash and a potential fifteen-thousand-dollar payday. He was four months behind on child support and needed to fulfill a promise he'd made to her. He usually made promises he didn't intend to keep, but not when it came to Jasmine.

Last July, Derek had had Jasmine for the weekend. The A's were at home but were playing a primetime game, giving Derek a free morning to stroll around Lake Merritt in Oakland. The marine layer was burning off, revealing a cool, hazy sunshine. Derek always enjoyed these times with Jasmine and tried to take it all in during these rare private moments.

"Daddy, I like it when we take walks in the morning," Jasmine had said, holding his hand as they watched two geese creating small wakes in the lake.

"Yep," Derek said.

"I wish we did it more."

"Same here, sweetie. But your mom's the boss, and she can get you what you need to grow up steady like her."

"That's what Mama says too, but I wanna be with you and Nanna more, even though Nanna smacks your head a lot."

"She does, doesn't she."

Derek rubbed the back of his head and winced. Jasmine giggled.

Derek's mom loved her granddaughter and spoiled her with love and Vietnamese cooking, something she didn't get with Pam. Pam usually made a variation of pasta, meatballs, fish sticks, and squash.

Derek and Jasmine finished their walk and found the bus stop that would take them back to the apartment he shared with his mom. When they boarded, Jasmine was excited her favorite spot was available, up front and opposite the driver. As they settled into their orange plastic seats, the bus lurched forward into traffic.

"I wanna do that," Jasmine said. She pointed up and across.

Derek followed her finger. Among the several placards advertising everything from injury lawyers to nonprofit tax help, Derek was drawn to one featuring a ballet dancer, dressed in a white leotard, tutu, shoes, and with her dark hair in a bun. She was on her toes, with the other leg and arm forming a perfect T. Even in a photograph, she displayed the grace of movement.

"Oh really? That's pretty cool. I didn't know you liked dance."

"I do. I watch on YouTube and copy what they do, but I wanna do it for real. Mommy says she don't have the money for it."

Jasmine dropped her chin to her chest and folded her hands together. Derek felt guilty. He was always playing catch-up in child support, and he knew Pam didn't have the money to provide any extra enrichment.

"Maybe I can help pay for some classes."

He meant to say it to himself. He was sure he couldn't afford it. He didn't even know how much classes cost. But as soon as he verbalized his thoughts, Jasmine's eyes went wide, her eyebrows went up, and her mouth opened.

"Really?"

"Sure. Anything for you."

"Thank you, thank you!"

Jasmine hugged Derek, and for a moment, he felt like a superhero. He'd do anything for his daughter, give her a unicorn if he could, anything to make her smile like that. But as quickly as his chest puffed out, he felt himself deflate, gripped by anxiety. He needed to make this work. Perhaps curtail his betting or at least make smarter bets and save it all to fulfill the promise.

Three months later, promises made and reiterated, he was in a bind. The classes and deposit started in a week. There were also expenses related to leotards, shoes, and other costs about which Derek didn't even know.

Pam had pulled him aside when she'd picked up Jasmine the day before.

"You know you're behind," Pam said.

"Yeah, yeah, I know. I'm working on it, okay" Derek said.

"I can't cover you. Are you gambling again?"

"Just some here and there so I can make good on those dance classes."

"Derek, do you hear yourself? You're gambling what you should be paying me for child support in hopes you can pay for classes you promised. You need to get a grip."

Derek turned and stepped away. He knew if he didn't, he'd lash out.

"I've got it under control. I'm working on some things, all right?"

And he was. With baseball season winding down, he was looking at some more stable work at a food truck. He hoped he'd get the news soon. But that didn't help right now.

"You're going to get it all to me? You know dance starts next week, and the money's due up front for the first week. If you don't pay it, I have to, and I don't have the money. I mean, I've been covering your ass for four months."

Derek felt the panic. He hadn't saved like he'd planned. He saved a little, then bet on a sure thing, only it wasn't. Then, he tried to double down on a couple other bets, and the further and further the summer continued, he'd gone deeper in debt.

"I'll get it, Pam." Derek looked at Pam, hoping she'd see the confidence of his face and not the terror in his eyes.

"You'd better. If I don't hear from you on Monday telling me you have the money, I'm going to the court."

Back at Club Maui with his betting sheet in front of him, Derek knew he had to go big, and he had to get it right. Poker wasn't his game, but he was putting his chips "all in." If they came through, he'd clear his debts and pay for dance. If they didn't...

On cue, Owen came around the corner of the bar from the back. A former ten-year NBA player who grew up in Oakland, went to St. Joseph's and Cal, Owen made several stops around the league's benches, including the Warriors. When he retired, he bought Club Maui, installed an outdoor patio, and made it a respectable local dive bar, complete with the neighborhood book on the side.

"There's my man, Derek," Owen said. "I can always tell if it's Sunday if you're sitting at my bar with the sheets in front of you. How are you doing, man?"

Owen gripped Derek's hand and pulled him in to slap his back.

"Good, guy" Derek said.

"C'mon back," Owen said. If there was such a thing as a gliding strut, Owen had perfected it as he led Derek around the bar. He had full control of his space and didn't have to duck moving through the doors in his bar. He knew he'd clear it by an inch. When they got to the back office, he reached into his drawer and took out a notepad. He put on his reading glasses.

"So, first off, do you have my eight grand?"

Derek shook his head. Owen stared at Derek over the readers.

"Man, I can't have you laying any more bets until you pay me what's owed."

"Last week was some bad beats, guy," Derek said. Derek's eyes darted everywhere but to Owen's face. "That friggin' Johnson fumbling when the Browns are running out the clock, only to have it returned ninety yards was a fluke. I had that game won, okay. And I've got some good action I want to lay down and will make up what I owe you and make me some more cash."

Technically, Owen didn't let anyone slide down beyond eight thousand dollars. From his position as a small-time bookie, it kept him from having to do the dirty stuff he hated. And he had a hard cutoff. But Derek was one of Owen's longest bettors, and even when he faced that limit, he always pulled himself out of his hole. Plus, Derek needed these bets today.

Owen thought about it, maybe recognized the desperation in Derek's eyes, then nodded.

"Okay, I'm only doing this 'cause you been with me forever, and you come through before. Just don't go too crazy. I can't have you losing no more. I got other fools behind me, and I can't have them harassing both of us."

Derek felt relief and felt good about the spreads, the money lines, the situations.

Owen licked his finger and pulled out his sheet.

"Whatcha got?"

Derek laid out his two NFL parlays.

"Big expectations. But no A's?" Owen asked.

"Not on the game, but how about I lay down another dime for Austen *not* getting the hit today, huh guy?" Derek used to feel bad about betting against the home team or local heroes, but his betting pragmatism had outweighed any hometown bias long ago.

"Oooo, don't be saying that shit again," Owen said. Owen read back the bets to make sure he had it all right. "But you ain't laying prop action, not when you in the hole like you are."

"I know, guy," Derek said. "But good things are ahead. I can feel it."

"Look, I'll take the parlays but not the prop on top."

Owen was sincere and concerned. Derek had a feeling maybe he'd gone a little far, but he was sure today was the day it would all work in his favor. If not, then he'd stop betting forever, pick up a couple shifts, and try to go straight.

"All right, all right. I'll take just the parlays. Appreciate what we've got," Derek said.

"I'll be rooting with you today. You win, I win," Owen said.

Owen's cell phone buzzed. "Aloha, Rick, how you been? Yeah, Austen's gonna get that shit done. Hold on a sec. Hey, Derek, we done, right? Close the door behind you."

When Derek returned to his red-vinyl barstool, his omelet and coffee were waiting. E turned the TVs to three different pregame shows while Derek sipped his coffee. These bets had to be right. He wasn't going to abandon Jasmine like his old man did, leaving the day after Derek's eighteenth birthday with the family's meager savings. No, Derek was going to get this right, send his daughter to dance, and be even more active in her life.

"I can't believe you bet against the Raiders, man," E said.

The morning shows were wrapping up, and the Raiders were lining up for the kickoff.

"That's our team. Who cares if they moved to Vegas."

"You know, they never travel well to the East Coast for a morning game," Derek said. "It's a fool's bet to take them, especially given the point spread."

"You've gotta have faith, D."

"Faith is a fool's bet."

"It's all a fool's bet," a voice further down the bar said.

"That's pretty depressing, guy," Derek said.

"It's fucking true," said this young bro at the end of the bar straddling the stool like a cowboy on a mule. He was wearing a bright-green A's tank top with bright gold trim, and Derek thought he was one of those young guys who'd usually be tailgating in the parking lot, getting in as many beers as possible before taking their drunk and belligerent selves to the game. Those guys were on the extreme. Either generous in buying everything that came their way or rude and obnoxious. Derek guessed he was the latter.

He was almost done with his beer, and there was an empty signature mojito in front of him. "We're all fucking mortal, and we're only here for a blip, so what's the point of worrying about things like the outcome of games?"

"True, but hey, looks like you're going to the A's game. That's got to be something," Derek said.

"Yeah, supposed to go with my family. We have this tradition of going together for the first and last game of the year, but my grandpa's sick, so I'm taking my friends instead. Just won't be the same."

"I'm impressed," E said. "Most guys your age would rather be with their buddies than with family for a game like today. It'll be a great game. Sun's out but cool on the field. And who knows? You might witness some history with Brett Austen hitting .400."

"Yeah, I need to talk to Austen. I have to share something with him about my grandpa." He took a last long pull from his beer. "It could make a difference."

"Good luck with that," Derek said. "He's got more things buzzing around him than flies on shit, okay."

"What if I wanted to get something to him? You work there?" The young man perked up. "Maybe you can help me."

"Guy, I don't even come close to having that type of access. You've gotta get a clubhouse guy or security or an usher or something, and even then, the odds are slim."

"I've gotta try." The young man stared back at the TV. "I think my grandpa would at least want me to try."

"Can't hurt," E said. "At the very least, enjoy your friends. Maybe they'll make sure you forget about your woes for a few hours. Tailgating before the game?"

"Yeah." He looked at the clock on the wall. "I'd better get over there. The tailgate's probably started."

He fished out a couple twenties and laid them on the bar. E was happy with the sizable tip and that this guy wasn't his problem anymore. Derek watched the man walk toward the door. He wasn't staggering but was deliberate with his steps. He hoped he wasn't going to be a problem in the stands later.

"Man, I'd hate to be his buddies. What a downer," E said when the man was gone.

"Yeah, there's something else going on there," Derek said. He looked up. The Jets recovered a Raider fumble on the twenty-six-yard line. "See, never bet on the Raiders when they travel to the East Coast for an early game."

CHAPTER 6

**Lizzie Hernandez
Daughter/Mother**

Dad expects me to be my best today, Lizzie thought. *Everything has to be just right.*

Lizzie stared into the mirror. When did her makeup routine shift from wanting to look great to keeping the effects of aging from horrifying others? These dark circles under her eyes were becoming a problem. She was against getting invasive plastic surgery, but maybe some Botox or injections might make her look less hideous.

Even though she was just going to her parents' house to watch the ballgame, it was so much more than that.

She moved on to applying mascara when her daughter, Heidi, stormed in crying. At twenty, Heidi didn't need much makeup with her plump cheeks and creaseless eyes and forehead. Makeup could wait. Lizzie held out her arms for her daughter.

"Mom, Papa's going to die today," Heidi managed to say.

Lizzie nodded and brought Heidi in for a hug. The tears flowed. Lizzie took a moment. She had to be strong for her daughter. Heidi's "papa," Lizzie's dad, wasn't going to last the next twenty-four hours. While Heidi was nearly old enough to drink, legally, these were the moments when she reminded Lizzie of the little girl who had taken a couple days to mourn a week-old goldfish. Kevin Rogers wouldn't want his "Little Lizzie Girl" to lose herself in her own misery. No, Lizzie Rogers Hernandez had to be strong for her family.

The last month had been a dark hole. As of last week, Lizzie's divorce was now official, just about the time when her dad's cancer was running out the clock. She wouldn't allow the idea that her divorce had broken her dad. Nope, Kevin Rogers's insistence on smoking Marlboro Reds for most his life was what had brought him here today, more than Eddie being a weasel and sleeping with some woman he'd met online. Now, in the final stages of hospice and back in his house, Kevin's doctors shared that he may go at any time.

"It's okay, sweetie." Lizzie stroked Heidi's soft black hair. For a moment, Lizzie was distracted by the vibrance of her daughter's youth. At forty-nine, Lizzie's hair lacked that same volume or natural color, one of the many things that had changed with her body since she was her daughter's age.

"The good thing is, we'll get to say goodbye to him."

"I don't know if I can," Heidi said. "I don't know if I can see him like that."

"You'll be strong, and it's better if you do. If you don't, you'll always regret it."

"I know. It's just so weird. We were supposed to go to the A's game today, and now we're going to his house to watch him die."

Kevin Rogers had been a lifelong A's fan and had made his children and grandchildren bleed green and gold. For most of her life, Lizzie remembered her dad buying tickets for every opening day and closing day. She smiled at those memories, piling into her dad's extended SUV and caravanning down from Sacramento with her brother's family for the game. She looked forward to those family gatherings more than Thanksgiving, certainly more than Christmas. There were no expectations other than the game, and even if the A's lost, the sights and sounds of the stadium made the trip worth it.

"I know," Lizzie said. "It's not the final day we were expecting. But we're going to have the game on in front of him, and you, me, Nana, your uncle Stephen, your aunt Leticia, and your cousins are going to be there."

Lizzie never really thought about this moment. In her mind, big Kevin Rogers was larger than life, almost an invincible hero but with the tenderness of a doting father. Except for her teen years, when it was a rite of passage to push parents' buttons, she'd adored him. He taught her self-sufficiency and confidence, insisting she take self-defense classes and change the spark plugs on her own car. He was always there for her. Even during her divorce, frail from chemotherapy, he had stood as a beacon of strength when she needed every bit of it to walk away from her relationship.

"Lizzie, you are two times greater than that man can ever hope to be," he told her when she'd finally kicked Eddie out. "I loved him like my own, but mark my words, you'll be in a better place in about six months."

Lizzie pulled back and held Heidi.

"This is our time to say goodbye, doing one of his most favorite things," Lizzie said.

"I just wish it wasn't today."

"I don't think there's ever a good day for it to happen, but it's a day you'll remember for the rest of your life."

Heidi nodded. Lizzie thought today was somewhat unfair. Here Heidi was, going into her junior year at UC Davis with the world awaiting her, yet instead of lying around in her apartment on a sunny morning with her roommates, she was off to visit her dying grandpa with her family.

"So, let's finish getting ready, then we'll drive over to your grandparents' house and watch the game from there," Lizzie said.

Heidi's smile returned, but it was just a mask. Lizzie knew the look well. Inside, they both remained devastated.

Heidi came in for one more hug. Her eyes were still puffy, but they'd be back to normal soon. Youth. Heidi turned back down the hall and into her room.

"All right," Lizzie said to her reflection. She'd need several self-pep talks if she was going to get through today.

Like her daughter, Lizzie thought this entire day was going to be strange. They were treating today almost like a Super Bowl party. They were dressing in green and gold. Lizzie was picking up sandwiches. Her brother, Stephen, was bringing drinks and snacks, and the family was gathering to watch a baseball game. Only, instead of her father sitting in his large leather recliner, he'd be in a large hospital bed in the middle of the living room hooked to several machines. Her mother, Carol, insisted that it was what her husband would want. It was the last game of the season, and Kevin would want to have his family together watching the A's.

Two weeks ago, Kevin Rogers had every intention of attending the final game of the season. He was determined to go down to field level, even using his walker and air tank and with remnants of COVID-19 still floating around. He wanted to sit with his family on the right-field side. He had the tickets and had begun to plan their day at the ballpark, driving from Sacramento to Oakland, using his disabled placard to get the family prime parking. He had hoped that although the A's wouldn't be playing in the postseason, he would still get to see Brett Austen live in pursuit of hitting .400.

Even at that time, Lizzie wondered if her dad's plans were unrealistic. The cancer and the chemo had ravaged his body. The entire day would likely tire him, taking precious days off his life. But, when a dying man says he would rather spend his last day at a ballgame rather than in his living room, you go to the game.

In the end, fate would keep him from the ballpark. Five days prior, while using the walker to get the paper in the driveway, Kevin fell over. When Carol, who was still sleeping at the time, didn't hear Kevin making his typical morning sounds, she raced outside to discover him in a heap. By the time the ambulance came, he was unconscious and having trouble breathing. Fortunately, he regained consciousness, but everyone knew that he had already attended his final A's game. When she and Carol brought Kevin home two days ago, they resolved to watch the game with him today.

Lizzie was putting the final touches on makeup when her brother called. She put him on speaker and returned to her mascara.

"Hey, Stephen," Lizzie said. "I'm just finishing getting ready, then I'm heading to Tony's to get the sandwiches. I should be there around noon. What time are you and the kids coming? What time does Robbie get in on the train?"

"Well, that's kind of why I'm calling. I just wanted to let you know that Robbie's using the tickets and going to the game with his friends."

Lizzie stopped putting on her makeup and stared at the phone, stunned. Robbie was a senior at Cal. Like Heidi, Robbie was navigating that transition from childhood and making his own decisions, good and bad; however, unlike Heidi, sometimes her nephew was the most selfish little prick. He had a knack for making decisions that benefited only himself.

"Are you kidding me?" Lizzie said. "Did you tell him that his grandfather is likely going to pass, and we're all going to watch the game together?"

"I did, but his reasoning is that grandpa would have wanted those tickets to be used by someone in the family, to watch the game in person, particularly today, and to watch Brett Austen."

"Wait, how did he get the tickets?" Her mom had transferred the tickets to Stephen to sell online. "You had to agree to transfer the tickets to him."

It was just like Stephen to let Robbie walk all over him. Stephen and Leticia had enabled and spoiled Robbie his whole life. Granted, Robbie was a genius and got good grades, which got him into Berkeley in the first place. But anything Robbie wanted, Robbie got.

"I did," Stephen said. "Robbie had a point. I mean, Dad would have wanted someone to enjoy the game in person."

"Oh God, Stephen. Whatever."

"Hey. Don't fucking judge me for how I parent my kid. He's an adult, and I actually think he has a point, so I gave him the tickets."

"Is he going by himself?"

"I think he's going with a group."

"So, they're going to party while his grandfather's dying?"

"Probably." Stephen chuckled. "Don't you think that's how Dad would have wanted it?"

It was true, her dad would enjoy having a few beers at the game. But still, they were supposed to be in Sacramento, watching the game on TV.

"Fine, everyone else coming? Or is there some other priority?"

"Hey, I'm going to forgive that because I know how this is stressing you out. But we'll be there. Just calm down, and remember to focus on Dad."

Lizzie pursed her lips. Stephen was right. She was a little out of line. The truth was that she envied Robbie. Today was going to be awkward. It was her dad's wish, but the idea of having a party and a vigil at the same time wasn't appealing. Lizzie had no doubt Robbie would have more fun drinking and cheering for the A's in the seats meant for her dad and his family. Well, at least Lizzie had wine.

"Yeah," Lizzie said, biting back a retort. Even as adults, she didn't let her younger brother win arguments too often. "So, we'll see you there. You're getting the snacks and drinks."

"You got it, boss," Stephen said.

Lizzie and Heidi finished getting ready. Lizzie smiled. In her jeans and ratty Mark McGuire jersey her dad had bought her thirty years ago, she was ready to sit in comfortable chairs and eat comfort food all day. Heidi, meanwhile, doubled down, wearing pajama bottoms and an A's hoodie she cropped off the bottom and the sleeves. Heidi looked good in anything she wore. They got into the car and headed to the deli.

"Did I hear Robbie isn't coming?"

"Apparently, Robbie thinks that grandpa would want him at the game," Lizzie said. Out of all the grandkids, Robbie had the closest kinship with Kevin over their love for the A's. Robbie was the one who paid attention when they went to the games. Instead of playing with his cousins at her parents' house, he sat and watched the games on the couch with his grandpa. When Robbie started attending Cal, and before Kevin was diagnosed, they attended a few games together, just the two of them.

"Typical," Heidi said. "But that means I have to bear the teens by myself."

Lizzie caught herself from reminding Heidi that she was just twenty and only two years removed from high school herself. At the same time, Lizzie knew that Andrea, a senior, and Bart, a sophomore, were a bit much. Both would be buried in their phones, Andrea checking and posting on Instagram and Bart playing one game or another.

"You know they'll just be looking at their screens," Lizzie said.

Lizzie sometimes felt terrible thinking about it, but she reveled in the belief that her Heidi had navigated the gauntlet of adolescence pretty well, while Stephen's kids were a part of the same dumpster fire. Yes, she loved her brother. He was her parents' child, and they shared many memories. But sometimes, she just shook her head. They had basically the same childhood, yet were so different in humor, temperament, and personality. While she was organized, astute, and grounded, Stephen was flighty, unrealistic, and impulsive. She was reserved. He was the life of the party. But, if anyone needed anything, she was there. He was there only out of obligation. Of course, he was still married to Leticia. Lizzie, well, she'd had Eddie.

"Hey, we'll be there for each other, okay?" Lizzie said. "We'll be there for grandpa and grandma, and we'll do the best we can."

Heidi rolled her eyes and shook her head. Lizzie smiled. There is a certain time of life when women are expected to share their disdain and annoyance at situations. When did it go from being a devastating weapon to a liability? That first job out of college? She was sure the patriarchy would find some way to knock that out of her in the next few years. Lizzie hoped it wouldn't. She liked Heidi's spunk.

Lizzie pulled into the parking spot in front of Tony's Deli. Her phone buzzed. Oh God, it was Eddie. She had managed to avoid him for three days, mostly because she didn't have the energy. But she knew Eddie had an affinity for the old man, and it was unfair to completely ignore the relationship they had shared for twenty-five years.

She pressed "Accept," and Eddie's face appeared on her screen as he sat on the couch in his apartment.

"Hey," Lizzie said. "Sorry I haven't gotten back to you. It's just a hard time, you know?"

"Hi, Dad." Heidi poked her head into the screen.

Lizzie pulled out her credit card and gave it to Heidi. "Go pay for the sandwiches while I talk to your dad. They're already ordered and under my name."

Whether it was the look in Lizzie's eyes, the tone of her voice, or any other nonverbals, Heidi understood Lizzie's message. *I need to talk to your dad privately.* Heidi took the card and got out of the car. Lizzie focused back on the screen.

"So, what's up?"

"How are you doing?" There was empathy and sadness in Eddie's eyes. He couldn't keep his penis in his pants, but he saw right through her. She understood that after this painful decoupling period, they would likely remain friends.

"I'm doing," she said. "It's going to be hard today. Stephen's going to be Stephen. Robbie's using the tickets with his buddies, getting drunk, and doing something stupid, and Stephen's totally fine with it. So, once again, I'm going to be the one to keep everything together for this final game with Dad."

"That's going to be tough. Your dad was a good man."

"Still is."

"You know what I mean." Eddie sounded frustrated, but he took a beat and showed grace. Part of why she loved him. "Listen, if at all possible, just forget about Stephen, Robbie, and all of them, and just be there for your mom, your dad, and Heidi. That's going to make it worthwhile for you. Don't get caught up in the drama. You draw value from being there for those closest to you, so just keep to that, and you'll get through it today."

Lizzie hated it when Eddie got her so clearly. Especially now. He had ruined what they had, and she hated him for that, but she loved him for these moments that provided her with such clarity.

"I'd like to ask you something," he said.

Uh-oh. "What?"

"I'd like to come over, if I can."

"No way."

"C'mon, he's like my own dad," Eddie said.

"Are you kidding me?" Lizzie felt the rage rise up and mix with her grief. "Yes, he felt you were his son, and you fucked that up, Eddie. You don't get to ride in at the end and comfort everyone when you've burned the forest down. Yes, you had this family, but that's done. You're not Stephen who gets fifty chances. You screwed it up, and it's over. You can come to the service, whenever that is, to pay your respects, but you don't get to be there today, not as part of the family. You just don't."

Lizzie felt the tears streaming down her cheeks and realized the pain she had tried to cover over the past six months bubbled up in her SUV. Thankfully, Heidi was still collecting the sandwich, but it wouldn't be long until she'd be out.

"Lizzie, I'm sorry for everything. Still, I want to be there for you."

"Stop, Eddie. You don't get that anymore. You made your choice when you cheated on me. You don't get to be that guy anymore, and I don't get to have you in my corner. You can't come over. I'm sorry."

Lizzie didn't give Eddie time for a rebuttal. She just pressed "End" on her phone and wiped her eyes. She pulled down the visor. Her makeup would have to be reapplied. Great.

Heidi loaded the sandwiches into the back of the car and got in.

"Everything okay?"

"Yep," Lizzie said. Without Eddie, Heidi would have understood Lizzie the best. And Heidi understood that it was time not to ask questions and to just be quiet and listen to the A's pregame show.

PREGAME

CHAPTER 7

Arrivals

"Good of you to join us, Dana," Dan Muir said. "Trouble picking the right outfit?"

Dana wasn't late, but Muir liked to poke at her. It was his little brand of sexism he liked to excise over some of the female talent. As the Baseball Broadcast Network's primary play-by-play caller, prepared and always early, he enjoyed limited immunity from perpetrating microaggressions.

Retorts flooded Dana's mind, like *I was on the phone with your wife, and she was having trouble getting stripper dust off your suits.*

Instead, she said, "You have no trouble being an ass." It was lame. Yet, she knew where she stood in the broadcast pecking order, and Muir was higher up the chain. If this Kansas City job was in play, she didn't want to come off as a problem child, even if it was justified.

Walking into the broadcast trailer, Dana and Clarkson adjusted their eyes from natural light to the luminated bank of monitors running across its length. In the span of fifteen seconds, they were bumped by no fewer than four production staff moving in and out of the trailer in preparation for the day's broadcast. But like a hurricane, the activity was centered around a calm, distinct, and rather large eye—Executive Producer Marv Palmetto. A walrus of a man, complete with a handlebar mustache that extended down his triple chin, Palmetto lorded over his kingdom.

"Good morning, Ms. Peck," Palmetto said. "Good work on the morning-show circuit today. That should get Kansas City's notice."

Palmetto smiled, then laughed when Dana returned a blank stare.

"C'mon, you know this a pretty small circle of professionals, and you haven't exactly been secretive about wanting to jump to the booth."

"Dana, you want the Royals job, huh?" Muir grinned, showcasing the smile that paid for his dentist's beachfront house in Honolulu. He stood against the back of the trailer reviewing his notes. Dana envied and wanted to emulate his work ethic. His notes were impeccable, and he had enough material to broadcast a fifty-inning game.

He was still a jerk.

"It's early, who knows? My agent's trying to set up a coffee tomorrow with Stan Love in LA," Dana said. Better to be transparent. Palmetto might have better insights into the job market than Jen Small.

"Well, good luck. This will be a great showcase game for you," Palmetto said. Sometimes, Palmetto was a little much, but he was always gracious and authentic.

"Meet him for drinks to increase your chances," Muir said with a wink. She caught it and grimaced. "There's only so many opportunities for women."

Dana clenched her fists. There was still sexism and misogyny in her workplace, but call it out too much, and she'd never get as far as she wanted, hell, deserved. Instead, she supplied a disapproving and disappointed stare and moved on.

"Where's your partner, Dan?" she asked. Unlike play-by-play men, in-game analysts only had to share their insights. The really good ones did their homework, but ex-players were mostly hired to bring their name and in-the-moment analysis. Tyson Porter was good. With an ounce of effort, he could be better.

"We still have an hour until Porter's call time and another half hour after that until he actually shows up," Palmetto said. "Plenty of time."

Porter had talent. He predicted balls and strikes with tremendous accuracy and drew in the most casual fan with simple explanations of player alignments or pitch selection. Word was that he was looking for a job back in the clubhouse but didn't want to pay his dues back in the minors. Dana could see him as a manager one day. He knew strategy and was certainly good-looking. It was those good looks that had led him to her bed eighteen months ago, but Dana knew he was a mistake the moment he left her room. They never acknowledged the encounter, but whenever they worked together, about fifteen times a year, she would sometimes get a late-night text for a revisit. Sometimes with his own dick pic. Ugh.

Dana, Palmetto, Clarkson, and Muir reviewed the high points from this morning's production meeting, including the questions to ask Austen. They also reviewed the flow of the game and where she might have an in-game standup or fan interview.

"Give me some good lead-ins," Muir said. He sat down on the desk as Palmetto settled into his chair. Dana turned to exit the trailer. "And good luck with the Kansas City thing. You know, they're looking for a lily-white virgin for their first-ever female play-by-play announcer."

Dana shook her head in frustration. What would it take for Muir, or any of these guys, to be taken down a notch? After all, it was perfectly fine for Muir, a married father of five, to fool around, but not for a single woman to do the same.

Clarkson looked at her, equally intrigued by what she would say or do.

"Thanks, Dan. If I get into the play-by-play club, do I get your list of best 'happy ending' massage parlors for every major-league city?"

Dan's face turned white, but she didn't linger. She pushed forward, Clarkson walking behind her. She felt a pit in her stomach. Sometimes, this business was just so shitty. You either had to look sexy or be told that viewers didn't respond to you. Or you were too sexy and considered a slut who wasn't right for viewers. Meanwhile, horrible stories of the men in her business making unwanted advances, taking advantage of the weird groupies, and all kinds of fireable offenses were commonplace. There were moments when she wanted to go on camera and burn it all down.

But she had worked so hard, sacrificed so much, and was going to make it on their terms, then reset the hierarchy to her liking. It was advice her mom had instilled in her as a single parent—the best revenge was reaching the top. So, she shut out everything else and worked. Nothing else mattered.

"Well, we'd better go set up for the Austen interview so we're ready for our one-on-one right after the press conference," Clarkson said. "I'll let Henderson know we're here."

Dana nodded as they walked from the trailer to the concrete tunnel burrowing through the stadium. By habit, she raised her phone to check her social media. Before she could scroll, the phone buzzed. Her mom was calling, not texting. That was odd. Over the years, Dana had trained her mom to text first and often. It was just too hard to find the right times for unsolicited phone calls. She was either working, on a flight, or not in the right head-space for a conversation. Plus, Dana's mom was retired. It was much easier to communicate on Dana's schedule.

"Hey Mom," Dana said. She made out what sounded like whimpers on the other end. "Mom? Is everything okay?"

Dana looked at Clarkson, who looked back, concerned.

"Mom?" Dana repeated. "Is something wrong?"

"Dana, I've screwed up so bad."

* * *

"Did you check out that Texas A&M game yesterday?" Brett Austen asked.

As part of his routine when he arrived at the stadium, Brett stopped by the clubhouse attendant's office. Jason, a short, skinny, intense bottle of energy, was one of the people Brett looked forward to seeing most when he came to work. In addition to taking inventory, washing uniforms, cleaning and maintaining the clubhouse, and running odd errands for the players, Jason was also a confidant. He kept secrets, didn't have an attitude, and gave advice when asked or needed. Most importantly, Brett and Jason rarely spoke about baseball. Their conversation centered around everything else; other sports, fantasy football, cars, movies, starlets, weather. It was the favorite part of Brett's daily routine.

"Brutal," Jason said. He was pulling down a case of Gatorade to place inside the dugout for batting practice. "Last-minute 'Bama field goal to win it. Sucked."

"Yeah, thanks for not spoiling it for me," Brett said. "I watched the replay last night. I wish I hadn't. When are the Aggies going to finally beat Alabama?"

"I'll be more surprised when they do."

Jason was the only person in the world who hadn't treated Brett any differently in the last month. Even his teammates had been avoiding him. Like a pitcher going for a no-hitter, the other A's walked around him gingerly or only offering a quick hello. They surely didn't talk about the average with him. He was no longer Brett Austen, teammate; he was Brett Austen, the story. Brett Austen, the anointed one to hit .400. And they couldn't talk trashy TV with a hitting deity. Well, at least the hitters didn't. The pitchers were a different breed, and his average was an affront to their profession. They were happy for him, sure, but they were also a little cold. He had figured out their shit.

He laid his bag on the leather recliner in front of his locker; well, more like a dedicated space, the benefit of being the star and veteran of the team. He took inventory. Since the A's had taken over the Raiders' locker room, he was afforded even more space, including the recliner, his own refrigerator, a small desk to sign the stacks of photos, and a spot next to the video room. On another playoff-contending team, he would be one of many stars on the roster and wouldn't receive this level of special treatment. Unless the A's went against their history and paid their best older player instead of reinvesting in the next season, he would say farewell to these perks. Brett shook his head. That was a thought for tomorrow.

"Hey Brett," a voice called from across the clubhouse. It was his manager, Frank Garza. "Hey, can you come over to my office when you get a chance?"

"Sure," Brett said. He looked at the clean white uniform with green letters and number five with gold trim. Would this be the last time for this shirt? *Not going to let these thoughts get to me.* That's how the demon worked its way into the brain, through sentimentality and expanding significance of the game. Nope, stick to the routine. See ball, hit ball.

Entering Garza's office wasn't so much entering a major-league manager's inner sanctum but a step into Margaritaville. One wall was an entire mural of a Caribbean beach scene, complete with light-blue water and palm trees. On another wall was a framed Jimmy Buffett-autographed Tommy Bahama shirt surrounded by pictures of Garza and his wife, Gina, at various Buffet shows, including a few with Buffet himself. One of the most recent was a picture of Jimmy Buffet with Garza on the field at a game in Miami. Even today, Garza looked like he was in full Parrothead garb, dressed in flip-flops, longboard shorts, and a faded T-shirt from O'Neill Surf Shop in Santa Cruz. His hair and mustache were more white than gray.

"Hey," Garza said from behind his desk. It still was a regular desk, all walnut and no coconut, and various papers strewn across it with today's stats. He had a large cup of his traditional Diet Pepsi in front of him. Brett sat down in the wicker-and-bamboo chair in front of Garza's desk. "How are you feeling today?"

"Ready to get this one in," said Brett, shrugging and leaning back into the chair, wanting to give off the most casual vibe in this most casual setting. A live version of "Son of a Sailor" came over Garza's tiny Bluetooth speaker. "Going to get my hit in and finish it off."

"You feel good about it?" Garza said. He leaned on his massive forearms over the desk.

Brett nodded. He didn't feel great about it. A hitter was fatalistic. Even this season, he failed six out of ten times he went up to the plate.

Garza nodded. As a player, Garza had sat on the bench more than stood in the field, and when his playing career ended, he worked his way back up the minors as a coach. When given the chance four years ago, Garza led the overachieving White Sox to the World Series in his first year at the helm. Let go by the Sox after last season, he joined the A's on a five-year contract.

"Hey, big day for Brett, right?" Jeff Dawes, the team's vice president of baseball operations, said after pushing into Garza's office. Dawes didn't enter a room as much as he conquered it. He was flanked by his PR lackey, Pete Henderson, and another man who looked familiar. "Brett, have you met Levi Mason in the commissioner's office?"

Brett now placed him. He was the guy to the right of the league commissioner whenever they announced a league initiative, labor deal, or something official. Brett thought Mason looked smaller in person than on TV, but he did have a very expensive suit. Brett shook Mason's hand.

"The league is very proud of you and your terrific season," Mason said, the lights reflecting off his head into Brett's eyes. "This is quite an accomplishment. I wonder what Ted Williams would be thinking."

"Open the freezer, and ask that frozen melon," Henderson said. Williams famously had his body and head cryogenically frozen twenty years ago. The comment drew laughs, with Dawes and Mason laughing louder, but Garza and Brett glared at Henderson. They had too much respect for the game and Williams, the legendary "Splendid Splinter," to make fun of idiosyncrasies at the end of his life. Brett was even more offended, being the closest to Williams's accomplishment in eighty years.

Henderson's smile drew thin, and he returned to his phone.

"So, you're planning to play today, even though you can sit and be above .400?" Mason said, looking a little nervous. "I mean, if you sit, it can be a huge boost to the league before the playoffs. You can make rounds to all the talk shows and really boost your brand."

Brett just glared at Mason. Whatever happened today, he wasn't going to be a monkey for the league.

"I mean, the league, the team, the fans, all of America will remember your number," Dawes said.

"No, they'll remember I sat it out," Brett said.

Dawes looked at Garza, who realized he had a part to play in this production.

"Look, I know what your answer is, but you don't have to play today," Garza said. "You can sit it out, and no one will care."

"I'm playing," Brett said. "Frank, I told you last night. I plan on playing, and I hope you manage the game and not me. I want to earn this and not back into it."

Dawes turned to Garza. "Has he heard about Kenny Roberts?"

Brett was perplexed. Roberts was the scheduled starting pitcher for today. Brett had pretty good success against Roberts this season, even going three-for-three when he had faced him two weeks ago.

"What's up with Roberts?" Brett asked.

"Late scratch," Garza said. "They're going to start Clint Shakely today."

"Fuck," Brett said. "It has to be *that* asshole?" Of all the pitchers, Shakely had had Brett's number. Over his career, Brett had a .214 batting average against Shakely, compared to his .325 career average. Ever since Brett's first professional game in the minors, when Shakely blew three pitches past him in a rehab assignment, Brett never shook off the humiliation Shakely had brought him. The demon would like this. It often showed up when he faced Shakely. Fortunately, he hadn't faced Shakely this season since he was acquired at the trade deadline from the Mets.

"Remember, you don't have to prove anything," Garza said. "And I can provide any cover you need. Just say the word."

"Well, now I certainly can't sit," Brett said. "If I sit, everyone will know I backed down, particularly Shakely. That little shit would look over at me every time my spot in the order came up and smirk, knowing he beat me without even having to face me. No, I can't give him that satisfaction, no matter what's at stake. I'll get him today. His curve ain't what it used to be. When it floats over the plate, I'll tag that to left-center."

"We're just saying to consider it," Mason said. "You have it now. Why risk it on some meaningless game?"

"Because this game is the game." Brett took a step closer to Mason and Dawes. "Not playing is disrespecting it, my teammates, and the fans. I don't want to hear another fucking word about not playing. I'm gonna play, get up to the plate, tag Shakely's weak-ass shit, and walk the hell out of here with my .400, end of discussion."

Brett surprised himself with his level of anger and frustration. Why can't the brass just leave him alone? Can't he just play ball like he's paid to play? Why does this whole thing have to be more than just him against a pitcher? This historic moment was his. It was *his*. Nobody else's. And why did Shakely have to be the one standing in his way?

Garza stepped in front of Brett. "You're right, Brett. You've got this, no problem. They're just looking out for what's best for you, and it's only a suggestion; right, fellas?"

Mason nodded. Dawes looked up from his phone, and Garza motioned them to leave.

"That's right, Brett," Dawes said. "You go out there and get that hit. If you'll excuse me, for some reason Tyson Porter wants to see me. Things we do for our broadcast partners."

Dawes, Mason, and Henderson turned and left Garza's office. Once they were gone, Garza turned back to Brett.

"Don't worry about them or Shakely. I've never seen a player see the ball like you have this year. If I've learned anything from you this year, it's always been about the process. The results come because of the process. And, boy, have you had results. Go in and watch some tape on Shakely. Let's make the Mariners regret that decision to start him today."

"Thanks. I appreciate you looking out. 'One Love.'"

Garza laughed as the first few bars of Bob Marley's song came on.

"'One Love,'" Garza said.

Brett wasn't two steps out of Garza's office when the demon spoke in his head for the first time in months: *Oh shit. Shakely? You should sit out. You can't hit that old man. And if you don't sit, this season will have been for nothing. A failure.*

"Shut up," Brett whispered back. He shook his head and kept walking.

"What's that?" Henderson was outside Garza's office, waiting for Brett. Like all senior front-office personnel, Henderson had his own weekend uniform—slacks, a polo shirt, and a sport coat. A walkie-talkie was in one hand and his phone in the other. Henderson was intense. Every movement had a purpose. And right now, his purpose was to push Brett to his next obligation.

"Remember, you have your pregame press conference, followed by your sit-down with Dana Peck in the dugout. You need to get ready."

Brett recalled how his mom would remind him of all the things he needed to do and chastise him for all the chores he forgot to do. He didn't like it when she did it either.

"Well, obviously I was preoccupied by the fucking league coming in here trying to tell me what to do. I'll be there as soon as I can."

* * *

Will climbed out of the Mustang, grabbing the vinyl roof and hoisting himself out of Paul's car. They were in the preferred lot reserved for members of the press, players, and front-office staff. Sometimes, Will wondered what it would be like to be like regular A's fans and tailgate before a game. He vaguely remembered the few times he'd joined his dad and another of his friends, Rob, for a pregame tailgate. He had played catch with Rob, the biggest man he'd ever known who ate the largest sausage he'd ever seen. With Paul and his media credentials, however, he had access to meal spreads of boiled hot dogs, fried chicken tenders, french fries, and more.

"So, mitt or no mitt?" Paul asked. He held his up high.

Will rolled his eyes.

"No mitt then." Paul threw it into the car before locking it. "Let's stop by the press box, see a couple people, and get some food before we go down to our seats. I need to thank some people for our tickets."

They went up the ramp, past the general gates, and to the press entrance. For Will, he'd been to a dozen games with Paul, and each time it was the same. Paul worked with the press office to get Will a credential. They'd check in with an intern at the press entry, and from there, the chains and barriers were tossed aside. Security and the ushers all knew Paul Buckley, and all he needed to do was walk confidently. Will was always impressed but squinted with embarrassment each time he heard Paul's "Catch of the Day" catchphrase repeated.

The press box was empty. Most of the reporters were either on the field talking to players or down in the press room waiting for Austen. The gates weren't scheduled to open for another forty-five minutes, and Will looked out at the grounds crew setting up for batting practice and some of the Mariners starting pitchers playing games of long toss as part of an off-day routine. The smells of food began to waft throughout the stadium. Will looked down press row at the computer bags, notebooks, and laptops laying around while their owners were talking to the best ballplayers in the world. What a life to come here for work every day, have the best seats in the house, and then write about it.

"Not all what it's cracked up to be," Paul said, standing next to Will. He placed a hand on his shoulder. "The pay is crap, you're away from home for at least a hundred and fifty days, including spring training, and you get yelled at a lot, sometimes for doing a good job. But...it still can be fun."

"Mr. Paul Buckley." Will recognized a familiar voice behind them. "I can't believe you're not covering the game today."

Will and Paul turned. Will was amazed Dan Muir was so short. On TV, he looked as tall as his analyst partner, Tyson Porter, but Will had to direct his eyes down to see the man whose voice he'd often heard for big games on Sundays.

"Nope, just watching the game with Will here. Will, this is Dan Muir, play-by-play maestro."

"Maestro, geez. Lay it on thick, Paul." Muir pushed out his hand.

Paul was the one who spent a half hour one day teaching Will how to shake hands with a firm grip and stiff wrist. Will gripped Muir's hand like Paul had taught him.

Paul looked around Dan. "Where's Tyson?"

"Either he's just rolling in, or he's down in the clubhouses trying to find an angle to get on the coaching staff. I swear, he wants to be anywhere but with us in the booth."

Paul clenched his jaw trying to keep his face neutral. "Who's your sideline?"

"Dana Peck. Didn't you work with her at ESPN?"

Will watched Paul's face go a little flush, his grin a little too forced.

"I sure did. She's good people. She still trying to get a play-by-play job?"

"Yeah. In fact, did you know Sasser in Kansas City is retiring?"

"I knew it was coming, but he's announced?"

"He's announcing today, but anyway, I hear they're going to move some people around, and there will be an opening for the pregame studio and to call some games. Dana's salivating for it. You know what? You should try for it. You'd be great. You have a national name and a catchphrase. I mean, if you're sick of Sacramento."

Will watched Paul. He looked up, like it was a consideration. Oh, hell no. Will wasn't moving to Kansas City. Paul must have recognized the fear in Will's face. He put his hand on Will's shoulder.

"Nah, not for me. Besides, I'm getting married, and it's better to stay around home."

Phew.

"Wait, what? The great bachelor Paul Buckley is going to get married? Congratulations."

"Thanks. Tracey's a great lady. A great mom to Will, and I'm honored she accepted my proposal."

"That's great. I mean it. There was a time when I thought you'd be single forever."

"You weren't the only one. But moving back home, losing one of my good friends, and getting older just gave me more perspective on what's important in life, and I just got into that place where I was open. And, well, I fell in love unexpectedly."

Will turned to look at the field but caught Paul glancing at him. Will cringed. Yeah, Paul was Will's dad's best friend. Yeah, now Paul was banging Will's mom. Yeah, it was a little weird to talk about with Will around. Paul always transitioned out of these conversations quickly.

"Well, I'm not actually working today. I was hoping to catch Pete Henderson and thank him for the great tickets, but I guess he's dealing with the whole Austen hurricane. We're just going to grab some food before heading down to the field. Will wants to get some autographs before he meets a girl he likes."

Will's stomach sunk. What the hell? He felt betrayed.

"All right, little man," Muir said. "Like father, like son."

Will closed off and stepped back. His conversation about Amanda was private, and Paul was throwing it around like it was nothing. Also, Paul wasn't his father, and Paul wasn't correcting Muir either. Will felt small, like his identity and his father were being rewritten in the context of Paul Buckley. Was this how it was going to be? He was already struggling to find his relevance in high school, but now he would be defined as Paul Buckley's stepson, a footnote to Paul's minor celebrity.

* * *

"What happened?" Dana asked. She stared down the hall toward Clarkson who had also stopped. Dana waited for her mom's crying to subside.

"I was such a fool, Dana. I trusted him and..." Kathleen Peck began to cry again. Her voice cracked, and she didn't sound like the strong woman Dana knew her to be. Dana mouthed to Clarkson, *I'll catch up.* Clarkson turned and moved toward the press elevator, leaving Dana alone in the vast concrete tunnel.

"Is this about Richard?"

Kathleen let out an affirmative grunt through the sobs.

Richard was Kathleen's boyfriend, one whom Dana had never met. In fact, Kathleen had never met him in person in nearly a year, though she swore that he was real. They texted, wrote adoring emails to one another, and chatted over video. Though he worked on an oil rig in the Gulf of Mexico, they talked almost every day, and she was happy to have some companionship. In truth, Dana was happy her mom had found someone. Ever since she had divorced her father twenty years ago, Kathleen had had a long string of boyfriends that never panned out.

Dana waited for her mother to compose herself.

"What happened?" Dana asked again.

"You're going to think I'm so stupid."

"Mom, I won't think you're stupid. Just tell me."

"Well, it started a few months ago. He was short some money..."

Dana's thoughts went sour. "What? Why did you lend him money?"

"Because he was working offshore on the rig. He switched all his accounts away from American banks, but when he tried to enter the US to finally come and visit me, they flagged him. So, he asked for some money to just stay in New Orleans while he got this settled. I mean, he had no money. It was all tied up in this international legal bureaucracy. So, I lent him a couple thousand to stay."

Dana knew where this was going. She leaned against the cool concrete wall.

"Well, then he hired a lawyer to get him out of this mess and needed more money, so of course, I sent it to him. I mean, we've been talking for a year, and he was in trouble. And he had lots of money and would pay me back as soon as he had access to it. Well, that one was about twelve thousand."

"That one?" Dana had a pit in her stomach.

"I know. I'm such a big idiot, which is why I didn't tell you any of this because I knew you'd be upset with me. But I knew him, or I thought I knew him, and I loved him, so I did it. Well, then he told me the FBI had frozen everything and was keeping him in New Orleans, and his lawyer said he could solve this, but he needed more money to do so."

Dana had had enough of this wreck in slow motion.

"Mom, how much money did you give Richard?"

"Total?"

"Total."

"Around a hundred grand."

Dana felt her stomach clench, her throat close, and the ligaments in her neck tighten. She felt a full panic overcome her. So many questions.

"How do you have a hundred grand to give away?"

"Well, I have the rest of your grandfather's life-insurance policy and my retirement savings. I know, but Richard promised to pay it back."

Dana leaned against the wall, then lurched forward. She was going to be sick. She remembered when her mom decided to retire five years ago. She had been the office manager for a small landscaping company in Bloomington and managed to save a modest amount. But she never touched the proceeds of the life-insurance policy Dana's grandfather had left, because that was the nest egg that would allow her to stay in her house and be able to enjoy a long retirement.

"How did you even get access to it?" Dana asked. "Don't you have it tied up in investments. Why didn't your financial advisor keep you from doing it?"

"Matt tried, but Richard needed my help, so I insisted." Dana would need to reach out to Matt Daniels, Kathleen's financial advisor. "Remember, Richard and I have been dating for a year. I trusted him."

"You've never actually met him in person, Mom."

Dana regretted what she'd just said. Her mom was conned. "Richard" had cultivated this relationship for a year before he had pulled this scam. He had lavished her with gifts, and Dana had even read some of the adoring emails he had sent her mom. Shit, even Dana thought Richard was a good guy. He knew what he was doing, and who knows how many other lonely women he'd swindled.

"Where's Richard now?"

"His email has been closed, and the cell phone is no longer in service. I was worried, so I called his lawyer's office. The office is real. But when I called, they had no record of Richard Chase as a client or that his lawyer even worked there."

Dana admitted Richard had thought of everything. When Kathleen had first mentioned Richard Chase, Dana had checked up on her mom's new boyfriend. He had a digital footprint. He was attractive, in his early sixties, with a full head of salt-and-pepper hair and a white beard. His Facebook profile had him as a foreman on an oil rig in the middle of the Gulf. Now, Dana wondered if she should have done more.

"Shit," Dana said. There was no easy fix.

"Language," her mom said. "But pretty much. I don't have practically anything."

"Have you called the cops?" Dana asked. "Can they do anything?"

"Yes, but technically I gave money willingly, so there's nothing they can do. I guess the bank account where I sent the money has been closed."

Reviewing the facts in her head, the red flags were everywhere. Her mom was smart, but this was a blind spot. In searching for a companion, Kathleen Peck had left herself wide open for this classic long con that appeared in movies and true crime. They happen all the time.

"So, do you have any money?"

"Enough for some living expenses, but that's it. My safety net is gone. I'm going to have to sell the house. God, I'm such an idiot. I wish you were here."

There it was. The gauntlet had been thrown. Of all days and all times, this was it? This was the moment that she'd see as the turning point of her career—a historic game, a job opening, and achieving her dream of calling play-by-play for a major-league club. She had worked so hard for this to happen for her, and now, what was she supposed to do? Go to Illinois? She was supposed to be in Los Angeles. Why did this have to happen to her?

For all of her life, Dana never had to worry about her mom. She was strong and capable, and even when her dad had left after the divorce, Dana knew her mom was going to be just fine. Kathleen's strength meant Dana could be selfish and career focused and not have to worry about life in Bloomington. Now, that might all change.

"Mom, it's going to be okay," Dana said. "But look, I have to go. I'm working. I've got a big interview, like right now. Can you text me Matt's number? I'd like to reach him and get his take on the situation."

Dana really wanted to call him and yell at him for allowing her mom to get scammed like this.

"Yes, I'll do that." Her mother's tone had changed to one of interest. "Who are you interviewing today?" Kathleen was a mother to the end, happy to pivot to her daughter's accomplishments, even in the midst of such a personal crisis.

"Brett Austen," Dana said. "He may hit .400 for the season."

"Oooo, that sounds like fun. I'm so proud of you, Dana."

No matter the level of crap she experienced, the affirmation from her mother always made Dana smile.

"Thanks, Mom, but I gotta go. Everything's going to be okay."

"Dana, love you."

"Love you too, Mom."

Dana pressed "End" and let out a big exhale and shook her head. This wasn't the person Dana knew as her mother. Normally, she projected strength, confidence, and independence. But the balloon had popped. Kathleen sounded neither strong nor confident, and her independence was wired to some con artist in the Caribbean. The quiet quiver in Kathleen's voice acknowledged the uncertainty of what lay ahead. This wasn't just a bad date or a man she'd caught in a web of lies. This was a treachery. Her identity as a saver and as someone who earned every cent of her independence and made sacrifices along the way had been obliterated.

What the hell am I gonna do? The meeting of her life could be in Los Angeles tomorrow, and the Wild Card Series would be a direct audition for her dream job. There was no way to fit a trip to Illinois into those plans.

CHAPTER 8

Warm-ups

As Fred Stephenson punched in for the final time as an usher, the memory of the loud *ka-chunk* sound the old punch-card system at the Coliseum made him smile. Now, he placed his ID card under the infrared scanner like he was checking out at Target. He felt like that old system, the analog making way for the digital.

"Hey, Fab-Five Freddie," said Denny, a fellow usher with whom he had worked the last three seasons. A child of the nineties, Denny was one of the last people who knew MTV when they actually played music. "It's your last day, and what a day it is. Such a great day to be alive."

Fred smiled. Denny had one of the most positive attitudes he had ever known. As a veteran of two tours in Afghanistan, he still held the spirit of someone who had lived at Disneyland and was parlaying his experience and outlook into a first novel based on the brotherhood he had developed with his fellow soldiers.

"It is. I'm going to miss your hopeful outlook on life, my friend," Fred said. "It got me through this year."

"We've gotta live in our present, man. We have to embrace the relationships we have, honor those we've lost, and continue to push forward toward new adventures. I'm so excited for you. We'll have to share one last pint after the game. You're leaving tomorrow, right?"

"Yep. My son and his wife are packing up my place right now."

"They don't mess around, do they?"

"Well, the escrow closes in a couple days, so it's more about the buyer than John."

"Still, it's going to be a shock to the system, for sure. I remember whenever I was deployed, it was one day in Santa Cruz, the next in Baghdad. It's a bit of a shock."

"I'm sure."

"Well, here's hoping today brings no in-the-stands drama for your last game." Denny tilted his head and looked to the sky. "I'm sure there will be plenty of drama on the field. Brett Austen is going to hit .400."

"What makes you so sure?"

"C'mon, we've been watching it all year. It's gonna happen. Just a matter of when."

"I hope it's early."

Denny shook his head. "No way. I want the tension to build throughout the game with every at bat adding more significance. I want it to be the last thing that happens for our season. I can feel the electricity already."

"I hope you're right. 'Cause I don't want to be leaving this place on a ho-hum note."

They were standing in the guest-services bullpen, just beyond where they'd clocked in but down the hall from the underside of the outfield bleachers and luxury boxes. In a few minutes, Fred, Denny, and the rest of the guest-services staff would hear general announcements on anything the club had planned for the middle of the game, changes in security protocols, or any other information the brass thought they should know.

The ushers gathered around their chief, Rich, who gave them instructions. Fred smiled, and even after three years, he couldn't believe Rich was the big boss. Rich was at least thirty years younger than Fred. In fact, Fred had trained Rich sixteen years ago and knew every mistake Rich made that first season. Rich was almost fired in 2006 for practically starting a fight when some Yankee fans were heckling a player. It was Fred who had pulled Rich away before he'd made a huge mistake, and Fred had ended up also having to clean up that mess.

Thankfully, Rich had grown a lot since that day. Today, he had on a crisp white polo and a white guest-services hat. Years of working in the sun had given Rich a dark tan, though it was lighter around the eyes where he typically wore a pair of wraparound sunglasses. He waved his hands in the air to gain everyone's attention.

"So, we all know the importance of this game," Rich said when all one hundred and fifty ushers were gathered into the room. "There's going to be a lot of extra attention paid every time Brett Austen is at bat and in the field. Everything he does today is going to be seen and magnified, so there's going to be more cheers, more requests for autographs if he comes out, more hoping he sends a ball as a souvenir into the stands, things like this. So, make sure there's no scurrying down the aisles, and keep everyone at their seats the best you can, especially you, Fred, as you're right on the line in right field."

Fred nodded.

Rick continued. "Also, it's the last game of the season, so expect more drunks. They want to leave it all out in the parking lot, so we're going to see more wobblies today and maybe even a little aggression. We've got extra security, so don't hesitate to call in reinforcements. Finally, I want to make sure we say good-bye and recognize one of our own. This is Fred Stephenson's last game with us. As many of you know, Fred started with the A's in 2000, the year of Giambi, the Big Three, Miguel Tejada."

Denny slung his arm around Fred, and Fred felt other hands on his shoulders. Normally, he didn't like this level of affection, but today it was welcomed.

Rich continued. "Fred trained me, and he trained many of you. He knows this stadium better than almost anyone. We all know he's had a tough go of it the last couple years, but he kept coming to work with the same smile, wisdom, and willingness to help. I'd certainly not be here if it wasn't for him, and I'm sure many of you would agree. So, let's all give a cheer to Fred now, and after the game, come on back, and we can give him a proper sendoff."

The group cheered.

See, Fred, everybody is going to miss you.

"And I'm going to miss them, Marjorie," Fred said under his breath.

Fred smiled and nodded in acknowledgement. He felt a burning brewing in the back of his eyelids, but he wouldn't let this moment overwhelm him. After all, he had a three-hour game ahead of him.

Rich looked at Fred to say something. Fred looked around at his fellow ushers.

"Thanks, Rich, for that," Fred said. "And thanks to y'all for the love, support, and grace you've given me these last twenty-two years. Particularly this last one. Boy, it was tough, and I leaned on you, and I thank ya. It's bittersweet. It's my last game, but I'm so glad to end it on this high note with all you good people. Have a great one."

* * *

Dana felt helpless sitting in the media room, awaiting Austen's press conference. With her own life, she felt she had some control. For years, her only obligation to her mom was to call her once or twice a week and catch up. She knew she should have been around more, but her career and her dream to become a play-by-play announcer always came first. But now? With a real problem? She couldn't blow off the Wild Card or a potential foot in the door for her dream job. But she knew her mom needed her too. She had no idea what she was supposed to do next. Dana tried to focus. Now was no time for distractions. She still had her job to do. She needed to interview Austen. She'd worry about her mom later.

"Everything okay?" Clarkson asked, grabbing a seat next to Dana. He and camera operator Huey French had finished setting up the cameras for the on-field pregame interviews.

"Yeah, it was my mom. She's got some things going on at home in Illinois." Dana shook her head. Her mind was swimming with how her mom could recover and the assistance Dana would need to provide. But she had to shake it off for now. This may be the most important day of her career. She pulled out a mirror to touch up her makeup and hair before Austen arrived. "Let's get through this interview."

Clarkson moved on. "Hey, I just heard that Kenny Roberts is a late scratch for Seattle. Clint Shakely gets the start."

"Wow," Dana said. Roberts had a respectful 15-7 record this season, and they needed the win. "Do you know why?"

"I can only think because Austen can't hit Shakely," Clarkson said. "He's got, what, a .220 career average against him? But maybe they want Roberts for the Wild Card. In any case, ask him a little about his history with Shakely. I'm sure that will bring a reaction."

"I'm sure of it," Dana said.

"Dana Peck."

A nasal, high-pitched voice from behind prompted Dana to close her eyes and ask for patience. She wasn't a fan of Sal Grant, Austen's agent. After her interview with Brett Austen blew up a few years ago, he cautioned all of his clients to tread lightly. Their answers were always rehearsed, never authentic. She understood. Sal was paid well for making sure his clients maximized their contract worth.

"Sal," Dana said. "Big day for Austen. Bigger day for you if he gets the hit, goes on the free-agent market, and gets a ten-year deal."

"But he's going to get paid well regardless."

And so will you, Dana thought, looking over his designer linen suit that cost more than her salary during her first year in the business.

"I heard the league asked Garza to sit him. I heard they called you to convince Brett to sit on the average. Any comment?"

Sal's smile was always plastic, so it was hard to see any break in his demeanor, but his eyes twitched for a moment.

"Don't be ridiculous. Where did you hear a thing like that?"

Dana stole a quick glance to Clarkson; his wide smile showed his transparency. Clarkson's source inside the league shared that calls were made to Garza and Sal, even to the A's management, to convince Brett not to play.

"I have it on good authority the league wants to ride this story and parade him around the late-night and morning talk shows to help promote the playoffs. They can only do it if he hits .400."

"They didn't call me," Sal said. "Can't say anything about Garza. But we know Brett. The surest way to guarantee he does something is to tell him not to do it. We all know he's playing today, and he's going to get that hit."

Sal leaned in toward Dana's ear. She nearly flinched to get away from him, but the room was so packed, she was afraid she'd knock into the reporter with the *Tribune*.

"So, what's up with Tyson?" Sal asked. "I hear he talked with Jeff Dawes a little bit ago."

Dana wouldn't be surprised if Tyson Porter was angling for something with the A's coaching staff. Without any real experience, they could sign him on the cheap. Before she could speculate, Pete Henderson, the PR guy, blew into the media room, the cool smile just a veneer to hide the manic perfectionist inside. Dana thought of him as the kid in class who disrupted the curve.

"Austen's a little late, so he'll be just a few minutes," he said to the assembled reporters. "Sorry about that."

"Well, it isn't the first time an athlete has taken his sweet time to get to the interview," said the beat writer from the *Chronicle*. Both Dana and Clarkson looked at their phones. How would this affect their time with Austen?

"I know," Henderson said. "There are lots of demands on him today."

"Any comment about the switch to Shakely instead of Roberts?" a reporter from the *Oakland Review* asked.

"Will have to ask the Mariners' PR people," Henderson said.

"Is it because Austen can't hit Shakely to save his life, and they don't want to give him .400?" asked a radio reporter from the local sports station.

Grant piped in. "Most of that was early in his career, when Shakely was with the Angels. He hasn't seen him much since Shakely went to the Mets."

Clarkson leaned in to Dana's ear. "And the Giants, the Marlins, the Nationals, the Diamondbacks. Shakely's the ultimate hired gun. He's a cancer in the locker room, but they can't resist his left arm, so he stays in the league."

An intern, a skinny kid probably not old enough to drink, passed out the game notes. Dana nodded to the kid with curly hair and scanned for anything that might help in her interview. Before she could dig deep, Dana felt a buzz in her hand. She checked the screen. Another text from her mom.

Mom: *I'm so sorry you must deal with this today and my stupidity.*

Dana: *It's okay Mom, we'll get through it. Working on some things.*

Mom: *Okay honey. I just feel so betrayed and lonely. I'm sure you'll get it all to work out. Talk to you later. Love you.*

With each word, the waves of guilt collapsed on her. Dana wondered if she should fly to Illinois. After all, her mom needed some emotional support. And, she had that mild heart attack five years ago. But with her dream job on the table? She admitted, she still should fly to LA. Her mom would understand. Still, that realization made her feel worse.

"Great, he's here," Henderson said, and Dana looked up from her phone.

Whereas Henderson moved in constant angles, Brett Austen walked in like a flowing stream of water. He entered and smiled first at Henderson, then Sal, before sitting down at a table in front of a large wall adorned with A's logos and sponsors.

"Sorry I'm late," Austen said. "Anything new?"

The reporters laughed. Dana rolled her eyes and tried not to think about her mom.

* * *

"What up, Nguyen?" The booming voice met Derek when he entered the stadium commissary.

Derek turned, always amazed at one of the biggest non-pro athletes he had ever seen. While Derek was thin, compact, and in his late forties, Roy had the physique of a prison enforcer and the demeanor of Mr. Rogers.

"There he is, my favorite degenerate," said James, Roy's partner in the commissary. James was the one next to Roy's zero—tall, lanky, and with leathery skin. In decades past, he may have had a cigarette hanging from his lower lip. Now, his gravelly voice shared how he had spent his breaks.

Derek was always amazed how the two of them existed in the same cramped space, day after day, managing the inventory of lemonade, beer, water, peanuts, and licorice. They moved through the room like choreographed dancers amid the chaos.

Derek interacted with Roy and James almost every day, though Roy only worked A's and Warriors games and split time between food concessions at the Coliseum and his co-owned food truck on the Embarcadero. Derek often made a point of visiting Roy's Super Sandwiches at least twice a month for gourmet, gut-busting grilled cheese sandwiches on his way to working a Giants game. Roy and his business partner were looking to expand to another truck, and Derek hoped those constant visits might result in a gig on the second truck.

"It's just another day in paradise," Derek said, a common refrain.

James looked around. The harsh fluorescent lighting illuminated the concrete box and industrial restaurant equipment. He raised his arms. "Well, if this is paradise, I'd hate to see hell."

"Hey, guy, how are the games?" Derek asked. "Jets score?"

"Jets are up ten-zero now, but the Raiders are driving," Roy said.

Roy was also a valuable resource during Derek's shift. He had a front-row seat to all of the NFL action with two TVs focused on two games and his smartphone set against a box of sanitary gloves streaming another. Roy was Derek's sports ticker, feeding Derek updated scores every time he came in to restock.

"Wow, seems you've got more riding on today, Derek," Roy said. "Doin' okay? Able to handle this action?"

"Nope," James said. He was a man of few words. "Action can't be handled."

"Yeah, yeah." Derek dismissed him with a wave, still fixed to the Raiders-Jets game on TV. He watched a twenty-yard run for a touchdown to cut the Jets' lead to three.

"Ah, I'm jinxing them by being here," Derek said. The more money Derek put down on a game, the less he enjoyed watching. The universe didn't want him to watch his bets progress, and he didn't want to suffer by hanging on to every play and score. The anxiety was one of the reasons he bet while working. Most of the day was spent walking up and down concrete steps in the stands with only occasional glances at scoreboards and updates from Roy. If he had to watch at home or the bar, Derek didn't know what he'd do.

"Whatcha hawking today?" Roy said.

"Lemonade. Lots of families on a warm day. I'll be sticky, but I'll get paid." Like all vendors hawking the aisles, Derek worked on straight commission. The more products he sold, the more money in his pocket. He tried selling it all, and while alcohol was always a big seller, he didn't earn as much per unit as he did with lemonade. On a warm day like today, with plenty of families in the stands, this was the best chance for a payday, maybe three hundred and fifty dollars. And with a few fudged spoils (discarded cups counted as spills), he might push that to four hundred. He needed every dollar today to get his daughter into dance.

Derek pulled down a tray and strapped it around his neck while James loaded it up with cold lemonade.

"Going to be hot," James said, already at his spoken-word quota for the day. For Oakland, hot was high eighties and in the sun.

"Yep, and a big crowd to cheer on Austen," Derek said. "Got a good feeling about today." Derek smiled and placed the sweaty cups in his tray.

Meanwhile, Mike, "the Peanut Guy," placed his bags of peanuts in his carrier. In the world of vendors, Mike was semi-famous. From his hand, a bag of peanuts found its way up rows and across sections to its consumer with unquestioned accuracy.

"Hey, guy," Derek said. "Big game today. Ready?"

"Always," Mike said. "Last baseball game of the year, unfortunately, and I'm just getting used to being cashless."

Like all things in modern life, smartphones and Wi-Fi had revolutionized the fan experience. There was no longer the communal passing of money down the line and product heading back. Now, it was just a phone or a swipe.

"Oh, Raiders just scored," Roy said.

Derek looked over and groaned. He was sure that the Raider game was a sure thing, and watching them score put a sense of dread inside him. What would happen if he lost not one parlay but both of them? Owen would cut him off or worse. Pam would report his delinquency, and without baseball, he didn't have the income that came from a game nearly every day.

The dark and oppressing "Imperial Death March" from the *Star Wars* movies blasted on his phone. It was Pam.

"Yeah," Derek said.

"At the Coliseum today?" Pam asked.

"Yeah, big game."

"So, the dance payment is due tomorrow. How close are you to sending me money."

"Pam, I can't deal with this right now. I've gotta go out and sell. I'll stop by tomorrow and give you the cash. Promise."

"All of it?"

"Really, Pam? I'm trying to get it to you."

"I need it all, Derek. I've got bills, and I've drained everything I've got covering for you. You need to come through. Come on by the salon tomorrow around noon. I've got a free hour to meet up."

"I'll try."

"You'll do, Derek. Or else I have to call the court."

Pam hung up, and Derek closed his flip phone. He needed today to go his way.

Before Derek turned to leave the commissary, Roy pulled Derek aside.

"Hey, I talked to Verne. He said we're a go to get another truck, and he's willing to give you a chance managing it."

While Roy was the face, the culinary inspiration and chef for Roy's Super Sandwiches, Verne, was the business. He managed the books, the schedules, the marketing, and everything non-cooking related.

"That's great, guy," Derek said, slapping Roy's meaty shoulder. "I need a steady gig, especially now that the Raiders left town, and my knees aren't getting any younger."

"I know, right? One thing Verne wanted to know. I mentioned you're connected to some bookies, and he was concerned that you're a deadbeat gambler. I've seen you lay down some big numbers, but you've got it all under control, right?"

"Oh yeah, of course," Derek said. His attempts at confidence felt shallow. "I've got a system, and I take some losses, but I get a lot of wins."

"That's what I said to Verne. Can you meet us on the Embarcadero at two tomorrow?"

Derek nodded. This was promising. But his positive vibes sank when Mike let out a whoop.

"Raiders intercept inside the red zone," Mike said. "Derek, your whole theory about the Raiders not performing on the East Coast isn't working out too well, man."

The tightness Derek felt in his throat, lungs, and chest was nothing new. When a sure win was snatched away by a fluke fumble and score, or when a player heaved a shot from halfcourt that ruined the point spread, or all the bets went bad in a single moment, the acid coming up his throat and the deflation of his lungs always hit the same way. Those other times, it was manageable. Most often, only *he* suffered the consequences. The idea that he wouldn't see Jasmine again was too much to take this early in the day. He put a hand on the table to brace himself.

"You, okay?" James said. "You don't look so good."

* * *

Brett smiled and answered all the questions from the dozens of reporters crowded in a room originally designed for the media to get in a bite to eat before the game. Yes, he had an egg sandwich for breakfast. No, he wasn't worried about Clint Shakely pitching today. Of course, he was going to try and get the hit. And no, sitting was not an option. He was going to get the hit, or he wasn't. When a random reporter Brett didn't know asked if he used "slumpbusters," a term where a struggling baseball player sleeps with a very unattractive woman to break a bad streak, Brett nodded to Henderson, and the press conference was over.

The toughest part of hitting so well this season wasn't the ability to get a hit consistently or seeing the pitches well or even getting lucky with a bloop single, it was all the obligations and distractions off the field. There were national interviews and press conferences. There were community obligations, stuff he enjoyed but still was part of the job. There were profiles. There was a lack of anonymity. It wasn't like Ted Williams in 1941, when only print reporters hung around before and after the game, and that was it. It wasn't even like 1994, when Tony Gwynn had the last real shot at hitting .400 before a strike brought that dream to an end. Now, it wasn't even called "press." It was called "brand exposure," and he dealt with impressions and clicks. Sure, the tools were better, the travel had certainly improved, but maybe it was easier when Teddy Ballgame did it.

Henderson led Brett out of the room.

"Man, it seems like everyone wants to know why I'm playing and not sitting," Brett said. "I don't know how many times I have to say this game is meant to be played, not for ballplayers to sit on statistics."

"I know," Henderson said. "Just looking for their angle."

They don't think you can man up and do it, Brett. They think you're going to fail. You're gonna be remembered as the guy who choked.

"They think going .399 is choking," Brett said, rebutting the demon.

"Nobody's saying that," Henderson said. "Now, we have your sit-down with Dana Peck."

Don't believe that fuck. Their stories are going to be about your failure. And now, Dana Peck's going to school you.

Brett shook his head. The demon was going to be bad today.

"So, how long do I have to dance with her?" Brett asked.

Henderson was leading him down the final tunnel to the dugout where Dana and the Baseball Broadcast Network cameras were waiting.

"About twenty minutes. They need enough for the New York pregame show and cutaways during the game."

"Anything I need to worry about?"

"Nothing you didn't just answer ad nauseum. Just keep your animosity toward Shakely at a minimum."

"Why? He's a dick."

"Well, yes, but it doesn't play well."

Especially when he strikes your ass out.

Brett slammed his hand against the wall as they moved out of the runway toward the dugout and into the sun. Brett wished the demon would shut up.

"Don't worry, you'll be fine. You've done hundreds of these," Henderson said.

They turned the corner, and Brett wiped away his frustration and put on the smile everyone expected. The camera was set with Dana already mic'd up. Her producer and cameraperson said a quick hello before supplying a small mic for Brett to slide under his uniform and pin to the lapel. Sal Grant was behind them, his face buried in his smartphone, no doubt lining up deals for his other clients.

Brett walked over to Peck, who wore a cream-colored blouse under her light-blue pantsuit. Her auburn hair bounced as she stood up and greeted Brett. While he had met with her several times, that first interview was the only one he remembered. Brett knew he had been wrong. He was young, dumb, naïve, and arrogant. But he'd learned a quick lesson—women can be attractive *and* smart and dedicated to their jobs just as much as their male counterparts. He had to always be on guard.

"Good to see you again. Thank you for coming on."

"No problem." Brett took her hand and shook it firmly, then sat on the stool near the on-deck circle with the camera focused on him with the batting cage in the background.

"No offense, but I won't miss this part of this season," Brett said. "The constant media stuff has been a little tiring."

"I can only imagine," Peck said. "That press conference was packed."

Brett took a breath. Now it was time to play the media game. He had a hot mic. Everything was now on the record. He had learned the hard way that the camera and microphone pick up everything and can be cut, taken out of context, and pushed onto the internet without explanation. His blowup with Dana a few years ago still lived on YouTube, and he was reminded constantly on social media with memes of that poor judgment. It was time to be vanilla.

Peck gave a nod to her producer and the cameraperson to confirm they were ready. Henderson and Sal also stood at attention, intently watching. Brett thought they were like stage parents, watching in the wings, anxious that the performances weren't going to meet expectations. Once the cameraperson gave sign they were rolling, Peck directed her attention to Brett.

"So, do you have tomorrow's breakfast planned?"

Seriously? Brett thought. Tomorrow was only a few hours away.

* * *

Like most athletes after years in the spotlight, Austen was much more guarded since Dana had interviewed him that time long ago. Not many people were going to pierce his protective armor. She felt bad. She had destroyed his innocence toward the media. But if it meant that he didn't treat her and her female colleagues like pieces of meat, at least to their faces, it was worth it. She smiled at her concession.

It wasn't Dana's best interview. In fact, it was tame and lame. Even the way she started it off with the breakfast question was tepid. Dana was distracted. Not only with her mom, but she knew what Palmetto wanted, and it wasn't anything controversial. Just get the canned answers everyone expected and move on. She caught herself on the brink of boredom as she asked about his process, his rituals, his approach, the pitches, his place in history, disappointment if he didn't get to .400. These were all questions he'd been asked a hundred times.

"Clint Shakely is now pitching today," Dana said. "You've never been able to hit him well. Does that make you reconsider playing today?"

"Not at all. Shakely has had my number, but that doesn't mean it can't change. Plus, to let that stat dictate my actions and approach is an insult to everyone I've played against before. I'll be ready."

"Didn't you face him in your first professional at bat? I mean, this goes back to your very first meeting."

The fire in Austen's eyes flared. She wondered if he'd blow up again at her. Instead, he took a long blink. When his eyes opened, they were cold and lacked the emotion she had seen a moment earlier.

"Well, you gotta remember, he was an established veteran and, like you said, it was my first game. He was an All-Star. The best way to turn it around is to get a hit today."

"I bet, out of all the pitchers, he brings you the most doubt."

"Nope, no doubt here."

"None? No worries that the one pitcher you struggle against is the same one who stands in your way of reaching .400?"

Austen turned his head. "That's an interesting question. I'm not worried. I have no doubt. Doubt in this game is a killer. If you accept you're going to fail a few times, then you remain confident in your ability. If you lose that, then failure feasts on doubt, and you find yourself in a slump."

"So, you haven't had doubt?"

"Not this season, no. Doubt is the enemy. I have no time or room for it."

"Thanks," Dana said. That was the answer she needed. She motioned she was finished.

"They don't ask questions like you do, Dana." Austen smiled. He was being sarcastic, she knew, but that smile was pretty good. To the unjaded, his charm rendered people defenseless. "I hear you're up for a job in Kansas City. Best of luck to you."

Austen knew? Who didn't know about her interest in this Kansas City job? He caught her surprise and smiled. It was a playful jab. She wasn't the only one who had sources.

CHAPTER 9

Preparation

Lizzie opened the door to her parents' house to see Carol Rogers on her hands and knees scrubbing the carpet. The demure seventy-two-year-old was working herself into a sweat. Lizzie closed the door and looked down at her mom at the base of her father's hospital bed in the middle of the living room.

"You didn't have to clean the house, it's just us," Lizzie said.

"Well, I spilled on the carpet, and it needed cleaning, so..."

"But, Mom, this house is spotless. You don't have to do any of this."

"Oh, Elizabeth, what else am I going to do? Watch your father or watch TV? I can't just sit here."

Carol's frustration gave way to love as she stood, smiled, and spread her arms wide to greet her daughter and granddaughter. Compared to Kevin, Carol could get lost in the shadows. A woman of Japanese descent, Carol wore one of the many A's jerseys Kevin had bought her over the years. Today, of course, it was Austen's number five in kelly green, which framed her dark-silver pixie cut. After six months, Lizzie still wasn't used to this hairdo. In most of Lizzie's memories, Carol wore a short, shoulder-length bob that never aged her. When Kevin began losing his hair to chemo, she shaved hers too, and when it grew back to this length, Kevin said he liked it this way, and she kept it.

"I'm just saying, save your energy. It's going to be a long day."

"Having you two here gives me all the energy I need," her mom said.

Carol looked at the sandwiches in Lizzie and Heidi's arms, and her eyes and mouth opened wide.

"Oh, big sandwiches." Carol was determined to make the day more joyous than somber. "Bring them over to the kitchen so we can slice them."

"Grandpa always liked the big sandwiches," Heidi said.

"Still does. I'm not going to let him have them today, though." Carol winked. It was her brand of optimism. Practical, with a glimpse of hope. Carol went to the pantry and pulled out bags of chips, pretzels, and other snacks, which Lizzie took to mean that Stephen was bringing a couple servings of potato salad he had bought at the store on the way over. Stephen and his wife, Leticia, never cooked, and if it was a potluck, they brought the minimal amount of food they found at the store. It was no wonder the whole family was overweight. Their idea of being frugal was getting a value meal at McDonald's. In fact, Lizzie wouldn't be surprised if Stephen brought a couple twenty-piece Chicken McNuggets as snacks.

"Wasn't Stephen going to handle snacks today?" Lizzie asked.

Carol nodded and kept pulling down the salty treats.

Lizzie shook her head. "You always cover for Stephen. You'd have thought he'd figure it out by now."

"Elizabeth, Stephen's a grown man now, and he's not going to change. Better to acknowledge it and move on than to be disappointed when he doesn't meet your expectations."

Heidi's eyebrows went up in amazement. Lizzie was also surprised by her mom's rare moment of candor. Normally, she would just make an excuse, but perhaps she was already emotionally drained and didn't have the capacity for any more of Stephen's bullshit.

"Besides, today is for your father. I want to make it the best for him," Carol said, her voice cracking.

Carol put the chips on the counter and grabbed the lip of the granite countertop. Her head dropped, and she breathed deep; however, the strength Carol wanted to portray broke down into sobs. Lizzie walked over and took her mom in her arms.

"It's okay," Lizzie said. "You don't have to be strong today. We're here for you."

Carol wasn't one to accept comfort often. She was always the one giving it. But as a fellow mom, Lizzie knew her mother needed that hug, and Carol's tears began to flow. Lizzie nodded to Heidi to retrieve a box of tissues. When she returned, Carol took the tissue and wiped and blew her nose, though she stayed in Lizzie's arms.

"I'm just starting to think of life without your father. It's been nearly fifty years with him, and the idea of not having him near me is... I just don't know what to do."

Lizzie had been with Eddie for twenty-five years, and when she had made the decision to leave him, the loss of her partner and best friend was the hardest part of all, a loss she was still mourning. How hard it must be, Lizzie thought, to know the love affair between her mom and dad was only going to stop because of cancer and death, not broken trust and rejection.

Carol took Lizzie and Heidi's hands and led them to the entertainment unit and a washed-out photo of her and Kevin. They were standing, holding hands, eyes locked on each other with the sands of Waikiki Beach and the Pacific Ocean behind them.

"Your father, your grandfather, had seen me for a total of seventy-five days before this picture was taken," Carol said. "Of course, in between the first week he met me and when he came back to Hawaii was thirteen months. He met me on his way to Vietnam, then he stayed on his way back, and by the time he left the islands again, we were married, and I was joining him on the mainland."

"I still can't believe that story," Lizzie said. "What if it didn't work out? You were in the Bay Area with nowhere to go."

"There was never a doubt, Elizabeth. I knew even before he left for Vietnam. That week before he left was the best week of my life up to that point. I was just eighteen years old, but then it was like time stood still but moved so fast while I was with him. Then, he left, and I had never known such sadness. He wrote these long letters every week, and it confirmed what I already knew. He was the man for me. He wrote to me about everything, even the horrors he saw. And I think it helped him. He was always honest with me and, somehow, I was never repulsed by what he had to do. I just loved him and wanted to do whatever I could to support him. So, when he came back, we were more in love than ever, and he asked me to marry him two days later."

"How did Grandpa feel about a *haole* taking his girl to the continent?" Lizzie asked.

"Oh, Daddy wasn't pleased at all. I mean, for one, he had a small store in Ala Moana, and he counted on me to help run it, and now he was out a trustworthy employee. Plus, this white mainlander taking his little girl? But, in the end, my mom convinced him that it was going to happen regardless of what he said or did, and if they wanted to see grandbabies, he had better get on board."

Carol turned back to Kevin. The last six months had taken a toll on him. His barrel chest was as thin as some of the boys Heidi had brought home. His once-full, wavy head of hair was now bald with spots dotting across it. His cheeks sunk like sucking on a straw, but he was still there. His beautiful blue eyes were open and staring at Lizzie.

With a small move of his right index finger, Kevin motioned for them to come over. Lizzie led Heidi over to the side of the bed. The contradictory feelings of sadness, regret, joy, fright, and poignancy overwhelmed her. This was her dad. The man who had taken her out for ice cream and taught her how to drive. The man who had let her paint his toenails and gone to every dance recital and tennis match. He was the one who had been there for Heidi's birth and laughed at her Tickle Me Elmo doll. Yet, it took all of his vast strength to wiggle a finger, breathe through a mask, and look at them. The sounds of his wheezy breath were more intense now that he was awake.

Kevin opened his hand, and Lizzie placed hers in it. She felt his clammy fingers, calloused with fifty years of swinging a hammer and turning screws on home-improvement projects, grip her hand and give it a weak squeeze. She clasped her other hand around his and leaned down to look in his eyes. Those deep-blue eyes with which Carol fell in love. Those eyes that smiled at Lizzie when he'd tucked her into bed.

"Hi Daddy," she said. She stroked his cheek. There was recognition in those eyes, and it was almost too much to bear. Tears streamed down her face, but she had to keep it together for everyone. "What do you think? Will Austen get his hit today?"

Kevin nodded and smiled. He tried to talk, his words barely audible. She brought her ear closer to his mouth. "What's that, Daddy?"

"Gonna crush it," he said. The words came out lighter than a whisper. If the room had any sound other than the nearby machines and running refrigerator, she wouldn't have heard him.

Lizzie smiled and nodded. "Heck yeah." She laughed and wiped the tears from her eyes.

Kevin laughed too, but the act consumed a lot of energy, and he tried to take a deep breath. He closed his eyes to rest.

"Heidi, why don't you sit next to your grandpa and grandma, and I'll get the big sandwiches ready for everyone."

As Lizzie left, she watched Kevin's eyebrows raise at hearing "big sandwiches." Even at the end, he loved the big sandwich.

* * *

Will was still frustrated. He felt like he was being absorbed into Paul's oversized life, just at the point when he was searching for his own space.

"What's wrong?" Paul asked as they rode the elevator to field level. "You've hardly talked. Was the food okay?"

"It's fine," Will said with more sass than he'd intended. He kept staring forward, not wanting to acknowledge Paul.

"Wow, okay. Well, we can go find our seats, then you can go get some autographs."

"I'll meet you at the seats." Will knew he was being unfair to Paul, but he didn't care.

"Don't you want to know where we're sitting?"

"Right-field line? Behind the visitor's bullpen?"

"Yeah."

"Cool. I'll look for the crowd around you taking selfies."

The doors opened, and Will didn't wait for Paul's response. He pushed out into the concourse and toward the left-field line and the A's dugout. He knew this new identity crisis wasn't Paul's fault. Everything was just moving so quickly. Paul and his mom had started dating less than a year ago, were engaged in April, and planning to get married in a little more than a month with a small ceremony on the shores of Lake Tahoe. Where was he in this equation? And what about the memory of his dad?

For the last seven years, Will had been defined by his dad's death. At first, there was this sympathy and sadness. But over time, he and his mom had learned what life was like without his dad's physical presence. His dad was always around—the family pictures, the stories they told and retold, the everyday things that spurred a memory. But Will felt those reminders were slowly slipping away in favor of a new future.

Though it was still more than an hour before the first pitch, the Coliseum was already turning into a circus. The wall between the stands and the dugout was now packed with autograph seekers, mostly kids but also the occasional grown man with several baseballs in his pockets and various hats ready to be signed and later sold on eBay. Will stood at the fence with a ball and a Sharpie, just in case. Tyson Porter, the retired Blue Jays star, was on the field in a shirt and tie, joking around with some of the players. First Dan Muir, now Tyson Porter. If he met Dana Peck, he'd get the whole broadcast team. Will jammed himself into the left side of the crowd and held out a ball in one hand and a Sharpie in the other.

"Tyson," Will said, along with every other fan.

"Hey, I don't get to sign many of these anymore," Porter said, half joking. "People forget about us old guys pretty quick."

* * *

With his media obligations done, Brett rushed to the video room where he picked up an iPad loaded with the Mariners' pitchers, including Clint Shakely. While Cobb, Williams, and Gwynn didn't have the media demands, his film study of pitcher nuances and tendencies put him at an advantage. Of course, the pitchers did the same thing, but he was certainly more prepared. As he internalized all the data, it only prepped him for that one-on-one confrontation. In the moment, the stat sheets wouldn't help, only what his intuition told him.

He watched pitch after pitch from Shakely's last start, looking for arm angle, grip, and release point. Why had he given him so much trouble over the years? Brett should be able to hit him easy. He swiped and zoomed in. Wait, what was that? Brett rotated his fingers to rewind the pitch. He watched Shakely throw again. He squinted. Brett went to another Shakely sequence. Before he went into his windup, Shakely pushed his thumb on his ring finger to crack it before he threw the curveball. This was new. Was it a tipped pitch? He checked another sequence. Same minor push, another curveball. It didn't happen with every curveball Shakely threw, but it was there only for the curve. Same thing happened whether he pitched from a windup or out of the stretch. Brett pulled up a game from a month ago. No knuckle push. Must have been something Shakely unconsciously picked up and didn't know it yet. This was an opportunity.

Confident, Brett had to get onto the field and get in some thwacks. Time in the cage always got his mind right for a game. After warm-ups and stretches, he finally stepped in for some batting practice. Since he had left his house in Alameda, this was the first time he felt at home. There was just him, the bat, and the ball hurtling toward him. He relaxed, the tension in his shoulders and neck floating away. Neither his eyes nor his hands betrayed him. With few exceptions, each connection was square and true, the ball flying off the bat and spraying to different points in the outfield. Brett wasn't a power hitter. He had power. He had hit thirty home runs this season, but most of his damage came with hits into the gap. He batted second in the lineup. His average speed made him a liability on the basepaths, but the club needed to maximize his plate appearances.

Brett stepped back from the plate one last time and took in what may be his final batting-practice session in Oakland. He would miss this dump if he left. Brett looked around and saw the myriad of fans lining the wall for an autograph, all calling his name.

"Brett," said a female fan in her forties in a flirty voice. She might be interesting if he had that kind of fetish.

"Austen, over here," called a teenager wearing his Number-five T-shirt, curly hair poofed out under a green cap.

"Mr. Austen, I was at your first-ever game in Stockton. Can I talk to you?" That was a weird one, Brett thought. Rather than search for the fan, he turned back to the cage.

"We love you, Brett."

"You can do it. We believe in you."

"Hey, Brett, show 'em how we hit in Texas."

A chill went through him, but he shook it off.

Oh, Brett, you can't get distracted that easily, or I'm going to be in your head all day.

For his final pitch, Brett always asked the batting-practice pitcher, usually bench coach Gary Sampson, to throw the ball low and away. It was his favorite pitch to hit, and he typically tagged it for a double down the line. He pointed to his spot. Sampson nodded and went into his windup.

See ball, hit ball.

Take this, Shakely.

He swung. And missed.

Oh, Brett, today's going to be fun.

Brett drew an anxious breath, then laughed it off. "That won't do my average any good."

The players around him laughed too. A swing and miss happens occasionally, just not normally to Brett. He pointed low and away again. Sampson threw again. This time he tagged the ball right on the screws down the left-field line.

"That's more like it," Brett said and tipped his cap to Sampson.

* * *

When Austen swung and missed his planned final batting-practice pitch, Will gasped. He had never seen Austen swing that badly. There were sounds of surprise and a little laughter. Even when he connected on the next pitch, Will remained surprised.

"Even the greatest sometimes miss," JT Berman, the A's centerfielder said. He handed a ball back to a fan next to Will.

"Do you know if Brett is going to sign before the game?" another fan asked. He was wearing a bright-green A's tank top with bright-gold trim. "I need to give him something."

"Man, that guy is so busy," Berman said. "He's got interviews, press conferences, and needs to get his work in before the game. I don't know how he does it."

Austen jogged in and passed Berman and the crowd next to the dugout.

"Brett. Brett. Brett," said the guy in the green tank top. "I gotta tell you about my grandpa."

Austen ignored everyone and continued to walk into the dugout, across the tunnel, and into the clubhouse. Will just watched. He wasn't going to be among the crowd demanding his attention.

His phone buzzed. It was a direct message from Amanda. He had almost forgotten about her, and he chastised himself for being distracted by kid things, like getting an autograph. He opened the message.

Amanda: *Hey, just got here. U around?*

Will: *Yeah, where u sitting?*

He walked up the steps while he waited for her reply.

"Hey," a familiar voice said.

He looked to his right, and there was Amanda in her bright-yellow jersey, along with her parents and younger brother. Will had known the Wrights for much of his life. After all, Amanda was a classmate throughout elementary and junior high. He even remembered a couple birthday parties at her house.

Amanda smiled at Will with what he thought were the most perfect and flirtatious eyes. He smiled back with what he thought was his most dorky and goofy face. Such was the fate of a teenager still growing into his features.

"Hey, it's Will Jenson," the man to Amanda's left said. Michael Wright was dressed in all A's gear, including vintage A's satin Starter jacket from the late eighties to the worn A's cap with at least two dozen pins adorning the material like rhinestones to a country-western singer's jean jacket. Next to him was Theresa Wright, similarly dressed but wearing a hat that was more pinned to the top of her hair. Amanda's younger brother was smiling and hopping up and down, excited to see the players.

"Hello, Mr. Wright, Mrs. Wright," Will said, remembering Paul's advice and trying not to deliver bad puns. "Hey, Amanda."

"Amanda said we might run into you here. Sit down and visit, at least until somebody claims those seats," Mrs. Wright said, directing Will to sit in the row in front of them. Will looked at Amanda, who shrugged and raised her eyebrows, like she had played a joke on Will. He'd have to talk to her parents. Will peered back, vowing to get back at her later. It was a small attempt at flirtation. She smiled. It had landed. *Good job, Will!* he thought

Will went right to the playbook Paul had prescribed. He shared how much he'd enjoyed Mrs. Wright's English class the previous year and how tough his new English teacher, Mr. Dunaway, was. He was deferential to Mr. Wright, making sure he answered with "sir." Amanda rolled her eyes at his act. She saw right through it but played along.

"So, who are you with, Will? Your mom here?" Mr. Wright asked, his eyes still focused on the field. He smashed a handful of sunflower seeds into his mouth, some remnants sticking to his gray beard contrasting with his dark skin.

"Nah, I'm with Paul, my stepdad. Well, future stepdad." It was still strange to call Paul his stepdad.

"Oh, really?" Mr. Wright said. "Who's she marrying?"

"I told you, Michael," Mrs. Wright said. "Paul Buckley."

"The Sports guy on KARC? You didn't say that."

"Yes, I did," Mrs. Wright said. Both she and Amanda shook their heads in embarrassment. "So glad your mom is finding some happiness. She's such a nice lady."

"Thanks," Will said. He needed to break away and engage Amanda. Unfortunately, two couples in their thirties appeared and chased him from the seat. Deflated, he didn't know what to do next. He still wanted to talk to Amanda.

"Well. Tell your stepdad hello for us," Mr. Wright said. Apparently, Will's visit with the Wrights was over.

Will stood up and went back into the aisle.

"Daddy, I wanna hang out with Will for a bit."

"Not right now. We're here as a family."

"Maybe a little later," Mrs. Wright said. "Let Will get back to his stepdad, and we'll see how the game goes. You can text him later."

Will secretly thanked Paul. He had called how to work the parents. Maybe Will would get her number. That would be a promotion from DMs.

"I'll DM you," Amanda said.

Damn, no digits yet.

"Nice to see you again, Will," Mr. Wright said. "Say hello to Paul Buckley for me. Tell him your mom is the Alaska Crab."

Mr. Wright laughed, and his face jiggled at his joke. Amanda buried her face in her hands, and it took Will a second to get the joke. Oh, yeah, the catchphrase, "Catch of the Day." This was what he would have to look forward to for the rest of his life as the stepson to a local celebrity.

Final Tosses

Just focus on what's in front of you, Lizzie told herself. Right now, her attention was on the long serrated knife and cutting the three three-foot sandwiches into individual portions. She halfway listened as the Baseball Broadcast Network studio hosts discussed the final Sunday of games and the upcoming playoffs. Her ears perked up when they transitioned to Brett Austen.

"And, of course, in Oakland, we have Brett Austen trying to become the first player in eighty years to break through and hit .400 for the season," studio host Ray Ford said.

The bright blue of Ford's crisp suit drew her attention toward the TV screen. Ford was standing on fake infield grass in front of a large LED screen with two baseball legends—Mark Wheatley, a Hall of Fame first baseman for the Chicago Cubs and Atlanta Braves, and the recently retired and likely future Hall of Famer Esteban Ruiz, who won one hundred and eighty games for the Los Angeles Dodgers and New York Yankees.

"Well, he already has it," Wheatley said. He was a six-foot-four, muscle-bound behemoth when he played; however, his muscles had turned in the last ten years, and the buttons of his purple sport coat strained to keep in his gut. "He could have just sat today and had it. Now, he puts it at risk by going out there."

"He's been upfront. He was going to play today to thank the fans," Ruiz said in his clipped Dominican accent. "But, yeah, if he doesn't get a hit that first inning, then he has to chase a hit the rest of the game. It all comes down to that first at bat."

"Is it the right decision?" Ford asked.

"If it were me," Ruiz said, "I wouldn't play. I'd preserve that average. I mean, he's been eating egg sandwiches every day for four months. You don't want to make it all for nothing."

"The A's are out of the playoffs," Wheatley said. His large hands waved across his body as he became more animated. "Today is rather meaningless. Nobody would fault him for sitting. But then again, Brett Austen is old school. He says the fans bought tickets expecting him to play, so he's going to play."

"Would you?" Ford asked.

Wheatley shook his bald, shiny, black head and smiled. "No. Of course, I'm much more selfish than Brett Austen. It would be different if the team was playing for something, for sure. But this is historic. Eighty years of history."

"But you'd have your manager tell everyone it was his idea," Ruiz said with a chuckle.

"Oh, definitely. Make it the manager's decision to hold you out. He can take all the heat. That's why you pay them. I'd definitely make it seem like it was the manager's decision."

Lizzie watched Heidi lean in toward the bed and laugh.

"What did Grandpa say?" Lizzie asked.

"He said, 'Wheatley's a coward,'" Heidi said.

Lizzie smiled.

"Our own Dana Peck sat down with Brett Austen to talk about .400, his approach at the plate, what this season means to him, and his future breakfast plans."

Lizzie smiled and went back to cutting sandwiches. While her eyes were focused on the turkey, Italian, and pastrami sandwiches in front of her, her ears were on the Austen interview.

"So, do you have tomorrow's breakfast planned?" Dana Peck asked.

"Oh, definitely." Brett smiled and laughed as though that question hadn't been asked one hundred times before. "In fact, I'm dreaming of a Belgian waffle with blueberries."

"I'm sure," Peck said. "What has been the most difficult part about hitting at such a high level for so long?"

"The biggest thing is staying focused," Brett said. "I don't mean at the plate, because I really try to stay focused for every plate appearance, but the preparation to get ready for that at bat is the harder part. When you're going as well as I have this season, it's easy to take a mental day off, not watch film, not eat right, not study the pitchers. But I realized that this whole thing is a result of an obsession with process."

"So, you think you can do this again next year?"

"I didn't say that. I know this is a special season. Things have just come together the right way to have an extraordinary year. But I think I can have another good season next year if I keep my focus on the daily work and preparation."

* * *

There were better assignments than Section 104 behind the visitor's bullpen down the right-field line. Fred had been offered the high-end sections behind home plate for years. That was where dedicated wait staff catered to the ticketholders' every need, tickets were used as tax write-offs, and most were owned by corporate partners and given away to impress their clients or reward high producers. Certainly, at those price points, there were fewer instances of violence. But Fred also thought those sections were rather stale. With more expensive seats and familiarity came more entitlement and complaints about everything from autograph seekers to other fans distracting from the experience.

After twenty-two years with the A's, the last ten on the lower cross aisle of Section 104, this was Fred's neighborhood. He enjoyed being one of the first people to welcome the fans to the game. It was one of Fred's favorite parts of the job. Sometimes, it was helping a couple to their spot on a date night or greeting a longtime fan with whom he'd built a relationship. The best was helping families with children and the sense of awe they felt in this big space.

Of course, Fred also had to deal with the sneaks, the fans who had tickets for upper decks but tried to move down. He was called a "seat Nazi" a couple times, just for doing his job. He got it. Tickets were expensive, and when seats were empty, why not let someone else sit there? But that wasn't his decision. Who knew why those seats were empty? Could be that the fans were getting food. Could be they were late to the game. But his job was to help people to their own seats. If they wanted to move closer to the action, there was an app to upgrade. In his section, fans needed to have the right tickets.

Fred looked out onto the green grass. The Mariners were on the field getting their work in before the game. At home plate, the batting cage was out, and the sound of the crack of the bat came every ten to fifteen seconds. Players were on the field playing long catch and watching fly balls. Some were hitting off a tee and more were talking with coaches and other personnel.

"You're going to miss this," Denny said from one section over.

"I am," Fred called back. "Don't get me started."

Fred had become friends with a few of the regular season-ticket holders who sat in his section. Some had even nicknamed him "Mayor of One-oh-four," a moniker he embraced. As mayor, a few of the season-ticket holders became family, and he and Marjorie had even attended a couple weddings. He watched children grow into adult fans in the seats in front of him. Beyond the games, it was the relationships he built with the people he interacted with almost every day for half the year that he would miss the most.

"Fred," a voice called.

Fred turned to see his good friend Winnie Price. He had worked with Winnie and her husband, Jerry, at the post office for more than fifteen years. When Winnie and Jerry had retired five years after Fred, they became regulars at A's games. When Fred moved down into their section, he knew right away that he had found his spot. Each game was a reunion.

"Winnie," Fred said and went into their hug. Whether they had just seen each other the night before or a couple weeks since the last homestand, Fred and Winnie hugged in greeting as if they hadn't seen each other in years. Recently, the significance of these hugs had become more poignant. When Jerry suddenly died two years ago, Fred and Marjorie were there for Winnie as she navigated his death and adjusted to life without him. So, when Marjorie got sick last year, there was no question Winnie would be there for them. Sometimes she stayed with Marjorie when Fred came to games. Other times, she brought dinner and conversation. She helped take Marjorie to appointments, and Winnie was the first person outside his family whom he had hugged at the hospital when Margie passed.

"How are you doing, Fred?" Winnie asked, her hands still clasping his. She wore a white windbreaker over a green A's logo T-shirt. Her signature green visor shaded her eyes. Her dark sunglasses contrasted with her white hair. "It's your final game here."

"It's not necessarily my final game. Just the last one as an usher."

"You know what I mean," Winnie said. She smiled, trying to hold back tears. Her emotional response almost broke Fred.

"Well, I'm glad you're here."

"Wouldn't miss it for the world. Brett's going to make history today." Winnie smiled and gave Fred's hands a squeeze.

"Exactly. He's going to do it today, isn't he?"

"He sure is, and on your special day."

"That's very kind, but I don't think... No, he's not thinking of me." Fred smiled.

Fred took Winnie's arm and led her down to her seat in the third row. While Jerry had been gone the past couple seasons, Winnie still paid for that extra seat. Sometimes, she'd bring a friend, a child, or a grandchild. Sometimes, she just had the empty seat for Jerry's spirit. Fred expected that many of those family and friends had asked for her extra ticket today. Still, the seat next to her sat empty. He suspected she wanted Jerry to be here for this one.

As Winnie sat, Fred looked back up at the stands. He smiled to himself as the young woman he met on the BART train came down the steps toward him. She smiled and waved, her inhibitions dulled by a couple drinks in the parking lot. And just as he had suspected, she was one of only two women with six men, their chests puffed out on bravado and beer. Fred was going to have to deal with this group throughout the day.

"Hi," she said. "Remember me from BART?"

"Of course, good to see you and welcome," Fred said. He prided himself on being cordial and polite. "Can I see your tickets? Do you need help finding your seat?"

She pulled out her phone and pulled up the ticket and showed it to Fred. As he suspected, their tickets weren't in the lowest section but just about ten rows further up. They knew this. They just hoped the woman's charm and cleavage might manipulate Fred into better seats. She smiled before a tall guy with a tight designer V-neck, gold chains, and pink shorts nudged her.

"A chance we can move up?" he said. "I told Karina that most of those seats aren't filled even in a sellout. What if we wait until the second inning or something and see who doesn't show and then take whatever's left?"

"Can't do that, sir," Fred replied. He went to the boilerplate messaging that he gave out hundreds of times a year. "Those seats aren't mine to give. You have great seats here. While those seats are temporarily unoccupied, we need to make sure our guests have direct and unimpeded access to the seats they bought."

Tight T-shirt's brow furrowed.

"I told you it wouldn't work, Eric," the young woman, Karina, said. "Let's just sit in Robbie's family's seats."

They turned to Robbie, a young man who was wearing a bright-green A's tank top with bright-gold trim. Fred recognized him.

"Robbie? You're Kevin's grandson, aren't you?" Fred said and smiled. "I was wondering if I'd see you and your family. Is Kevin coming?"

Karina and Eric dropped their heads and filed into their seats, along with other friends. Robbie, the young man in the tank top, frowned and shook his head.

"No, he's in hospice. He's in his last days."

"Oh, I'm so sorry," Fred said. He felt worse than he would have a year ago. Ever since Marjorie had died, he'd had these same uncomfortable conversations when someone was caught unaware of the despair of certain loss he was feeling. And even though he had weathered them all, he didn't know what to say. "He's a good man, a big fan, and I know how much he loves going to these games with your family."

"Thanks. Two weeks ago we thought it might work out, but things took a bad turn, I guess, and I wanted to be here anyway. This is where I remember him best, you know?"

"I understand. Look, short of upgrading you all, let me know if there's anything I can do for you, okay?"

Kevin's grandson stepped forward and pulled Fred aside.

"Thanks. Well, I mean, I need to get a message to Brett Austen. Brett was my grandpa's favorite player, and I want to share something with Austen. I know, it's kind of stalker-like and all, but I think my grandpa would be grateful."

"As you know, Austen's very busy today and not much public access. But I'll see what I can do."

The grandson looked over to the left-field side and then back to his friends.

"Well, maybe I'll just get drunk and rush the field," the grandson said, then laughed.

"Oh, I wouldn't do that." Fred laughed back. "Some of our security folks played linebacker and defensive end."

"True. That's all I'd need." Robbie nodded, then sat down in the aisle seat.

Fred turned his attention back to the rest of the fans filing in. As always, the next half hour was a blur, checking tickets, leading fans to their seats, directing people back to their actual seats, and getting ready for the game.

Fred always felt exhausted during the pregame rush but was satisfied with his job by the time the ceremonial first pitch was thrown. He was always grateful for the national anthem. For the most part, fans stopped their activity to pay respects to their country, which allowed him a couple minutes to catch a breath and reflect. First, he thought of his country and his boss for thirty-three years. The United States wasn't perfect, but it was good enough. And, like any organism, the country was still trying to find meaning. He thought about Denny and other service members who had sacrificed and put themselves out there. Of course, all thoughts led back to Marjorie and the memories of her and her church choir singing the anthem. He remembered playing a role in that performance, convincing the A's to consider them.

Fred, see? You have pulled some strings in the past for us. You can do the same for that nice boy.

Fred thought about Robbie and what he had said about getting a message to Brett Austen. He wondered about the help he would want from someone if Marjorie had a final wish. He'd want effort, even if it didn't create a result. He'd want to know nothing else could be done.

Maybe he was working today not just to see Brett Austen's final day and say goodbye to this chapter but to help Robbie send a message. Fred was resolved. He was going to help this boy get a message to Brett Austen. He didn't know how, but he would pull some strings. It was his last day, after all.

* * *

"We got what we needed. Thanks," Palmetto said. Dana was back in the truck with Clarkson and French. "Good work. Liked how you drew out the Shakely aspect."

"Thanks," Dana said. "Hey, I've got some stuff with my mom that's come up."

"Everything okay?"

"Don't know yet. I have to make some calls."

"Today? During the game?" Palmetto looked at her in disbelief

"I know," Dana stammered. She was just as flabbergasted by the news from her mom. "But I have to sort some stuff out for her. It's just complicated. I've just got to figure it out."

"Well, you better figure it out fast."

"Thanks, Palmetto," Dana said. "Need anything else?"

"Nah," Palmetto said. He shook his head.

Wondering if I'm dedicated enough because I'm a woman, Dana thought.

"We'll start you out near the A's dugout and then go from there."

"Sounds good," Dana said, biting back the unspoken rebuke she thought Palmetto had delivered. She walked out and called her mom. Voicemail. She must be on the phone. Dana checked flights. There was a direct flight out of SFO to Chicago, leaving at 6:00 p.m. She could be in Bloomington by morning. But did she really want to?

* * *

Will felt some pride that he didn't make a complete fool of himself with Amanda and her family. He walked along the concourse with confidence. Maybe it was the break getting the autograph or the natural high from his interaction with the Wrights, but his identity crisis with Paul had dissipated. He found his section, and it only took a few seconds to find Paul. Will descended the steps to their seats. Paul was sipping a beer and eating a hot dog. Will sat down on the aisle seat.

"Did you get any good autographs?"

"Berman and Porter," Will said.

"Tyson Porter?" Paul laughed. "Did you tell him you were my stepson?"

"No." Will scowled. Why in the hell would he tell him that?

"I'm just saying that I know him and that it would have been cool if you wanted to drop my name."

Will shook his head. It was all about Paul. Will didn't need to be reminded that Paul knew everybody in sports and that everybody knew Paul. Every time the three of them went out for dinner, to the movies, even to Will's robotics competitions, there was at least one person who stopped Paul and said hello. Often, Paul knew them too, and soon Will was left to look around to distract himself while Paul laughed and carried on. While he wouldn't mind climbing up the social ladder a bit, maybe as Amanda Wright's boyfriend, he liked the anonymity of being at a ballgame and not being bothered by people who wanted to be in Paul's presence.

"Did you see that girl?"

"Amanda? Yeah. Talked to her parents."

"Good. Did you do what I said?"

Will nodded. As much as he didn't want to admit it, Paul was right about connecting with the parents.

"Great. They're more likely to be okay with letting her leave their seats to hang out with you if they like you."

"Yeah."

Paul turned his attention back to the mound. "Now, what are the odds that this dude bounces the first pitch?"

On the mound, a man honored for his service to one of the area hospitals during the pandemic waved to the crowd and prepared to deliver the ceremonial first pitch. He was a hero to those he'd helped, but he was certainly not an athlete.

"Oh, the odds of bouncing it just went way up," Paul said.

The nurse went to the rubber on top of the pitcher's mound.

"Big mistake to go to the rubber. If you ever get asked to throw out a first pitch, do everyone a favor and just go to the base of the mound and toss a nice, easy ball to the catcher. Don't do what this guy's doing."

The nurse pantomimed a big-league pitcher, from shaking off imaginary signs to spitting to looking to first base to watching an imaginary runner. Just as predicted, the nurse's ball made it halfway before it hit the ground and rolled the last ten feet to the plate. The catcher picked the ball off the ground and gave a patronizing pat to the nurse.

Despite himself, Will laughed with Paul.

* * *

Lizzie finished placing the twenty-four segments of the sandwiches on the ceramic platters her mom used for entertaining and placed them like minute markers on a clock. It took her three platters to get them all displayed, but she wanted to make it seem festive, even if they were there just to watch her dad die. Lizzie wondered if anyone had an appetite for food. She sure didn't.

Meanwhile, her mom dumped chips into their own bowls, and the two of them displayed them on the island. They knew that whatever Stephen brought over would be minimal, and they would simply have a small corner for him. Right on cue, Stephen knocked on the door and walked in.

"Hey there, A's fans," Stephen said. He was wearing his own black A's jersey that their dad had given him twenty years ago. Stephen had gained a few pounds since his twenties, so he wore it unbuttoned with a black T-shirt molding his belly. "All right, let's get it started."

Lizzie thought this whole situation was so macabre. It was a celebration of their dad's favorite player on his favorite team.

It was a celebration of joy for the end of the season. But it was also a precelebration of life and the beginning of a vigil. Behind Stephen was Leticia, Andrea, and Bart. Leticia was dressed all in black, as though ramping up for mourning season. And, as expected, Andrea and Bart were staring at their phones as they walked into the house. Carol was the first to greet them and went down the line, hugging Stephen, Leticia, and the kids.

"Good, the game's about to start," Carol said. "You don't want to miss the first pitch."

Lizzie followed Carol in the hug line. Bart and Andrea gave cursory embraces, while Leticia lingered. Heidi stood by Kevin's side, still grasping his hand. Lizzie loved her girl.

"Hey, what's Eddie doing here?" Stephen said as he casually carried in two opened bags of chips, salsa, and guacamole to the kitchen. Either they brought what they already had at home, or they had opened everything on the way from the store.

"What?" Lizzie asked.

"Eddie still drives a red pickup, right?" Stephen asked. "It's parked across the street. Why did you let him be here?"

"He's not here," Lizzie said. She was surprised Stephen knew what kind of car Eddie drove. He was so oblivious to anything not in his direct line of sight.

"Well, I think his truck is on the street. Go check for yourself."

Lizzie shook her head and rolled her eyes. Stephen thought this was all one big joke, and she knew as soon as she walked out the door, he would start laughing like he'd just pulled off the prank of the century. God, Stephen annoyed her. And it wasn't like the big sister, little brother annoyance that siblings get. No, this was more. Lizzie walked outside, her curiosity getting the best of her. She walked down the entry past the garage obstructing her view until she got to the curb. She looked left and, sure enough, there was Eddie's red Ford F-150 with Eddie in the front seat. Lizzie was reminded of the frustration she felt when Heidi was two years old and decided to paint her antique armoire with pink nail polish. She closed her eyes, ran her hands down her face, and let out a large sigh.

"Fuck my life," she said.

* * *

Some players put on hip-hop, others hard rock, others just a mix of their favorite music. For Brett, it was the only time he listened to spiritual, meditative music of reed instruments, light piano, or ancient tribal instruments. He had found this randomly on some streaming service a couple years ago. He wanted to be transported to his subconscious, and the yoga station provided that space. In these moments, he put himself in the batter's box, his mind focused on the pitcher's release point and the ball leaving the hand, the spin as the ball began its trajectory toward him, and the movement as it got closer. With each beat of the music, he dropped deeper into this mediation, focused only on the arm and the ball. He would transfer this state to his presence at the plate, calming his brain, blocking out the distraction of the crowd, the noise, the situation. See ball, hit ball. Clint Shakely.

Brett... Brett...

Brett closed his eyes tighter, trying to keep the demon out of his head. He exhaled and returned to his breathing, gaining a sense of calm and an aura of mindfulness surrounding him like a forcefield, keeping him focused. When it was time for lineup introductions, final warm-ups, and the national anthem, his mind was finally right. Outside the dugout, he allowed himself to glance across the stands and see the show of support. The fans were all there for him. They held signs that said, "400 reasons I love Brett" or "Austen for President" or "Brett > Ted." He even smiled at the "Brett, please stay in Oakland" sign a young girl held above her head. Brett smiled and waved, and the girl jumped up and down, excited at just being noticed.

Brett grabbed a ball in the dugout, found one of the many Sharpies hanging around the dugout for this purpose, signed the ball, then came back out and tossed it to her. Of course, this action only incited greater excitement from everyone else, and the crowd pushed further down toward the railing. By design, the crush of fans was interrupted by the singing of the national anthem, so everyone had to return to their seats.

As the Encinal High School Choir sang, Brett allowed himself a little smile. This was going to happen. He was going to get the hit. He was going to be talked among the greats. This was his season. This was his moment, and he was going to take it. The demon wasn't going to get the best of him today.

"O'er the land of the free, and the home of the brave."

He looked over at Shakely in the Mariners' bullpen.

A cold chill came across Brett.

Brett, you're gonna fail.

* * *

Derek used this first walk around to scout potential customers. The product he hawked that day determined his marketing strategy. Peanuts were for the traditional baseball fans. Spend extra time on the sunny side of the stands to increase ice cream sales. Cotton candy for the younger kids, licorice ropes for the older kids. Lemonade was always a bestseller on days like today.

Typically, Derek started off in the left-field bleachers and moved his way down the third-base line cascading from the field level seats up to the second and third decks. He never worked out, but he was sure his calves were the envy of 90 percent of the suburban dads guzzling down the sixteen-ounce, seventeen-dollar beers. He thought about getting a personal tracking device or watch to track the calories he burned going up and down those stadium steps. But that wouldn't even account for the extra fifty pounds of ice, liquid, and other items strung over his neck and back.

In his pregame routine, the goal was to be behind home plate for the national anthem. It was always his favorite part of the pregame pomp and circumstance. As refugees at the end of the Vietnam war, Derek's parents had brought him to the Bay Area not knowing what to expect. But they were forever grateful for their American opportunity, and this instilled an eternal patriotism. Particularly after 9/11, everyone, including hawkers, was expected to stop, remove their hats, and pay attention to the song. For him, it meant a special time to appreciate this opportunity, regardless of his current situation.

He liked to stand behind home plate but in the back of the first level, where the shade under the cold concrete was nearly thirty degrees cooler than in the sun. When the high school choir was done, Derek put on his light-black hat. He smiled, but his mind soon shifted.

The Bucs have got to cover today.

THE GAME

CHAPTER 11

Top of the First

	1	2	3	4	5	6	7	8	9	R	H	E
SEA										0	0	0
OAK										0	0	0

[Dan Muir over Ted Williams highlights in black and white] On September 28, 1941, the last day of the regular season, Red Sox legend Ted Williams capped his historic season with six hits in eight at bats during a doubleheader in Philadelphia, boosting his average to .406. It was the last time any major leaguer hit over .400.

[Dan Muir continues over Brett Austen highlights in bright color] That may change by the end of the day as Brett Austen of the Oakland A's has the chance to make history against the Seattle Mariners. Austen is sitting on .40033 and could take the day off. But like Williams more than eight decades ago, he's in the lineup to make sure there is no doubt about his accomplishment. And if he does, he will be among the greatest hitters of all time.

[Prerecorded interview with Brett Austen] I'm not competing against Ted Williams or Tony Gwynn or Ty Cobb. I'm facing the Seattle Mariners and their pitching staff, beginning with Clint Shakely. And so, my focus must be on them and the ball. See ball, hit ball. If I do that, I'll be talking about that history later.

[Dan Muir in broadcast booth with Tyson Porter] Good afternoon, everybody and welcome to Oakland, California. I'm Dan Muir, and with me is my partner, Tyson Porter, and Dana Peck reporting from the stands. Tyson, Brett Austen wants to treat this like any other game or at bat. But this is not an ordinary game. The atmosphere is electric, and it's all focused on one man.

[Tyson Porter] It's hard to think of anything else. Personally, I think with the environment as charged as it is, the smart move is to sit and preserve this accomplishment. But as a former player, I get it. You go for it. And we know Brett Austen. He's dialed in, and if anyone can get a hit today with all this pressure, it's him.

[Dan Muir] And a late scratch for the Mariners. Instead of Kenny Roberts, Seattle will roll out crafty left-hander Clint Shakely, who's probably the only pitcher in baseball to have success against Austen. Smart move, Tyson?

[Tyson Porter] Maybe to get out Austen but not for the Mariners to win the game. Shakely's success against Brett Austen notwithstanding, his stuff isn't what it used to be. I think it's a downgrade for Seattle as they battle for homefield advantage in the Wild Card Series. Then again, Clint Shakely is intense, and with his competitive fire, he'll bring it, especially if it means denying Brett Austen his chance at history.

Brett's chest was tight. It was harder to breathe. Somehow, the sight of Clint Shakely's name on the pitching line always knocked him off balance.

Oh, Brett, you should have sat today. This ain't like the other games, is it?

The demon was getting louder.

Brett stood out in his position in right field, the loneliest spot in the whole place. Brett was serviceable in the field, but it wasn't why he was in the major leagues. He relied more on JT Berman to cover some of his inadequacies. Out here in the great expanse of right field, he sometimes lost focus, but it was better than being the designated hitter. Most of his worst hitting days had occurred when he was placed in the DH spot. It was why, despite his mediocre defense, they kept him in right field.

Even with all his meditation, his focus, Brett felt anxious. This feeling wasn't like anything he had ever experienced. He had been in important games before. When his team needed a big hit, he'd come through. But this was different. This wasn't about the team. They were just playing out the year. There were no team moments in this game, just his. And now, all eyes were on him, and it was throwing him off. Even now, with A's pitcher Ruben Terranova blowing the first pitch by the Mariners' leadoff hitter, he felt the 43,000 pairs of eyes bearing down on him.

It all comes down to that first at bat. You better get that hit, Brett. You're going to let everyone down, and they'll finally know what kind of fraud you are.

* * *

Fred, what a beautiful day to be your last game.

"Sure is, Marjorie," Fred said to himself, reflecting on the ideal weather and perfect circumstances. If this was his final game working this section, he'd have it no other way.

Fred's thoughts turned to Kevin and his grandson Robbie. Whether it was the large presence of him doing the chicken dance and shown on the Jumbotron or his soccer-style chants and songs he sang for almost every player, Kevin had always made an impression in his limited appearances at the Coliseum. Fred was always sure he welcomed Kevin back to the neighborhood, many times with his family beside him.

It was about the time that John and Carla were moving to Sacramento that he found out Kevin and his family lived there. Kevin gave his honest assessments about the neighborhoods, schools, and abundance of outdoor activities available within an hour's drive. Throughout the game, Kevin shared everything from hikes to restaurants to floating down the lazy American River in a raft to the Sacramento Kings.

"Best kept secret in California," Kevin had said.

Fred looked over at Robbie and his friends. While Karina, her boyfriend, and their other friends were laughing and giggling, Robbie's expression belied a resignation to the sadness and mourning he would feel in the coming days. Robbie was here to honor his grandfather and bring his spirit to the game. But unlike the times that Kevin had attended these games, Robbie wasn't having a good time.

Fred, you need to help that boy.

Fred nodded. He felt a connection to Robbie. Whether it was Fred's own experience with having a loved one wither away or the opportunity to leave the A's with an altruistic gesture, he knew what he needed to do.

Fred climbed the steps to Robbie's seats. When he stopped at Robbie's row, he bent down.

"Hi. I'm seeing what I can do to get a note to Brett. It's my last day, so I'm going to pull in some favors. Got a piece of paper? Write what you gotta say, and I'll see what I can do."

"Really, you can do that?"

"No guarantees, but I'm gonna try."

Robbie's eyes brightened, and a smile went across his face. He turned toward his friends and called down the line.

"Hey, anybody got some paper and a pen?"

"Let me look in my briefcase, dumbass," Karina's boyfriend, Eric, said. Fred shook his head. He didn't like Eric.

"I think I may have something," Karina said. "What do you need it for?"

"I need to write a note," Robbie said.

"To who? Your lover?" Eric said.

"Shut up." Karina shook her head. "You're being an asshole. Here it is."

She pulled out a planner from the clear plastic bag that took the place of purses and backpacks.

"Here we go. And I've got the envelope from an 'I'm sorry' card Eric wrote me a few weeks ago."

Karina smiled as the rest of the group said "Aww" and laughed at Eric.

"What the hell, Karina?" Eric's face flashed red.

Fred laughed.

"All right, so write what you need to say, and I'll see what I can do," Fred said.

"Okay, I'll get to it." Robbie smiled with the excitement Fred often saw when players tossed a ball to a child in the stands.

* * *

"Ice-cold lemonade here," Derek called, walking up the steps, the tray slung around his neck and the wet, cold plastic cup making his fingers numb as he raised it high. He had two left. He would go up this aisle, then head back to the commissary to restock.

He was in Denny's section on the sunny side of the field. Derek expected to sell more lemonade here than in any other part of the park. But Derek had to scan the crowd, looking to meet eyes with anyone who may want the cold, sugary-tart beverage. He met eyes with a man whose haircuts cost more than Derek's rent. He was with his girlfriend or daughter—sometimes Derek just couldn't tell—and whispered to her. She looked over at Derek and nodded, and the man held up two fingers. She went back to her phone. *Daughter*, Derek thought. *She's only here because Daddy asked.*

"What do you think? Does he get it?" the man asked as they completed the transaction.

"I don't know, guy, but the money's on him getting to .400 today," Derek said. That was a good, honest answer. He didn't have to say he wanted to bet against Austen.

"Really, that says something. The bookies in Vegas know their shit," the man said. "But I thought he struggled against Clint Shakely."

"He does, but Kenny Roberts is pitching."

"Nah, man, late scratch. They're putting up Shakely."

Derek looked at the scoreboard and confirmed it. How had he missed this big news? This changed everything. For some reason, Austen was a mere mortal against Shakely and had been for his whole career. Derek thought it was a lock. Austen wasn't going to get that hit, unless the A's got into the Seattle bullpen. Derek felt the itch, that excitement that comes from sitting on something big. He needed to place action on an Austen hit right now. The gods were demanding it. Why wouldn't Owen just let him place this prop bet?

"Oh, crap, the Raiders couldn't pull it out."

Derek followed the man's eyes to the large screen above the stadium showing the early NFL scores. There it was. Jets seventeen, Raiders fourteen. Derek smiled. More confirmation today was his for the taking. How did the other games turn out? Before the scores changed, the transaction came through with a beep. Derek handed the two lemonades over and looked up at the scoreboard again. The scores were gone.

Derek cursed himself. Now that he knew most of the early games were completed, he needed to know the status of his bets. He looked up to the top of the steps and found Denny, one of the ushers. Without any lemonade to spill, he bounded up the steps two at a time.

"Hey, can you look up some scores for me?" Derek asked Denny, a bit breathless.

"Sure. You got a big bet coming through?"

Derek didn't answer verbally. His eyes said it all. "I need to know. Panthers, Bucs and Rams, Bengals."

Denny scrolled over his phone. Derek tried to stay calm.

"Let's see. I've got Panthers twenty-three, Buccaneers ten."

"Hell yeah," Derek said. One more game and he'd be up six grand. "Okay, Rams?"

"Hold on. Looks like it's still going. I'll refresh."

"Score?" *Oh my God.* Derek hated this part. Once his mind got wrapped up in the action, usually at this time on Sundays, it was nearly impossible to find relief until the uncertainty was resolved.

"Rams up five, but Bengals on the thirty-yard line. Two seconds left."

Derek felt elation and relief. He had the Rams with three points. Unless there was a catastrophic bad beat on the final play, Rams covered, and he had the win.

"Pass incomplete. Rams win twenty-six to twenty-one."

Derek was already on his way to the stairwell. He felt good about his chances now. He was just two thousand dollars down to Owen, which was almost like playing even. He still had his afternoon parlay with the Bears, Cardinals, and Dolphins, and if he hit that, then he was on his way. The gods were indeed smiling in his direction. Like Derek, they wanted little Jasmine to have dance lessons and not take her away from him. He needed to make that Austen bet before he came up to bat.

"Well, someone's in a good mood," Roy said when Derek put his tray on the counter.

"Bets are looking pretty good today, and if all works out, dance classes for Jasmine." Now that he knew Verne was concerned with his gambling, he couldn't let on he was playing to get even. "I feel so good, I may make one more bet."

"Are you sure you want to do that?" James grumbled.

"That's right," Roy said. "Don't you always say, 'Keep on your streak, and don't break the routine?'"

Ordinarily, that was Derek's mantra. Stick to the routine. Keep the bets. Stick with the plan, and don't chase the action. It was what had kept him mostly above water all this time. When he chased, that's when he got in trouble. But this was no ordinary bet and no ordinary circumstance. This was his chance to be the hero in Jasmine's life. This was some relief from the constant pressures he always faced.

"I know that, but the way the games are going, it would be wrong not to pull the trigger," Derek said.

James was skeptical. He pushed more lemonades forward for Derek to put in his tray. He mumbled his disapproval. Derek shook his head. What did this guy know?

"What are you going to bet then?" Roy asked.

"You're not gonna like it," Derek said.

Roy's eyebrow went up, and he squinted.

"Did you see that Shakely's pitching today? Austen never hits him well. Add that to the nerves? I tell ya. In. The. Bag."

"Oh man, you can't do that," Roy said. "That will jinx it, for sure."

"I told you you weren't going to like it. Particularly the way I'm feeling and the way I'm playing today. Plus, the odds are just too good in the bettor's favor."

"Mistake," James said.

Derek strapped on the tray and felt their disapproving stares. No support for a fellow working stiff trying to make this one score and get back on his feet. He needed this. He ignored his doubts and the red flags in his brain. All his thoughts were of Jasmine, and that was justification enough for the risk. He might pay for a whole year of dance up front and not have to worry about it again.

Derek went into the tunnel, but he didn't call Owen. Owen said he wouldn't take this bet. No, he hated to do it, but he had to call Carlos. Derek didn't like placing bets with Carlos. For Carlos, bookmaking was just one of his business interests, along with small-time drug dealing, human trafficking, and some enforcement of debt collection. Whereas Owen felt for his clients, Carlos reveled in their misery. He paid. He collected. He didn't have a cap or a ceiling, but if you didn't pay, his moves were swift and violent. Derek rubbed his nose and flexed his fingers. They were the victims of the last time he had crossed Carlos. Once, he had to stay home for two weeks without collecting any paychecks. He put that memory to the side and dialed.

"There's the playuh," Carlos said. Derek couldn't decide if it was the cell service of Carlos's mouth of gold teeth that made his voice thin.

"Hey, guy. I've got a good feeling, and I wanna place some action."

"Is that so?" Ray said. "What you got?"

"I want to lay a grand that Brett Austen doesn't get that hit,"

"Hey, isn't the game already started?" Carlos said.

"That's why I came to you," Derek said.

"Hmm. Vegas had it at plus-four hundred before the game. I'll give you plus-three hundred now, then we settle up tomorrow."

"You usually give a couple days," Derek said. He should hang up now.

"Hey, you want the bet or not?"

Derek took a breath. He couldn't admit to anyone, least of all himself, but this was the moment he loved the most. He could turn back at this moment, and nothing more was at risk. But the moment when a gambler pushed those chips in with confidence and without hesitation was almost sexual.

"Yep, put it down."

"All right," Carlos said with a giggle. "We'll meet up tomorrow at noon, win or lose. Same spot."

Derek pressed end and groaned. He wasn't a fan of the West Oakland BART station. To Carlos, it made sense. It was the main hub for all BART lines. From that station, lines went under the Bay to San Francisco, down the edges of the East Bay, or to the suburbs of Walnut Creek. There were several ways to hop on a train and get lost. And while gentrification had led to some areas being cleaned up, the homeless and drug addicts continued to be a constant in this mostly industrial part of town. On the other hand, Derek felt he would be going to BART in triumph to pick up the remaining cash before getting square with Pam. It would all work out.

Confident, he reveled in his early glory. He walked up to the next section of stands, doing mental calculus of all the winnings coming his way. At the end of the day, he might even have enough to take his mother out for dinner. No ramen tonight.

* * *

After Chris White flied out to JT Berman to end the first, Dana set up with French in the third-base photo well next to the A's dugout. During the production meeting, they had agreed to come out of the first break straight to her to introduce another snippet of her interview with Austen.

"Thirty seconds," Palmetto said through Dana's earpiece.

She nodded. Austen was scheduled to bat second. French angled the camera with Dana in the foreground and Austen standing with Berman, the leadoff hitter, swinging the bat and watching Clint Shakely.

Dana was ready. Just off camera, the buzz of her phone vibrating on the camera well diverted her attention. "Mom" flashed on her screen, and her mind drew back to the hundred grand, Richard, and her mom's request to fly back to Illinois.

"Dana! Look alive. Hey!" Palmetto yelled into Dana's earpiece, so much so, she put her finger to her ear. "Coming in five, four, three, two, one. Go."

For a second, Dana was dumbfounded about what she was supposed to do, her mind fixed on the phone. A second was an eternity. Palmetto was in her ear again.

"Dana!"

A quick blink, and her attention came back, as if someone had pressed play.

Bottom of the First

	1	2	3	4	5	6	7	8	9	R	H	E
SEA	0									0	0	0
OAK										0	0	0

[Dana Peck] Back in Oakland in the bottom of the first inning. Brett Austen will try to secure his .400 season while batting second. There's been a lot of talk about whether Austen should risk his .40033 average. When I talked to him earlier today, he addressed why he's playing.

[Prerecorded Brett Austen interview] I'm paid to play. The fans buy tickets to watch the A's and see us try to win. Today will be packed, and there will be a lot of folks here to watch me hit. So, I'm playing today for them. Besides, I don't back into anything, and if I sat, I'd be saying .400 was more important than the game. That's not how I'm wired. So, I'm going to go out there and get my hit and silence the critics.

[Dana Peck] So, you're going to get the hit?

[Brett Austen, smiling] What do you think?

[Dana Peck, live] As Brett Austen came in today, he told me he was going to try to keep today the same as any other game. He wasn't going to change his approach. He was going to keep doing what he'd been doing all year long, mainly "See ball, hit ball." Dan?

[Dan Muir] Thanks, Dana. And we'll see if he gets his hit off of veteran pitcher Clint Shakely, whom Seattle acquired at the trade deadline from the Mets, despite his abrasive reputation.

[Tyson Porter, laughing] It's more than a reputation, Dan. He's not here to start a knitting group.

"And we're clear," Palmetto said in Dana's ear. "What the hell was that freeze?"

"Sorry, phone distraction," she said.

"C'mon, Dana, get your head out. Can't let that happen again. You looked like a rookie. You're better than that," Palmetto said. "We'll come back to you in the bottom of the next inning, unless he gets a hit."

Dana agreed. She had to stay focused. She still had a job to do. But she also had a mother in crisis. She blew out a deep breath and shook her head. She could think about her mom later. She needed to focus on the game, on her possible meeting with Kansas City, and then she could figure out how her mom would survive with no retirement.

* * *

"Eddie, I told you not to come here," Lizzie said. She stood in the street with Eddie still in the cab of his pickup. Lizzie wondered if he was scared to leave his metal cocoon and face her.

"I was just going to stay here and listen to the game and be close by if you needed anything," Eddie said. "I wasn't going to come in unless you needed me to."

Lizzie shook her head. "Oh my God, Eddie. I just... I just can't." Lizzie felt herself beginning to break down.

"Liz, I'm here for you," Eddie said. His eyes showed the warmth and compassion she had seen when they'd first began dating and throughout the good years of their marriage. He began to open the door of his truck, but the sound of the latch broke that spell.

Lizzie thought about the moments when his clothes sometimes smelled different, or he had to meet a client unexpectedly at night or on the weekends. At first, she blew it off, then she thought she was growing paranoid. After all, they had a good marriage. They didn't fight often, and they still enjoyed making love. Still, her doubts and suspicions persisted.

One night as he took a shower, her paranoia got the best of her. Lizzie checked his phone and scrolled through his photos to see pics of a naked woman. Lizzie tried to tell herself it was just downloaded porn. She knew why Eddie sometimes took extra time in the bathroom. She almost put the phone away when the phone buzzed with a text from "Josh." Eddie had never mentioned a "Josh," yet he was texting her husband a lot. Lizzie scrolled through the texts and found more pics of this woman, even a video of her calling for Eddie to do intimate things.

Lizzie had almost wretched. She wasn't paranoid. Her best friend had betrayed her and lied about it. Her life had been a lie, perpetuated by the man she had vowed to love and trust for the rest of her life. Her despair turned to anger, and she resolved to confront Eddie. She walked into the bathroom, his phone in hand with a picture of "Josh." Eddie was still drying off, and the flaccid penis before her never looked so disgusting.

In that moment, Lizzie thought there was a chance to save her marriage. She was committed to the life they had together and wasn't ready to discard it so easily. Yet, when she confronted him and Eddie accused her of invading his privacy, Lizzie broke. This wasn't the man she thought she had married, a man who would be accountable, who would put her concerns over his own, who would see her hurt and put her above his selfishness. Maybe she was naïve to think that was possible in the first place, but that was what they had or thought they had built for twenty-five years. She'd never look at him the same. The door to reconciliation closed, and she had put a lock on that door and broken the key. It was over. He had made his choice. And that made today, when she needed his comfort the most, even harder. Eddie was no longer the person to hold her and tell her everything was going to be okay.

"Eddie, we're divorced. You broke me. And you think I'm going to forget what you did to me, how you humiliated me, then forgive you and let you come be a savior to me on one of the worst days of my life? You gave up that right, and you can't be here."

"But what about Heidi? What if she wants me here?"

"Not today, Eddie. You're not coming in."

"Fine, I'll stay out here."

"Why?"

"In case Heidi needs me. Or anyone else."

"We're not going to need you. You're not a part of this family anymore."

Lizzie watched her verbal blow connect. She wanted him to hurt like she was hurt, and Eddie deflated. He sank down to the curb and buried his head between his legs. Even when he had pleaded for her to take him back during the divorce, she had never seen him utterly retreat into himself and become smaller. During the divorce, she felt he was fighting for the status quo. He didn't want to be the divorced guy, and he liked their life together. But now, Eddie finally understood what he had lost. His infidelity had severed his support system. Lizzie felt a little sorry for him. His parents were long dead, and he wasn't close to his sister who lived in New York. She was pretty sure that "Josh" wasn't interested in this type of comfort either. She, Heidi, Kevin, Carol, even Stephen and Leticia were his family, and that was gone too.

Lizzie knew she would regret this. "Eddie, you can stay parked out here on the street. And *if* Heidi wants, I'll send her out with some sandwiches and chips. You can talk to her. But that's it. You're not coming in. Not today."

Eddie nodded. Lizzie shook her head. They had been so good together, yet they would never be good together again. She had barely even considered what life would be without him before she was hit with the news of her father's progressed cancer a week later. At that point, she considered any potential feelings of self-pity or moving on as selfish. She had pushed them down in order to be strong for her father, for her mother, and for Heidi.

"Hey, Liz." Stephen popped out from the side of the garage. "Austen's about to bat."

Lizzie nodded and then looked back at Eddie.

"I'll see if Heidi wants to come out and say hi," Lizzie said and turned.

"I love your dad," Eddie said. "If there's a way to convey that to him, I'd appreciate it. And give your mom a hug for me."

Lizzie didn't know what to say. She just nodded and kept walking, every step wanting to turn and invite him in. The early autumn afternoon felt more like an extended summer, but Lizzie's arms clung to her body as she walked up the driveway and back into the house.

The scene before her at least gave her comfort. Heidi was still next to her grandpa, holding his hand. Stephen was on the other side. Lizzie's mom was sitting between Andrea and Bart as they explained memes and Instagram to her. Leticia was in the back, helping herself to some of the wine she had found in the fridge.

"I'll take some of that," Lizzie said.

* * *

You should have sat, Brett. Now, you'll just be a footnote, known as a failure who could have been great.

The demon was relentless. Brett had been here before. There were a couple minor slumps this season, a couple games without a hit, but he would follow that up with a good string that returned his average back to the stratosphere. He battled the demon back then by focusing on the fundamentals, waiting for his pitch, seeing the ball, and connecting.

Standing on the on-deck circle, Brett swung his thirty-six-ounce Louisville Slugger, his arms loosening with every swing of the bat. Brett was a traditionalist when it came to his bats. Some liked to have skinny handles to create better bat speed. He tried that for a couple of weeks during spring training a few years ago, but the result was an infield littered with splinters and a weak ground ball to the shortstop or the pitcher. Nah, Brett knew these bats as an extension of his arms. Like Goldilocks picking out her afternoon-nap spot, this bat felt right.

Batting leadoff, JT Berman's role was to get on base any way possible. His compact frame made it tougher for pitchers to hit his strike zone. He had a great eye for the ball coming out of the pitcher's hand, and he was fast. Batting left-handed, Berman only needed to slap at the ball and put it in play to get a head start on reaching first base before the ball. Brett liked Berman ever since he had come up as a rookie three years ago. That year, Berman hit .310 and helped the team stay in contention for the playoffs all the way into September. Berman was a key piece to their plans to make the playoffs this year, but an injured hamstring made this another lost season.

"All right, let's get on them early," Garza said. His gruff baritone pierced the amplified white noise of the crowd.

Berman stepped across the plate and into the batter's box. Because of his "make contact" approach, he didn't dig his cleats into the dirt like many other hitters. His steps were light, as though he wanted to get out of there as soon as possible. He looked at Shakely and swung the bat in a windmill before securing a loose grip around the bat. His wrists twirled the bat in a circle behind his head. He stared at Shakely. Shakely went into his windup, and just as they had seen in the warm-up, the ball came out quickly. Shakely's pitch was low, but Berman committed to the swing and lowered the bat head to slap the ball. The ball skated meekly to Shakely, who fielded it off the mound and threw to first base for the first out. A groan came down from the crowd, disappointed their leadoff hitter didn't reach base. But just as quickly, the melancholy tone shifted to exuberance and anticipation. The low, rhythmic bass-guitar riffs over a hip-hop beat blasted through the Coliseum speakers, prompting fans to stand and cheer.

Brett had chosen "Lose Yourself" by Eminem in the minors. The song pumped him up every time it came on. And the title drove his approach at the plate. Lose yourself in the battle, dedicate every thought in your head to the pitcher on the mound and the ball coming out of his hand. Cut out all distractions and focus on that connection with the ball.

With each beat, Brett bobbed his head and shook his shoulders, and the crowd got louder. He looked up, and fans reacted to the beat, their voices rising a decibel with every step.

"Now batting," the announcer's voice boomed, "right fielder, Brett Austen."

The roar hit a crescendo. Brett relished this moment. The music, the beat, the crowd. He looked around to take it in. Who knew if he'd ever see this again? Sports were like that. There were so many common uncommon moments. One thought the adoration would last forever, and there was always the next time.

Eventually, though, there was no next time. At some point, there is a peak of performance before a slow slide to irrelevance.

This is your peak. It's all downhill from here.

The crowd was still on its feet, applauding and yelling for Brett. Before he stepped into the batter's box, he looked up and scanned the stands. He gave a quick wave and put his fingers to the edge of his helmet for a quick tip of the hat. Somehow, it grew louder. There were times in baseball history that were replayed over and over. Cal Ripken's continuous-game streak, Jeter's final game at Yankee Stadium, and anything David Ortiz did in Boston. Brett wished the overwhelming noise would go on forever. The smartphones were out, documenting the moment.

Enjoy the applause. They'll deflate quicker than a hiccup when you don't get this hit.

Brett slammed his helmet with his hand. "C'mon, Brett, get back in it."

"Jesus Christ, done milking the moment?" Mariners catcher Wilson Tomlin said in his crouch.

"Yeah, just had to make sure everyone had their phones out," Brett countered. A little trash talking helped supply some levity and relaxation as he stepped into the box.

Forty-three thousand recordings of you failing.

Unlike Berman, Brett liked to dig his toes into the dirt. He wanted his feet firmly planted in the ground. He didn't rely on the slap hit and his speed to get on base. He liked his line drives and doubles to the gap. Once his feet were set, he swung his lumber like a windmill twice before pulling his arms into position.

As Shakely went into his windup, Brett lowered into his crouch, ready. The ball came out of the left hand, the rotation of the seams spinning quickly for a red dot on the top end of the ball. In a split second, he recognized it as a fastball. But it was heading right for his head. Brett ducked out of the way, feeling the slight breath of the ball moving past his ear.

There's the arrogant prick we know and love. He's got your number, Brett.

"Ball," the home-plate umpire, Carl Davidson, said.

The cheers of a moment before turned to thunderous boos, sharing their collective anger of the brushback pitch. Austen shared their disdain and glared at Shakely.

"Don't you try to show me up, asshole," Shakely yelled at Brett.

"Shut up, old man, and pitch," Brett said. "I'll send you to the retirement home."

"Fuck you."

Davidson stepped out from behind Tomlin and looked to Brett and Shakely. As umpire, he had to keep control of the situation.

"All right, that's enough. I don't want none of this bullshit."

"He's the one who came in at me."

"Brett, I'm sure you don't want to get thrown out today, of all days."

This is your last chance. Get ejected and the madness ends. No one will know you've lost the edge.

Brett nodded and tried to refocus. He had to block out the demon. This was his chance. This was his moment. This was his at bat, his season, his career, his life. He had a right to meet this moment, and goddammit, he was going to embrace it. He tapped his cleats with the bat and adjusted his batting gloves. Shakely was trying to knock him off his game. Brett breathed deeply.

"Told you not to milk the moment," Tomlin said. "He doesn't like that."

"How do you put up with that guy?" Brett asked as he began to dig back into the box.

"We just deal. We need his arm."

"But he's a fucking asshole."

"He's *our* fucking asshole. Now get back in the box so he can strike your ass out."

Tomlin's comments were gentle, and Brett didn't take offense.

Brett locked back in. Okay, so he knew the tip for the curveball, he had seen the fastball, albeit a little too close. He had to watch for the changeup and the slider and maybe his sinker, though that was Shakely's worst pitch, and he inconsistently threw it. Brett looked back at Shakely. Same routine. The windup and the pitch, a slider that sliced across the plate toward him. It wasn't an ideal pitch, but it was going to be a strike. Unfortunately, Brett was late, and the ball jammed his hands on the inside of the bat.

The ball popped behind him and to the back fence out of Tomlin's reach. Foul ball.

The count was one-and-one.

Okay, slider, fastball, and the tipped curveball. Although he'd fouled that off, Brett saw another pitch. Back into the box. Another couple twirls of the bat. The sign, the pitch. Another fastball. Outside. Two balls, one strike.

Okay, he was ahead in the count. He didn't think Shakely would come back with another slider. So that meant fastball or changeup or the curveball. Shakely went into the windup. Brett waited. Looked like a fastball that was going to be right down the middle of the plate. As Brett's swing began, the ball began to dip. Crap. Sinker. Brett tried to check his swing, but it was too late. The ball hit the dirt, but his bat crossed the plate. Strike two.

Brett looked at Shakely. Shakely gave an arrogant smirk. It was a good pitch, and Shakely was pleased it was working. Shakely had his good stuff, which made Brett's task even tougher. Brett stepped back in.

Shakely's got something extra special today. You should have sat.

"Didn't expect that, did ya?" Tomlin said.

"Nope, but it won't surprise me again," Brett said.

Shakely in the windup again. The fastball again, but this time, it wasn't a sinker; however, that slight hesitation caused Brett to take a mediocre swing. Instead of a line drive, he hit a weak grounder to second baseman Rex Bishop. Brett dropped his bat and ran hard to first but knew it was futile. Before he got halfway down the line, Bishop had tossed the ball to first baseman Dustin Reese for the out.

Told ya.

Brett blew out his mouth like a blowfish as he cut off his run and jogged back to the dugout. He didn't look at Shakely. He didn't want to give him the satisfaction. It was always disappointing to hit into an out, but the collective groan and subsequent pity applause from the crowd left him deflated. He came down the steps of the dugout. Garza was there.

"Next time, Brett," he said.

"Sinker's working," Brett said. "That's not a good sign."

"We'll see," Garza said.

CHAPTER 13

Top of the Second

	1	2	3	4	5	6	7	8	9	R	H	E
SEA	0									0	0	0
OAK	0									0	0	0

[Dan Muir] Sometimes milestones don't end in a blaze of near-glory but in a feeble groundout to second. For the first time since mid-June, Brett Austen's average has dipped below .400, now at .39966. Tyson, Seattle pitcher Clint Shakely made quick work of the A's in that inning.

[Tyson Porter] Yeah, Dan, Shakely looks like the Clint Shakely I faced about ten years ago. He's got velocity, movement, and he's painting the corners. He's also bringing his nasty attitude. Remember, he was a late add today because of his success against Austen but also to rest Kenny Roberts for the Wild Card Series. He's an innings eater and is in there to keep the bullpen fresh for the playoffs.

[Dan Muir] And as we saw in that first inning, Shakely will not be grooving a pitch to Austen.

[Tyson Porter] There's no love between those two. When it comes down to it, Shakely may just bean Austen in the rest of his at bats to ensure he doesn't get to .400.
[Dan Muir, laughing] That would certainly live up to his reputation.
[Tyson Porter] No, Dan, I'm serious.

The screen on Will's phone refused to change. There were no notifications. No incoming DMs or texts. Between pitches, Will kept looking down, wondering if he missed something.

"Why do you keep looking at your phone?" Paul asked. "The game's up here."

"Amanda was going to DM me when she could hang out."

"Don't worry, she'll text you. It's only the top of the second"

"Easy for you to say. She's so out of my league."

"Look, you're likely more interesting than her family today, and she's going to need a break from them. Don't worry, she'll reach out."

When Will looked back from the phone to the field, his view was blocked by two men in their thirties, both with wide grins. It was a common look when he was around Paul. As they kneeled in the aisle, Will rolled his eyes and looked toward Austen in right field. He wasn't amused. These fan boys were interrupting the game. In some ways, Will didn't understand why he was annoyed. When Paul was just Paul, the extra attention he brought was exciting. Will was celebrity adjacent. Now, he was going to be legally part of Paul's world, and for the rest of time, no outing was going to be without this same scenario played out with different backgrounds.

"Hey, Paul Buckley," one of them said. "You think we'll get to see a halibut today?"

Paul smiled like he always did, broad and accommodating. They bent down and took a selfie with him before moving on. Paul didn't mind the attention. He seemed to enjoy it. Meanwhile, Will stewed.

"Do you ever get sick of that?" Will asked when they left.

"What? People coming up to me? A little. Sometimes, I wish I'd never come up with 'Catch of the Day.' Although, it has helped me with some ideas for cooking fish over the years."

When Will first heard how Paul came up with the *Catch of the Day* catchphrase, he thought it was clever and funny. But after seven years and hundreds of retellings, the story was stale. The catchphrase started when Paul was out of college and working a job in Duluth, MN. He went to a restaurant, where they had Alaskan halibut in a white wine sauce as their 'Catch of the Day.' Paul thought it was just weird to feature an ocean fish as a midwestern catch. That night, while recapping the day's highlights, Paul was inspired and said on-air, "Ken Griffey with the Alaskan halibut in a white wine sauce, your catch of the day at Fisherman's Grotto on Fifth." The news anchor thought it was hilarious, so he kept using it. The phrase was born and followed him to ESPN and now back in Sacramento.

"I don't know if I'd rather be anonymous like I am at school or harassed like you are."

"It's not too bad. You get a few assholes, but for the most part, folks understand boundaries."

Will looked at Paul, who was oblivious. Being interrupted with a quip, stopped for an autograph, his name called out randomly on the street, was secondhand to him. But not for Will. Would he be expected to smile and ignore this constant attention and interruption? All he wanted to do was watch the game next to Amanda. If only she would DM him again. He turned the phone over and checked his Instagram. A new message from Amanda.

The world was now perfect.

Amanda: *Would like a break from my family later.*

Will: *Sounds good.*

He showed the message to Paul.

"See? What did I tell you?" Paul pointed to the seat next to Will. "And without your mom, we've got an extra seat."

For a moment, Will allowed himself a little grace toward Paul. He could have been annoyed that Amanda was intruding on their bonding time or bestowed what the great Paul Buckley would have done at his age in high school. Instead, he was being chill, and Will respected that.

"Hey, I probably need to go up to the press box and thank Pete Henderson for these tickets. Do you want to come with?"

More back slapping and introductions as Paul's future stepson didn't appeal to Will. Besides, what if Amanda wanted to meet up?

Will shook his head. "Nah, I may just wander the stadium for a bit. You go ahead, but please thank Mr. Henderson for me too."

Paul smiled. Will felt like he was being seen for the first time in the stadium.

* * *

Fred scanned and assessed his area. While he wasn't part of the security detail, he was supposed to alert them if anything seemed suspicious. He watched Robbie, Karina and their friends. While Robbie was sullen, his group was going to be obnoxious, for sure. The alcohol eased their conscience and consideration, allowing their narcissism and immaturity to take over. He watched the fans around them. One parent gave the group the stink eye while the other distracted their young children. Another set of regular season-ticket holders shook their heads at the behavior. Fred hated to see what might happen once the group noticed that Paul Buckley was sitting a few rows below them.

Fred should go and talk to them. And he needed to get the note from Robbie if he was going to get it to Austen. Fred always tried to be genial and disarming, a smile on his face the first time he approached these kinds of fans. Sometimes all they needed was a reminder that their behavior was distracting to other fans around them and to be considerate. Sometimes, a sterner approach, or even a call to security, was necessary. He hoped this wasn't one of those times.

Fred went up to where Robbie, Karina, and their friends were sitting.

"Hey, Robbie. Hey, Karina. I'm gonna need you guys to dial it back a bit. We've got families here and other fans, and we want everyone around here to enjoy themselves, so just keep it down, please."

"We're just having some fun," Eric said.

"And I want you to, but let's keep it so everyone can have fun, okay?"

"Yeah, shut up, Eric," Robbie said.

"You shut up," Eric said.

Robbie shook his head, along with Karina.

"Oh, um, I got that note for Austen," Robbie said, handing Fred an envelope. Fred examined it. It was bent and "Karina" was scratched out, replaced with "Brett Austen." "So, you're really going to get this to Brett?"

"I'm going to try. After all, it's my last day. Most likely, it will be put in with the rest of the fan mail. He'll probably get it tomorrow, at the latest, when he cleans out his locker for the year."

"My grandpa may not last the day."

"I understand, but again, I can only do the best I can."

Robbie didn't hide his disappointment. He took a drink of his beer as though it was the only activity he thought he could do.

"You're doing right by your grandpa," Fred said. "Regardless of what happens with this note. Now, a favor for me. It's going to be a great game today. I need you to help me keep your friends in check so everyone, including those around you, have a good time, all right?"

Robbie nodded. "All right. Thanks again. This is a big relief."

Fred tapped Robbie's shoulder and slipped the letter into his pocket. Fred considered asking Robbie what was in the note but decided against it. He knew the gist.

Fred walked back to his station in the center aisle and looked up to survey his section. Just three rows down and a few seats over, Fred's eyes were drawn to a couple in their early fifties with a two-year-old, a child Fred assumed was their grandbaby. Wasn't it just yesterday that he and Marjorie were bringing the twins to their first game? He always took one day off a year to enjoy a game with Marjorie and the grandkids, though they hadn't gone for the past few years. With the pandemic, followed by Marjorie's illness, it just didn't make sense. Maybe next year, he'd take John, Carla, and the twins and begin a new tradition, like Kevin had with his grandkids. Maybe one or both of the twins would take to the game, like Robbie.

That would be lovely of you to take the twins

Fred's momentary daydream came to an abrupt conclusion with the crack of the bat. By now he had an instinct. Over twenty years of being an usher and sixty years going to baseball games had ingrained in him that a foul ball was heading his way. Watch the fans. Watch their eyes. He didn't need to look up. Someone in his section was getting a souvenir. The trajectory went a little to the right, and he began to make his way toward the area where he thought it might fall. The ball began its descent. Some ducked. Some shirked. Some spilt beers. Some came into the aisles. A father in his thirties brought a glove and caught it. Fred went over the to the dad with his new souvenir. Protocol dictated that he visit the fan to check on him and present a QR code for a liability release and, if signed, a voucher for a free item from the concession stand.

"Great catch," Fred said.

"Thanks," the dad said.

Fred made a quick look back toward his section. These moments were a vulnerability. Foul balls were a distraction. Those extra sets of eyes supplied another layer of protection. He scanned and found nothing out of the ordinary. Everything was good in his neighborhood.

CHAPTER 14

Bottom of the Second

	1	2	3	4	5	6	7	8	9	R	H	E
SEA	0	0								0	0	0
OAK	0									0	0	0

[Dan Muir] Welcome back to the scenes of the Bay Area—the Golden Gate Bridge, the Bay Bridge, Alcatraz, Jack London Square, and of course the Oakland Coliseum, home to so many historic moments from the A's and the former Oakland Raiders.

[Tyson Porter] The A's need to get to Shakely early. He's the kind of guy who can get in a groove, locate his spots, and frustrate hitters if you let him. And judging by how he looked in that first inning, he's got his swagger, and Shakely's dangerous when he's got that going for him.

[Dan Muir] Shakely will face off against first baseman Gus Williams, followed by Ricardo Rivas and Ron Vasquez.

[Tyson Porter] On the surface, those three aren't ones who are likely to disrupt Shakely's rhythm. They swing early and often. Garza and the A's coaching staff need to emphasize patience and working the count.

[Dan Muir] Is that what you would do if you were on the A's bench?

[Tyson Porter] I'm just saying that's got to be the approach to Shakely. Otherwise, if he's able to disguise that sinker like he did to Austen in the first, it may be another one-two-three inning.

"Where's that fan interview?" Palmetto asked in Dana's earpiece. Dana was in the concourse while Clarkson scouted for fans to interview on air. Dana looked down as Clarkson walked up the aisle and gave a thumbs-up.

"I've got a family in the midlower deck. I talked to them, and they're willing to be interviewed on camera. There's even an empty seat," Clarkson said.

"Clarkson says he's found a family. Give us three minutes to get set up with French."

"You've got two," Palmetto said. "We've got to get this face-in-the-crowd shot this inning. Get there."

Clarkson led Dana down the section behind the A's dugout. When she reached their seats, Clarkson introduced the Wright family—Michael, Theresa, and young Myles. Michael's grin beamed through his graying beard and dark skin. Michael, Theresa, and Myles would be perfect for this shot. They had all the gear. Clarkson had scouted well.

"Our daughter, Amanda, is on the phone talking to a friend somewhere," Theresa said.

"Good to meet you," Dana said.

With Amanda's seat open, Dana sat between Michael and Theresa with French positioning the camera on his shoulder and kneeling in the aisle. Clarkson got on the radio with Palmetto, letting them know they had a good interview, and Dana talked with the Wright family. Dana learned that Michael had attended A's games since the early eighties and that they try to make at least ten games a year from Sacramento. Austen was Myles's favorite player, but he also enjoyed JT Berman, the speedy A's center-fielder. Theresa liked Joe Schmitke, likely in the final game of his career. They both went to the same college, San Diego State.

Dana liked to ask some easy personal questions and try to relate her own experiences during this setup time. It helped put her subjects at ease and make the conversation more personal and authentic.

"Coming to you in ten seconds," he said.

Dana nodded to the Wrights, letting them know it was almost time.

Palmetto counted down, and as he got to five, Dana sat up higher, put on a smile, and was ready. Dan Muir was in her ear.

"...where the local fans are excited at the prospect of watching Brett Austen make history. Our own Dana Peck is in the stands to introduce us to a few of them. Dana?"

* * *

Will admired all of the caps on display at the pop-up shop behind home plate. If he had the money, he would buy half of them. The designs ranged from the traditional A's logo to the Athletics' script to various incarnations of the elephant mascot. Some had the logo was embedded in a baseball or a diamond and in all colors. There were the wool fitted hats like the players wore, the adjustable cotton-blend caps, trucker hats, alternate and special-edition hats for Military Day or Breast Cancer Awareness Day or Independence Day. And there was the bucket hat he almost wore for the game today.

"Shopping?" Amanda said from behind.

Will smiled and turned. Maybe it was because she wasn't with her parents. Maybe he realized she was making a choice to hang out with him, but he felt like a cartoon, his heart pounding out of his chest, his smile wide, and his eyes big and lovelorn. He caught himself before he looked totally desperate. He had to keep it cool.

"Hey," Will said with a nod. "I thought you were going to message me."

"I was going to," Amanda said, smiling before looking past him toward the pop-up shop. "Actually, I need to get a hat."

"Well, here's the place to get them," Will said, waving his arm like a carnival barker. "As you can see, lots to choose from."

Amanda pushed Will to the side. While he was still growing, he was five foot ten with his shoes on, Amanda was still about four inches shorter, in contrast to only a year and a half ago when she was taller than him. Amanda leaned against the counter and looked at the huge array of baseball caps.

"What do you think I should get?"

"What do you want?"

"I don't know, that's why I'm asking."

"My mom told me once when we were at Disneyland, 'Don't think about what you want to wear today, think about what you'd wear in six months on a regular Saturday.'"

"So, you're saying you don't have one of those crazy Goofy hats at home?" Amanda smiled. It was beautiful. She turned toward the cap display. "In that case, what would I wear on a random Saturday in April?"

Amanda scanned the array of hats and looked at a forest-green hat with the black A's logo. "That looks like something I'd wear." Amanda pointed to the hat, and the vendor grabbed it for her. It was adjustable, so she sized it and placed it on her head, pulling the brim midway down her forehead. Will usually pulled his all the way down to the brow, but her way brought out her lovely brown eyes. "Thoughts?"

"Looks good." Who was he kidding? Even his sweaty bucket hat would be much more fashionable atop Amanda's head.

"Not too militant? It's almost like a camo hat," she said. "Don't wanna be the angry black girl."

Will was stuck about what to say. So much messaging, sometimes conflicting, had been drilled into his brain, he was somewhat confused as to how to respond to gray sarcasm. *Be honest,* Paul's voice encouraged in his head.

"Nope, your eyes show your kindness."

"Aw, that's sweet," Amanda said, her smile perfect. "That wasn't my question, but I'll take it."

"Truly, I think that hat looks good on you and will look good in April, May, June, even January."

"All right." Amanda pulled out a card from her wallet and paid for the hat.

Afterward, they walked up the right-field side.

"So glad you're here," Amanda said. "I needed a break. My family's exhausting. When we're at a game, they just talk baseball.

It's all strategy about positioning and different situations and pitches and hitters. Sometimes, like, I just want a backdrop to zone out, and they keep hitting me with questions."

"At least they're interested."

"I guess. The worst part of it is, I know the answers without even thinking."

Even as a freshman last year, Amanda made the varsity softball team and started several games at third base and was expected to start for the next three years at Kennedy High School. Even though he never attended a game, he strategically walked past the softball fields a few times to watch Amanda play. She was impressive at third base, the "hot corner." With so many bunt attempts, slap hits, and the shorter distance between bases, third base demanded super-quick reflexes and skill, along with a strong arm.

"That's not a bad thing. I mean, we can talk about that last Austen at bat and why he was late on the fastball."

"Oh god, you sound like them." Amanda smiled and bumped him with her hip, knocking him off stride.

"I'm just saying," Will said.

"I know. I should be thankful. I mean, I have both parents, and they're still married." Then she turned to Will and put her hands to her mouth. "I'm sorry. I didn't mean it like that."

"What? My dad died seven years ago, Or did you mean because I'm going to get a new stepdad? No, you didn't make it awkward at all." Will stared deadpanned at Amanda. Her eyes got wide. Then he busted out laughing. "Oh, I got you!"

"Ass." She laughed back. "And he was caught looking for the sinker, just in case you were wondering."

* * *

"Dana, good work on that." It was Palmetto back in her ear after she threw it back to Dan Muir and Tyson Porter. "We'll come back to you when Austen comes back to bat, which by the way Shakely's pitching, could be next inning."

"Yeah, it looks like Shakely's mowing them down. I'll be ready."

After Gus Williams grounded out to the shortstop, Ricardo Rivas was now up.

"Looks like it's going to be hard for Austen to get a hit against Shakely," Michael Wright said as Dana thanked the Wright family.

Dana smiled and looked over to the pitching mound. "Yeah, Shakely's dealing, his best outing of the year so far."

"We may have two historic events today," Michael said and pointed to the scoreboard to the number under the *H*. It read "0."

"Mr. Wright, are you calling a no-hitter after a single inning?" Dana raised her eyebrows.

"Just saying, that's all."

Dana walked up the steps, followed by Clarkson and French. She was always amazed by some of the people she met in this job. The Wrights were gracious and warm and conveyed it all to the camera. The interview had provided a needed mental break from thinking about her mom. Looking at her phone, Matt, her mom's financial advisor, still hadn't gotten back to her. A hard bump. followed by cold wetness shocked her back to her current surroundings. She looked up at the equally surprised face of a vendor with a tray full of lemonade cups; well, except for the five whose lids had popped off and spilled onto her.

"Hey, watch where you're going, missy," the vendor said. His long graying ponytail bobbed as he glared at her.

"I could say the same thing about you," Dana said. "You're the one with the lemonade around your neck."

Dana wanted to say more but was keenly aware of causing scenes in the cell phone era. She felt the smartphones turning in her direction to catch her in a bad position. There was certainly no scenario where a viral video of her chastising a vendor looked good. She was sure that Kansas City wouldn't want its radio play-by-play personality to be at odds with their food-and-beverage staff.

Dana looked down at her ruined blouse. The bright pink streak ran from one shoulder across her chest and to the side of her ivory sleeveless blouse. The sugary drink was becoming sticky on her skin. She rushed over to the condiments and grabbed a handful of napkins. There was no use. The colored dye had already penetrated and stained her top.

She had no choice. She'd have to change her shirt and get back to her spot next to the A's dugout by next inning, and she had no time to do it. "I need to get another top," Dana said.

"Oh, crap," Clarkson said, coming up from behind. "I'll get a PA do it. You got something in your garment bag?"

"I have the shirt I was going to wear for the Wild Card, but I really don't like someone going through my stuff."

"Why don't you go the press box, and I'll have a production assistant bring the whole bag to you. I'll talk to Palmetto and see our next shot."

"Okay. That should give me a chance to figure out what happened to my mom's money."

* * *

Derek didn't see the tall, pretty, well-dressed, distracted woman coming at him until several of his lemonades had burst wide open and spilled down her fancy outfit.

"Shit," Derek said. The cherry lemonade got the worst of it, most of it on the woman, who was trailed by a camera operator and another guy.

Derek turned. He recognized her and knew he would never win their argument. She was high rent, a small-time celebrity. Guys like him never won arguments with people like that. He couldn't afford to get fired, so he mumbled a quick apology and took inventory. Out of the sixteen lemonades he had just placed in his tray, he'd lost five of them. He thought about cleaning up the cups and continuing, but his shirt also didn't come away unstained. He needed to change into his backup bright-green shirt.

This was also an opportunity to pick up some extra cash. If he found six more empty cups and included those in his spoils, he had a chance to make an extra twenty dollars. As Derek retraced his steps back to the commissary, he found four cups. That would have to do. Of all the stupid things. Now he was losing prime sales time to replenish his stock.

"What happened?" Roy said as Derek came back in.

"You can guess," Derek said, pointing to the TV showing the game. "And it was that woman on the TV too."

"Who? Dana Peck?"

Derek nodded and was out the door and across the tunnel to his locker. Backup apparel was necessary in his position. Fan/hawker interference was common. From lemonade, coffee, beer to hot dogs, cotton candy, ice cream, dippin' dots, nachos, even bean pie, having to change was part of the job, but the bright-pink stain across his neon-green shirt meant this shirt was ruined, and he'd have purchase another at his own expense.

"Scores?" Derek said once out of the bathroom and back in the commissary with his backup shirt. James was checking out the replacement lemonades, and Roy was putting them in the tray.

"Not any different than ten minutes ago," Roy said. "I'm so glad you aren't here to be a pain in the ass. I don't think I could stand you gibbering the whole game."

"Meanwhile, I have Roy gibbering at *me* all game," James said.

Derek wanted to stay and continue needling James and Roy, but his run-in with Dana Peck had put him way behind. He hustled back to the stands to resume his route through the stadium. Derek had sold so many items over the years, he knew exactly where he should be at all times. He had a pace. He always kept an eye on the clock at the Jumbotron over the left-field foul pole. He shook his head. Bumping into that reporter had cost him some prime time. What if running into Dana Peck was a sign that his last bet was a mistake? He grimaced at the prospect of jinxing himself.

CHAPTER 15

Top of the Third

	1	2	3	4	5	6	7	8	9	R	H	E
SEA	0	0								0	0	0
OAK	0	0								0	0	0

[Dan Muir] Well, partner, we came to the park looking to see a historic hit, but so far, we've just seen two pitchers play catch with their catchers today.

[Tyson Porter] Both Shakely and Terranova have started off on target, locating their pitches and confusing the hitters.

[Dan Muir] The crowd certainly loves it. They're on their feet and dancing like it's a playoff game.

[Tyson Porter] You know, sometimes the A's have a reputation for light attendance throughout the year. But when they show, they're loud and active. It's a great atmosphere for baseball, one of the best.

[Dan Muir] Auditioning for a new job, Tyson?

[Tyson Porter, laughing] Any job in baseball is a good job, Dan.

Lizzie took another sip of wine. Her eyes were on the game, but her thoughts were in several different places. She continued to replay her interaction with Eddie. She was perplexed at his contentment of sitting outside in his truck.

"Is that Robbie?" Leticia pointed to the TV. The focus was on an old woman dancing to the music of ABBA's "Dancing Queen." The camera pulled back. "In the upper-right corner."

Well, it wasn't all of Robbie—his face wasn't in the frame—but his unique A's tank top was recognizable in their typical seats. Next to him, his friends were laughing and sipping beers.

"Yeah, I think so?" Stephen said. "Looks like he's having fun."

"More fun than here?" Lizzie asked. Her sarcastic tone thickened the air.

"Elizabeth, don't you start," Carol said.

"What? Mom, I'm just saying."

"Saying what?" Stephen asked.

Lizzie bit her lip. She reminded herself that today wasn't about the issues she had with her brother or how she thought it was wrong for Robbie to be at the game. He should be here. All of them were expected to be here. Instead, Lizzie focused on her third glass of Chardonnay. After her encounter with Eddie on the street outside, the first pour went down like a glass of water. She greedily took a second, and now she was sitting next to her mom on the loveseat watching the game with her latest glass. She knew that the buttery liquid was only a temporary solution to dull the senses, but that's what she needed. Eddie's appearance exposed open nerve endings she had purposely suppressed. Now, in her father's final hours, she couldn't risk breaking the thread by which she was hanging. She kept telling herself to focus on the game and the memories she had of watching baseball with her dad.

Her first memory of baseball with him was a trip with the Girls Scouts when she was ten years old. The game was the only thing her dad had talked about for weeks. Since moving to Sacramento two years before, he hadn't been to the Coliseum, and this was a chance to introduce his daughter to the game he loved so much. Lizzie recalled the excitement of that day, being with her friends and her dad. She didn't remember anything about the game, except for a moment, when there was a crack of the bat, and her father called, "Heads up!"

Lizzie had been eating a scoop of ice cream in a tiny plastic A's helmet. Ann, her best friend, squealed and dropped under her seat. Lizzie looked up and squinted, trying to understand what was happening. Fans rushed to her section, and she thought she might be trampled. She saw a ball coming from out of the sky toward her, then her father reached up and caught it.

"Ow," he'd said before transferring the ball from the right to left hand to shake out the pain. Everyone around him cheered. Her dad smiled as he tried to hand Lizzie the ball. Lizzie refused to trade the ice cream for the ball, but he offered to hold the upturned mini A's helmet while she ate. Lizzie later realized he wanted the cold cup on his hand. She was so proud of her dad. Lizzie thought he was a superhero, and for years she brought that ball to be autographed.

Lizzie shook away the memory and dove her hand into her purse to pull out a ball covered with the ink of dozens of blue and black signatures. Some were still vibrant as ever. Others had faded. Some in ballpoint pen, some with a Sharpie. There were even some scuffs from when Stephen had used it to play catch. She walked over to the side of the bed where Heidi was still sitting next to her grandpa. Heidi recognized the ball, smiled, and offered Lizzie her seat. As Lizzie sat down, her father slowly turned his head from the TV to her. As she showed him the ball, he squinted, and his lips turned upward, bringing life to his face.

"Dad, look what I brought." Lizzie placed the ball in his hand.

"Oh, wow, you still have that ball?" Stephen said. "I bet that's worth a lot."

"More if you hadn't played catch with David in the middle of the street when we were kids," Lizzie said.

Stephen laughed, recalling his neighbor. "Well, it wasn't my fault David couldn't throw."

Kevin shook his head and tried to laugh but didn't have the energy.

"I know. I realized my mistake," Stephen said. "And Dad made me wash cars every weekend for six months."

"Our cars were the cleanest for those six months. Right, Dad?" Lizzie looked down at her father, whose eyes were closed, his mouth slightly open. A wave of fear came to her. "Dad?"

Stephen stood up. They looked at the heart monitor. It was still beeping, but the spikes were weaker than they were a minute earlier. *Oh God*, Lizzie thought. *Is this it?*

* * *

Dana stood in the press lounge, ready to throw her phone at the concrete wall after she had hung up with Matt Daniels, her mom's financial advisor. He wasn't any help. He confirmed what she already knew. Her mother had been scammed, and there was very little likelihood that Kathleen was getting any of that money back. Still, Dana laid into him for not stopping it.

"I'm so sorry. She's a sweet lady, but she was the perfect mark," Matt said. "I told her I had my doubts and reservations, but she was totally taken by this guy. On the last call, I really pushed back. I suggested hiring a private investigator to look into him. She said that she trusted him and that hiring a PI would violate that trust and how dare I even suggest she betray that trust. Nothing I said made her change her mind. In the end, it was her money, her decision, no matter how much I advised against it."

According to Matt, Kathleen Peck was now on a severely fixed income and would need to find a roommate or a part-time job. *Or live with me*, Dana thought. Pangs of conscience swept over her. Scammers take advantage of lonely, old people who wouldn't be so lonely if their children paid them any attention. Maybe, if Dana hadn't been so focused on her career and not taken her mom for granted, this never would have happened. Her mom always wanted her to succeed and be strong and independent. And instead of returning that support, Dana took her independence and selfishly focused on the next job and the next move.

"Well, if it isn't Dana Peck?" came a voice from behind her. Dana recognized it, but it had been years since it was directed at her. In fact, the last time she had seen him wasn't on a date, per se, but attending a Christmas party together. They had left separately but chosen to forget the circumstances.

"Oh, wow. Paul Buckley," Dana said. "Are you covering today's game? You don't look like you are."

Buckley smiled and shook his head. The years had treated him well. Even in jeans, a light jacket, and a T-shirt, he was one of the most handsome men she had ever met. Buckley ran his hand through his hair, bringing back memories of their friends-with-benefits romance. Yes, he had sent dick pics, but she didn't mind at all.

He came in for a hug, and he smelled so good. She remembered he was now a local anchor, a step down in many ways from ESPN, but the rumor was he wanted to be closer to his parents in Sacramento. He was all she needed to take a break from thinking about her mom.

"So good to see you," Buckley said. "Not on the job today. In fact, I'm here with my future stepson, Will."

At first, she thought he was joking. Part of what made their relationship so great was their equal disdain of matrimony over career. They used each other for superficial physical and emotional needs—a plus-one at parties and weddings, a colleague to solicit career advice, a booty call late at night or when they were on the road together.

"Stepson?" she laughed with a hint of sarcasm. "You're getting married? The world must be coming to an end."

"I know. Pretty crazy, right?"

Dana's fantasy stopped cold, and she attempted a poker face to hide her surprise, disappointment, and dip in self-worth. What did this say about her and her priorities? He was more fucked up with relationships than she was with a network of women across the country more extensive than the Mary Kay company. And he was the one getting married?

"I'm sure there are hearts breaking wide open across the world."

"Right, that was part of my problem. It took me some time, but I found the right person who makes me happy in every way."

Dana was struck by his shimmering glow in the fluorescent light. Dana looked around. Buckley was alone. There was no little kid clinging to his leg.

"Well, where's the boy now? You left him alone?"

Buckley laughed. "Oh, right, he's fifteen, and he's meeting up with a friend right now. Kinda why I came up to see if Henderson was around to thank him for the tickets and to give Will some time to hang with this girl from school."

"Well, your influence is obviously apparent if he's already trying to pick up girls."

"Not exactly, but he has a good heart. I just hope it doesn't get broken."

"That's great, Paul. I'm so happy for you," Dana said. She looked at him. How could she resent him for having it all together when her life was blowing up? She wanted to be angry, but the change in him was remarkable. He always had a great smile, but it was a bit superficial, like it was painted on. But the Paul Buckley before her wasn't the pure veneer that she had seen many years ago. In the past, Paul saw his relationships as transactions. He charmed. He smiled. He did all the right things. In some ways, he was like Richard. This Paul Buckley was different. He stood before her relaxed, comfortable with being vulnerable, and happy. Whoever had captured Paul Buckley's heart had cut through all the shiny pieces of armor and made him more beautiful than ever. His eyes glanced down to her chest, and she thought he may be giving her the once-over, but then she remembered the lemonade.

"So, are you introducing pink-slasher film to the baseball-viewing masses?"

"No, lemonade. Ran into a vendor."

Buckley winced and nodded. "Something like that happened to me last year, but it was at a high school football game."

"I can't believe you're back doing local sports. That's crazy." Out of the corner of her eye, Dana saw the PA enter the long hall with her garment bag. Back to reality. "Thank God, she's here."

"I bet you've got a quick change," Buckley said.

"Yeah," Dana said. It was time for goodbyes. She took a beat and just looked at the man he had become. "Hey, Paul. I'm so happy for you. You look, and I sincerely mean this, you look happy, and that's just wonderful."

"Thanks, Dana. That means a lot."

Dana smiled. She hugged him one more time, not as a one-time lover but as an old friend. She kissed his cheek, then reached up and touched his face.

"See you around, Paul."

She grabbed the garment bag and rushed to the press-box bathroom, Palmetto's voice screaming in her earpiece.

CHAPTER 16

Bottom of the Third

	1	2	3	4	5	6	7	8	9	R	H	E
SEA	0	0	0							0	0	0
OAK	0	0								0	0	0

[Dan Muir] As we start the bottom of the third, the fifteen-year veteran Clint Shakely has dialed back the clock and is showing the electric stuff of old.

[Tyson Porter] Yeah, I didn't like digging into the box against him back then, and I'd hate to be doing that now.

[Dan Muir] We talked about Shakely's abrasive personality.

[Tyson Porter] And that was to his teammates. As opposing batters, sometimes we wanted to rush the mound from the on-deck circle as a preemptive strike.

[Dan Muir, laughing] And you know this from personal experience?

[Tyson Porter] I got myself into a few heated exchanges with Shakely over the years.

[Dan Muir] Certainly your signature admiration of the ball flight and bat flip after a home run didn't go over well with him.

[Tyson Porter] Dan, you're a man of art and culture. You've been to the Louvre. You have to stop and admire beautiful things. It's just that Shakely doesn't have the same tastes in art. And he likes to let you know when he disagrees with you. Sometimes with a heater near the ear.

[Dan Muir] But he's still in the league.

[Tyson Porter] He's a badass in every sense of the word. You hate it when you're opposing him. You put up with him when he's on your team because he's a bully on the mound and won't back down. But for the A's, it's important to stay in there. At some point, he's going to make a mistake or at least give you one good pitch to hit.

For the first time today, Will felt like himself. He wasn't Paul Buckley's future stepson, and nobody cared about the "Catch of the Day." Instead, he was lost in the world of Amanda Wright as she talked about her parents, playing softball, and her annoying brother. The game was just a backdrop. Then it all crashed the moment her phone buzzed. She turned to shield her screen from him while her thumbs busily typed out a message. She sighed, pressed send, and turned back to him. She rolled her eyes in annoyance and mock fatigue.

"Everything okay?"

"Boys are so dumb."

"Hey," Will said, his hand to his chest in mock shock. "I'm offended."

"Hate to break it to you, but your gender is dumb. Do you know Darren Foyle?"

"Yeah, he's the stoner skateboarder."

"Yeah, so I went out with him because he seemed, like, totally chill, but he's not at all. He wants to know what I'm doing all the time. He's exhausting."

"He's your boyfriend?" Will's chest tightened, dreading her answer. He should have listened to Paul.

"Not really. We've just hung out a couple times. My dad hates him, which is kinda fun. And he's damn cute."

Will's fantasy world crumbled. How dumb was he to think that Amanda would fall for him at a stupid baseball game? Their time at the cap stand seemed so effortless. He was just himself, and she was, as always, perfect. But the reality had set in. He wasn't going to sweep her off her feet and come to school on Monday with her on his arm. It didn't work like that for him. It happened for Paul. It happened for Darren Foyle. But not him.

Paul had warned Will not to get his hopes too high. What did he say? Just to have her get to know him as a person? What fun was that? The endgame was never the "friend zone." He would always be stuck there. No amount of advice from a dad, stepdad, or anyone else was going to help with that.

"You okay, Will?" Amanda asked, shaking him from his self-loathing.

"Yeah, I'm good. I should probably get back to our seats."

"Oh, okay? I thought we were having fun."

Will was having fun, until the bomb had dropped. At least it was less awkward than watching Paul socialize with forty thousand people. He did have the extra seat, and Paul was up in the press box. She was much easier to look at than him.

"Do you want to go to our seats? We have an extra one since my mom didn't come. Paul's up at the press box anyway. It will be totally chill."

Amanda weighed the options, then texted something on her phone.

"Sure, my folks say it's cool for a little bit. I wasn't kidding when I said I needed to get away from them. They're sometimes too much."

"Believe me, I get it," Will said.

They walked down the steps to Will's seats. Paul still hadn't returned.

"Great, he's not back yet," Will said.

"Seems like you don't like your new stepdad."

"It's not that. It's like I just disappear when he's around. Everyone wants to talk to him, and it's like I'm a ghost."

"Well, he's pretty famous. Good looking too."

"Don't remind me."

"How did your mom meet him again? They totally don't seem like a match."

"They grew up together. My mom, my dad, and Paul. I guess my mom and Paul dated in high school, but she and my dad got together after college. Paul was one of my dad's best friends, and they went camping together every year for, like, twenty years. Anyway, my dad died in a car wreck coming from Paul's house. After he died, Paul promised to take care of my mom and me. Paul made it his mission to do dad stuff with me—camping, playing catch, ballgames, and that was really cool. He also was a comfort to my mom. At some point, the promise to my dad became a romantic relationship for my mom. And I can't get over that."

"Oh, wow, I didn't know all that."

"I know, right? Some kinda soap opera."

"Well, at least he's there for you, right?" Amanda put her hand on his knee. Her touch was like ten thousand volts shooting through his system. He tried to remain cool.

"Yeah, I guess."

"I mean, I know a lot of kids whose parents don't give a shit."

"True."

"I guess, just give him a chance."

Like on cue, Paul slid into the seat next to Amanda.

Will blew out a big sigh. He needed some lemonade.

* * *

"Lemonade," Derek yelled, holding up the yellow liquid. "Ice-cold lemonade, heerah!"

He scanned the crowd looking for potential customers. When he had a moment, Derek eyed the game and the scoreboard. He smiled with confidence each time Shakely mowed down an Oakland Athletic with precision, but his focus was on the sales in front of him. He looked for hot-and-sweaty kids without a beverage in front of them. Then he'd raise his voice, change the inflection, and look at the kid with his kindest eyes. He knew if the kid smiled and salivated for the tasty beverage, he was halfway there. That trick worked up to ten years old. Then, Derek would just give a nod, try to act like the cool uncle or guy on the street to say, "You want this lemonade. It's cool. It'll make you feel good."

It was easier before phones. Now the kids just stared at the screen instead of having nothing else to do but watch the game.

The trick worked on his way around to the right-field side. He was close to selling out another tray when he spotted a teenager, his girlfriend, and his dad, though the man looked familiar, like he'd seen him before, but not at the stadium. The dad put up his hand. Recognition penetrated his brain. It was the ESPN guy Paul Buckley.

Derek nodded to the boy. "Lemonade?"

"We'll take two," Buckley said. He pulled out his card. Derek scanned the card and handed the lemonade down the aisle. The boy didn't look anything like his father. Maybe he'd grow into his dad's features. And the girl was definitely out of the boy's league. But maybe she liked him for the money. Derek was sure Buckley pulled in good coin.

"There's your catch of the day," Derek said to Buckley, who gave a polite, but strained, smile. The boy rolled his eyes, and the girl shook her head and took a sip of her lemonade. Yep, she was way too good-looking to be with that kid.

Derek moved on. He was still behind pace for what he should be selling, and with the game moving a bit quicker than normal, that meant less time to sell. Also, since it was a good game, he didn't get the boredom sales, when fans just bought because it was something to do. He spied another fan a few rows up and hustled over. On the aisle was the kid he had met at Club Maui. He recognized him because of that distinctive tank top and those eyes carrying a deep sadness, but the kid smiled in recognition of Derek coming up the steps.

"Hey, Club Maui," the young man said. Derek was surprised he wasn't more intoxicated. "You were there this morning."

"Hey, guy, sure was. I see you found your group. Good for you. Hope you're enjoying the game."

Derek took the card from one of the young man's friends, swiped it, and handed it back with the lemonade.

"Oh yeah, things are good, man. I even convinced that usher over there to get a note to Austen. He needs to know about my grandpa."

Derek smiled and raised his eyebrows. He didn't have time to decipher the garbled nonsense coming out of the mouths of drunks. He needed to sell more lemonades. With a fast game, he was sure the demand would only go up, and he needed every cent.

CHAPTER 17

Top of the Fourth

	1	2	3	4	5	6	7	8	9	R	H	E
SEA	0	0	0							0	0	0
OAK	0	0	0							0	0	0

[Dan Muir] After a quick three-up, three-down inning for Shakely to end the third, we're heading into the fourth inning here in Oakland. Both pitchers have faced the minimum.

[Tyson Porter] This is a baseball purist's dream—a pitcher's duel. I wouldn't be surprised if we started to see the managers playing some small ball, get a man on base, and try to disrupt the rhythm of the pitchers. Seattle has the top of the order coming up. Expect Tom Cooper, Mario Martinez, or Nelson White to wait for their pitch against Terranova.

[Dan Muir] Hey, folks, imagine coming to the ballpark to work for more than twenty years. This after being a postal worker for thirty.

[Tyson Porter] Sounds like a dream.

[Dan Muir] At the stadium the A's are recognizing a longtime usher, Fred Stephenson. Stephenson has worked for the Athletics as an usher since 2000, and today is his last game.

[Tyson Porter] And what a game to be your final one. All the best to you, Mr. Stephenson.

Fred was a little embarrassed. He thought the tribute prior to the game was enough recognition. But when the PA announcer said, "May I have your attention, please," Fred looked up at the large scoreboard to see his own face staring back.

Ladies and gentlemen, please direct your attention to the right-field stands. Today marks the end of an era for one of the Oakland A's' top ambassadors. For twenty-two years, Fred Stephenson has roamed the aisles in right field as a member of the guest-services staff. He's seen his share of Oakland A's highlights from the twenty-game winning streak to Brett Austen's hitting tear. He's helped fans to their seats for more than 1,700 games and provided good cheer to millions of A's fans over that time. Today is his final game. Please help the Oakland A's recognize Fred Stephenson for his twenty-two years of service. Thank you, Fred.

Fred looked around. People were giving him standing ovations. He didn't understand why anyone thought this was an accomplishment. He performed his job every day, like any one of these people. He showed up. He did the job. He went home. Still, Fred was touched, and he wiped tears from his eyes as he watched his Section 104 neighborhood recognize him. Like all the ballplayers he had witnessed after a memorable accomplishment, he pulled his cap from his sweaty gray head and waved it. He turned around and felt the cheers envelop him. When he turned back, there was Rich, his boss. Behind was the A's PR guy and a photographer

In recognition of Fred's fine service to the A's and the Oakland community, he is being presented with a baseball signed by every player on the Oakland A's roster. Congratulations Fred, and good luck in your retirement.

Fred looked out onto the field. Each Oakland Athletic, including Brett Austen, turned toward him, clapping and tipping their caps. He had seen all of their Coliseum debuts, whether they were visitors or an Athletic, a veteran or a wide-eyed rookie. He had been here for all of it, and here they were, recognizing him, just some retired postal worker looking for something to do. He was a part of their story as much as they were his. Outside the typical milestones of life, this was the greatest moment he had ever experienced.

Told you they'd do something special.

"Well, Fred, we told the players you were retiring, and they lined up to sign this ball," Rich said. "We're all so proud of you and thankful for your service to the organization. I know I wouldn't be here if it wasn't for you and your mentorship all those years ago. You'll be missed."

"Thanks, Rich," Fred said. "This means a lot."

Fred took the baseball and looked at the signatures covering every space. There was Joe Schmitke, Don Dinsmore, JT Berman, and Frank Garza. Of course, Brett Austen took the sweet spot between the stitching. In terms of monetary value, the A's weren't good enough for it to be worth anything huge.

In fact, if it just had Austen's signature, it might be worth more. But to Fred, this memento would require prominent placement in his new home. After standing with Rich for a photo, Fred felt the stiff rectangular paper, triggering his duty to Robbie. And if he was going to make the ask, he might as well do it now with all the goodwill floating around.

"Hey, was wondering, since it's my last day and all, could you do me a favor?"

Rich raised an eyebrow as if public recognition in front of the crowd and a team-signed baseball wasn't favor enough.

"I mean, thank you for what you've done here," Fred said. "This is something more than I ever dreamed of. And I appreciate everything, truly. But I need you to put a note in Brett Austen's locker. It's important he sees it."

Rich remained skeptical.

"Is this note from you?"

"No, it's a fan whose grandfather is dying."

"Do you know what it says?"

Fred shook his head. "All I know is it's about his grandfather dying, and he really wants Austen to see it. Can we do that?"

"Is that the favor you're asking for on your final day? To deliver a message, not even from you, to the biggest A's star of a generation?"

Fred nodded. Part of him didn't know why he was putting himself on the line. But underneath the doubt, he knew this was right. He felt it.

Rich considered the request. If it was any other usher on any other day, Fred knew Rich would say no. But for some reason, whether it was the grandpa sob story or Fred, Rich's rigid heart loosened just a fraction, and he took the note.

"God, this is some ratty paper. Are you sure it's legit and not some psycho trying to get something out of Austen?"

"It's absolutely true," Fred said.

"All right, since you're gone after today, and I won't have to deal with any other yokels for six months, I'll do it. But only because you're you, okay?"

"Yes, sir," Fred said. "Thank you, Rich."

* * *

Clarkson looked up from his phone and turned to Dana.

"Palmetto wants us to go interview that usher."

He nodded up to the scoreboard, where an older black man was tipping his cap.

"I thought we were doing this later," Dana said.

During the production meeting, Palmetto had remarked that they would talk to Fred Stephenson in the sixth or seventh inning.

"Muir just mentioned it on the broadcast, so the time is now. We gotta hustle. The way these pitchers are sitting them down, we don't have much time."

Dana trailed Clarkson and French as they speed walked through the concourse. Despite having changing and cleaning herself off in the press-box bathroom, she still felt sticky from the lemonade. She was frustrated. Yes, running around during the game was her job, and she was grateful for it, but it was all this other stuff. Running into the lemonade guy, seeing a former lover and finding out he was getting married, the opportunity to call games for a major-league club. And then there was the situation with her mom. There was just not enough time to process everything, let alone make these critical decisions.

I just need this week, she thought. *That gives me some time to figure out Kansas City, do my job, and understand Mom's finances.*

With that resolve, she descended down the aisle with French and Clarkson to Section 104. The Mariners had runners on first and second with no outs and Ronnie White at the plate. Dana was a bit relieved. They would have enough time to get in a few questions. Dana shifted focus and looked at her notes from the production meeting that morning: *Retired postal worker. First season in 2000. Wife recently died.* All she needed were the basic questions.

The usher was already standing with Pete Henderson. Palmetto had texted him at the same time he'd talked to Clarkson. She heard the crack and a murmur. Terranova induced a ground ball to Dinsmore who turned and threw to second baseman Rolando Vasquez and onto first for the double play. And just like that, there were two outs.

"Are you all about there yet?" Palmetto said in Dana's ear.

"Just got here," Dana said.

"All right. I see French's camera. We're coming to you in thirty seconds."

"We've got thirty," Dana said to French and Clarkson.

Dana turned to the usher and took a breath. Time to transition and make this genial man feel comfortable.

"Hi, I'm Dana Peck."

"This is Fred Stephenson," Henderson said.

The usher looked at Henderson. He didn't need anyone to speak for him.

"Hi, Ms. Peck," Stephenson said. "Welcome to my neighborhood."

Dana smiled at why he was a beloved member of the guest-services staff, thinking this will be a good interview.

"We're coming to you in ten," Palmetto said.

Dan Muir's voice was pumped into her earpiece.

[Dan Muir] With two outs in the fourth inning, we go down to Dana Peck who's speaking with a remarkable member of the A's guest-services staff. Dana?"

[Dana Peck] Dan, I'm here with Fred Stephenson, an usher with the A's for more than twenty years. He's worked more than seventeen hundred games in that time and is a beloved member of his staff. Fred, I loved what you said when I introduced myself. You said, 'Welcome to my neighborhood.'"

[Fred Stephenson] Of course, this is my part of town. We're all friends here.

[Dana Peck] So, you've been here for more than two decades. What moments stand out for you?

[Fred Stephenson] You know, some of my best memories are in the stands. I've seen eleven marriage proposals. I even saw a woman go into labor right over there. Just like out there, life happens in my neighborhood.

[Dana Peck] So, today is your last game as an usher. What do you plan to do now?

[Fred Stephenson] Well, I'm moving tomorrow, and I plan to spend time with my grandkids and my son and his wife and maybe next year sitting on the couch and watching games on the TV. Maybe I'll come back for a couple too.

[Dana Peck] What do you think of today's game for your final outing?

[Fred Stephenson] Can't ask for anything more. I hope Austen gets his hit, but it's going to be tough. Shakely's looking pretty good today.

[Dana Peck] Well, he'll get another chance in the coming inning. Thanks, Fred, for your hospitality in Section 104, and good luck in the future. Back to you, Dan.

[Dan Muir] The crowd is on its feet, cheering on Terranova. After giving up a leadoff single to Cooper, a walk to Martinez, he's one pitch away from getting out of the inning. Here's the pitch. Swung on and missed. Darrell Love strikes out. No runs, one hit, and one left on base, and in the middle of the fourth inning, we're still scoreless in Oakland on the Baseball Broadcast Network.

CHAPTER 18

Bottom of the Fourth

	1	2	3	4	5	6	7	8	9	R	H	E
SEA	0	0	0	0						0	0	0
OAK	0	0	0							0	1	0

[Dan Muir] As we come back to Oakland, the crowd is back on its feet. After a marvelous bit of pitching that gave some life to this crowd, Brett Austen returns to the plate, trying to get that hit to propel himself into the record books.

[Tyson Porter] Man, if this crowd wasn't alive before, they are now.

[Dan Muir] Before the game, Brett Austen talked about the fans and the lift they provide him.

[Brett Austen interview] I wouldn't be here without the fans. They allow me to do something I love for a living. During those times when I just didn't want to get out there or thought about putting in the bare minimum, I remembered that there were fans who were paying to watch me play baseball, and there's a responsibility there, you know? Maybe this is the only time they're going to see me. Maybe they've saved up to go to the game, or maybe the tickets were a gift. I have an obligation to do my best.

[Tyson Porter] That's why Austen's in the position he's in today. Some days, it's a grind to get up, do the preparation, and compete at a high level. Sometimes, you just want to phone it in. But the best, guys like Austen, don't take those days. Talking to the coaches and management on the field before the game, they see no difference in him today versus a random Tuesday in July.

[Dan Muir] Shakely delivers the first pitch. Berman pops up to the catcher, and just like that, there's one away. Now, here comes Brett Austen for his second try to get a hit and secure that .400 season.

Brett walked to the plate, and the beats of *Lose Yoursself* propelled the crowd into a frenzy. This time, though, he didn't wiggle his shoulders. He didn't acknowledge the crowd. No, his focus was on Shakely.

Getting a little anxious, Brett? What happens if you don't get a hit this time?

Shakely's confidence was brimming after retiring ten straight batters and hoping to make Brett his eleventh victim. Tomlin was giddy.

"This last hit is going to be harder than you thought," Tomlin said as Brett dug his feet into the dirt. "My boy's dealing."

He's right. This ain't no coronation. No historic moment. How does that feel?

Brett tried to block out Tomlin and the demon. The time for pleasantries and small talk was done. Brett needed to jumpstart the offense. He had done it plenty of times during the season. There was the time in Toronto when they were down 4-1 in the ninth inning. But with a leadoff double, Brett single-handedly energized the team, and they batted around and scored six runs in the top of the ninth and eventually won 7-4. From second base, and in the dugout, he was uncharacteristically cheering and pumping everyone up. Because it didn't happen often, he used his cheerleading to great effect.

Right now, his attention was solely on Shakely. As he locked in, Shakely's vision zeroed in on Tomlin's signs. Brett stared back, trying to connect with Shakely to understand what pitch was coming. He hoped for the tipped pitch or a wayward fastball that he could send to the bleachers.

Shakely began his windup, and Brett breathed deep. From the left-hand angle, Brett recognized the red dot of the fastball coming his way. It was a little high but right in his wheelhouse to take a full swing and break open the score. But the speed was a bit faster than Brett had expected. He was late, and the ball careened into the stands just above the Mariners dugout. Foul ball. Strike one.

Oh my. Shakely's getting stronger. This isn't good for you.

Brett stepped back. He looked at Shakely, who grinned and raised his eyebrows. God, what an asshole. Why was Shakely so hard for him to hit? And now, with confidence and adrenaline, Shakely was in full command. Brett stepped back in.

"Man, that one was fast," Tomlin said.

Again, Brett tried not to acknowledge nor take that comment to heart. Just get one good ball to hit. Brett willed his arms and grip to loosen. The key was to keep relaxed. Don't let the moment overtake the technique. He breathed. He watched Shakely, who cracked his knuckles.

Wait, that was the tell for the curveball. Good. Brett had waited for this moment, and here it was. Focus on the curve and see if it drops into the strike zone. Focus on the spin. Watch the angle. The ball came out smooth. It was going to drop right into the strike zone. It wasn't going to hang, per se, but Brett was ready for it. See ball, hit ball. He swung.

The bat connected but skimmed the top of the ball, which dribbled toward first base. Shakely, following through toward third base, recovered. He moved three steps to his left, away from his planted food, causing him to field the ball barehanded, spin, and throw in one motion. It wasn't a routine play, there was a degree of difficulty to it. As Shakely spun and threw, Brett continued to sprint toward first base. He might be able to leg out an infield single and get his .400 after all. It wasn't the way he preferred to secure his achievement, but he would take it.

The crowd was on its feet cheering. It was going to be close. Brett watched as Seattle first basemen Dustin Reese strode to the bag and stuck out his glove, awaiting the throw. Reese stepped out, extending his leg and arm. It stretched further and further. Finally, Brett was one step away from the bag. He could make it. He was close. As Brett extended his foot to touch first base, Reese's foot came off the bag to catch the ball. But the ball moved past Reese's mitt and into the Mariners' dugout. The umpire called Brett safe, ruled the ball out of play, and awarded Brett second base.

Brett smiled and jogged toward second base. He did it. He got his hit.

The crowd cheered. Brett turned toward the stands as he slowed and walked toward second. He was about to take off his helmet and acknowledge the crowd, when the cheers turned to boos. Brett looked up at the scoreboard, and he knew.

E-1

Instead of giving a hit and error on the throw, it was being scored as a two-base error. Most times, grace is given to a player having to make a difficult play. If Reese had made the catch, Brett thought the play would have been ruled an infield hit. So why was it ruled a two-base error? Also, as it didn't count as a hit, his average dropped again. The boos continued.

As he stood on second, Mariners second baseman Darnell Love and shortstop Mario Martinez met him. Even though they were on opposing teams, they shook their heads

"Can you believe that shit?" Love said.

"Was it an error?" Brett asked.

"I don't think so," Martinez said. "Clint had to make a tough play. He had to regrip the ball. Maybe that's why."

"I thought it was a hit," Love mumbled. "You got screwed."

"Well, shit," Brett said. "I saw that pitch well too. Just topped the sucker."

"Yeah, almost made it a no-doubter," Love said. "And now some out-of-shape official-scorekeeper hack in the press box makes that decision for you. Ain't the game great?"

"That guy never liked me when he wrote for the *Chronicle*," Brett said. He shook his head. Damn sportswriters. Even when they retired to scorekeeping, they still held grudges.

The universe doesn't want you to get the hit, Brett. You put your faith in the wrong place. Now, you have maybe one more chance. You're screwed.

Brett took off his batting gloves and slid them into his pocket. He watched Willis step into the batter's box. The crowd grew a little more boisterous. After three and a half innings of virtually empty basepaths, now they were shaken awake by the controversial call and their hero on base.

Like he did in Toronto, Brett raised his hands, imploring the crowd and his teammates to return the energy. The crowd took his cue and cheered. Let's put focus back on the team and take away from this obsession with the hit. That's what he had done throughout the season.

The demon had set up camp inside his brain. He felt it. Throughout the year, there were always moments of doubt. But he trusted himself to get through the game, through the at bat, and to do his best. But there was no tomorrow. There was no way to make up for a bad day today. There was at least one and possibly two more at bats, and doubt was creeping in.

This is the pinnacle of your career. It's never going to be this good again, and if you fail, you'll be remembered for not being good enough.

Even his attempts to pump up the crowd and his team didn't work against Shakely. Willis hit a long fly ball to the left-field corner, where it was caught at the warning track by Ben Morales. Shakely got Gus Williams to strike out for the second time, and at the end of the fourth inning, it was 0-0 with no hope for a big offensive day.

Brett jogged back into the clubhouse. He was offered condolences by his teammates and coaches.

"Bullshit call," Garza said. "That should have been a hit. The scorekeeper has never played a game of ball in his life."

"It was close," Brett said.

"Should have given you the benefit of the doubt."

Brett went to his small cubby, replaced his fielding glove with his batting gloves, grabbed a quick swig of water, and started back out.

"Still got one or two more at bats to get it back."

CHAPTER 19

Top of the Fifth

	1	2	3	4	5	6	7	8	9	R	H	E
SEA	0	0	0	0						0	2	1
OAK	0	0	0	0						0	0	0

[Dan Muir] As we get back to Oakland, there's some controversy in the press box. The official scorer is sticking by his decision to score Austen's dribbler an error on Shakely, dropping Austen's average again from .39966 to .39898.

[Tyson Porter] Kinda surprises me, Dan. The home scorekeeper typically scores plays in favor of the home team and particularly star players. But I guess not in this case.

[Dan Muir] Apparently, there was a shouting match between the A's press man Ron Henderson and the scorer in between innings.

[Tyson Porter] We all know who has the power in that relationship.

[Dan Muir] Apparently, like usher Fred Stephenson, this is the scorer's last game.

[Tyson Porter] Well, if it wasn't before, it certainly is now.

Like everyone, Derek had stopped everything and watched Austen's at bat. From his vantage point on the second deck near the left-field foul pole, Derek felt a punch to his gut when Austen was declared safe. It was the end of the line. He'd need to win the final parlay and beg Owen to pay him tomorrow morning so he could pay off Carlos and part of his back child support. But there wouldn't be enough for the dance class, and he imagined the look on Jasmine's face when she realized her disappointment.

The chorus of boos shook him from his self-loathing, and when he looked up and saw the error, he closed his mouth tight, holding back his scream of jubilation. He was still in it, and this error was further validation. This was the day. This was the moment he'd look back on realizing everything had changed. He wasn't chasing the score. From now on, he owned his narrative.

On his way back to refill his tray, he ducked into the stairwell and called Pam.

"Yeah, what's up? Shouldn't you be working?"

"Yeah, I am, okay, but is Jasmine there? I wanna say hi."

"Why?"

"Because I'm getting her those dance classes."

"You have the money?"

"Not yet, but I will." Derek's confidence soared. "Let's just say, I'm having a great day, and it's all coming to—"

"Oh my God, Derek. Listen to yourself. You're delusional. You have a problem."

"Look, after today, I'll be clear, and I've got something brewing with some regular hours helping manage a food truck. After that, I'll be fine. I'll be able to be square. I'm going to do what it takes. I promise. Just let me talk to her."

"No."

"Why not?"

"Because I'm protecting her from you. I know you're going to make a promise you can't keep, and I'm going to have to pick up the pieces. No, you can talk to her when I get the money."

"Pam, I'm trying to do the right thing. I'm not abandoning my daughter. I'm not like those guys who just spread their seed and don't care about what happens next. I want to be a part of her life. Yeah, so I have a side hustle that's a little dirty and unreliable, but I'm trying to change that."

Silence. Derek thought Pam had ended the call. He pressed the phone closer to his ear and plugged his other ear with a finger to block the sounds of the concourse. He finally heard Pam's light sobs. She sniffed and sighed.

"Derek, you need help. And I hope you get it, because she adores you, and I know you feel the same. But until you make Jasmine your first love, you'll never be able to keep your promises to her."

Derek shook his head. His anger flamed from within.

"What are you talking about, first love? I don't love you. Jasmine is my first love."

"I'm not talking about me or your mom. And the fact you don't know what's tops in your life doesn't give me hope."

Derek ended the call and rounded his arm to throw the phone against the wall but stopped short. He was catching all the right breaks on his bets, so why did he feel like everything was falling apart?

* * *

Fred looked at his watch. The game was making good time. They were halfway through, and it was only 2:15 p.m. Perhaps the game would end early, but Fred knew better than to verbalize this. He had twenty years of empirical evidence and experience of someone remarking on the fast pace of play and dooming the rest of the game to slow to a halt.

He had made the mistake himself when he'd first began working there. Oakland pitcher Tim Hudson was on the mound, forcing hitters to blast the ball into the ground to shortstop Miguel Tejada, who'd throw them out at first. The first six innings took just ninety minutes. Fred had turned to a fan and joked, "I might get out of here and see a *Law & Order* tonight."

The fan didn't crack a smile, only shook his head.

"You just ruined it," he said, pushing up the collar of his coat and settling in for a long, cold summer night in Oakland.

"What?"

"I'll just let you watch and reap what you sow." The man just stared straight ahead, hands folded over his gut.

Sure enough, Hudson hit a batter, walked another, then gave up a home run. Art Howe lifted Hudson for a line of relievers. The last three innings took two hours and what had been a one-zero lead for the A's turned into a nine-to-seven loss. As the game ended, the fan turned to Fred as he left and said, "Don't ever do that again."

Fred's memory was jolted by the loud boom of the ball coming off the bat, followed by the collective groan from the fans. He didn't need to look. The A's were now behind. Over his shoulder, Mariners first baseman Dustin Reese trotted around the bases. The crowd's energy was now deflated, the expectation for Austen's crowning achievement on top of an A's victory circumvented by a cranky Mariners pitcher and a home run.

Fred looked over to Winnie, her face in her hands. She shook her head.

"Winnie, it's only one run. We can come back from that," Fred said.

Sometimes, half of his job was giving the fans hope when they expected bad things to happen.

"Austen likely has a couple of at bats left. He'll come through. You'll see."

"You're too positive," Winnie said. "This is a game of failure. After twenty years of standing here and watching the game, I'd have thought you'd realize that by now."

"I've also seen the brilliant and miraculous too. I just prefer to look at those instead."

Winnie's white head bowed and shook, but when she looked up, her sweet smile appeared again.

"You're the most positive person I've ever met. Even after the last year you've had, you still keep that smile on your face."

Fred would miss Winnie. He placed a hand on her shoulder and scanned the crowd. Karina was smiling, more interested on what was scrolling through her phone than what had happened right before her. Eric had put his hands through his full dark head of hair while his friends were in equal display of disappointment and disgust. Next to them was Robbie, staring at Fred. Fred climbed the steps. He needed to update Robbie on his message to Austen.

"Hey, all," he said as he reached them. "Enjoying the game?"

"Except for that fucking home run," Eric said.

"Eric." Karina elbowed him.

"Austen just needs to get his hit," Eric said.

"Still have a couple at bats to go," Fred said. He turned his attention to Robbie. "I gave your note to my supervisor, who's going to try to get it on Austen's locker."

Robbie's eyes brightened. "Really? Thank you so much."

"No guarantees. I had to really lay on it thick with my 'last game' angle and all that. And it still has to pass a couple hands to get there. But hopefully, he'll have it when he gets to his locker after the game."

Robbie smiled and nodded.

"All right. Well, I hope Austen gets it, and it's after he gets his hit," Fred said. "Now, you guys just keep having a good time, but stay respectful of everyone, okay?"

Karina looked at him and smiled. "Thanks, Fred. We won't make your last day hard, I promise. Plus, this game is going by so fast."

CHAPTER 20

Bottom of the Fifth

	1	2	3	4	5	6	7	8	9	R	H	E
SEA	0	0	0	0	1					1	3	1
OAK	0	0	0	0						0	0	0

[Dan Muir] Well, folks, we do have a run here in this season finale between the Seattle Mariners and the Oakland A's, thanks to a home run by Dustin Reese to put Seattle ahead one to zero going into the bottom of the fifth.

[Tyson Porter] Reese tagged Terranova, and there was no doubt that ball was a souvenir. Now, the pressure is all on Oakland to push a run across and tie this one.

[Dan Muir] Tyson, unless Oakland can find a way to solve Clint Shakely, that may be all the Mariners need to secure the win and home-field advantage for the Wild Card Series.

[Tyson Porter] Indeed, all of Shakely's pitches are on point. He's never been fazed by the crowd or the moment. And for one afternoon, he seems to have even brushed back Father Time.

"Eddie's still out on the street," Stephen said. He closed the front door to the house and shook his head. "He's persistent, I'll give him that."

"Why don't you just invite him in?" Carol asked.

Lizzie looked dumbstruck at her mother who was filling her plate with more chips and guacamole. "Because he's my ex-husband. I don't want him here. I don't want our issues to distract from these moments with Dad."

"He's already distracting," Carol said and bit into a tortilla chip.

Ever since the third inning, Lizzie hadn't left her father's side. She'd positioned herself to hold his hand and watch the monitors and the game at the same time.

A quiet hush had descended in the house. It wasn't like before when her dad was conscious and listening to the sibling squabble and conversation and smiling. Everyone was happy to talk. Now, only the sounds of the broadcast and monitors hooked up to her father filled the room. Brett Austen's "error" only drew head-shakes, and the family groaned with Reese's home run.

Lizzie pulled on another glass of wine. Her mind was now numb and less conscious of the cliff toward which she was edging. If she didn't have another glass, she could deal with whatever happened. If her father passed, she was sober enough to comfort her mom and Heidi, call the right people, and move into this next phase. Another drink meant surrender and abdicating all responsibility.

She knew this edge quite well and often played on both sides of that knife. Most times, she found herself on the good side, stopping when she needed and sobering up enough to be the adult. Lizzie didn't want to appear out of control, a bad person, or a drunk. So, she stuck to one or two glasses of wine, and she was fine. But when Heidi was away at school or with friends and Eddie was out of town or "working late," or when she was on a work trip and by herself in her hotel room, she let herself go. A glass of wine easily turned into a bottle, or more, and she'd wake in the middle of the night with a headache, cottonmouth, and self-loathing for the rager-for-one she had thrown for herself. She controlled it. After all, she wasn't one of those alcoholics where one drink led to ten.

"Look, there's Robbie again." Bart pointed to the television. Robbie was laughing it up with the other young twenty-somethings, his spirits high and carrying on like nothing was happening here in Sacramento. Lizzie fumed, fueled by the alcohol. *Robbie doesn't care,* she thought. *He's disrespectful. He should be here. He should be wallowing in grief, like the rest of us, not being a drunk ass with his friends.*

"Why did you give Robbie the seats?" Lizzie asked. "I thought we'd agreed to sell the seats and turn a nice profit."

"Oh my God," Stephen said and rolled his eyes. "This again? Robbie wanted them, and he felt Grandpa would have wanted him at the game."

"Oh, would he? Would Grandpa want him to get drunk with his friends while he was here taking his last breaths too?" Lizzie's tone and volume increased as she spoke.

"Hey," Carol said. Usually, that's all it would take for Lizzie to back down. Stephen, however, never got the hint.

"Look, Liz, I think Robbie knows what he's doing. He's gone to as many or more games with Dad than we ever did. If anyone can say that Dad would want him at the game, Robbie can."

"This isn't like a Super Bowl party or other insignificant event at the house. This could be it. Robbie may never see his grandpa again, and he's off having a blast with his friends like there's a tomorrow. There isn't. We're here waiting for our dad to die."

"So, are you upset that he's not here or that you're not there?"

Lizzie stood up. "How dare you."

Lizzie walked to the refrigerator and pulled out a bottle of unopened Chardonnay. *Fuck this.* She knew alcohol was considered liquid courage, but she also thought of it as liquid hope, that if she just dulled the pain, fortune would stumble upon her, and she wouldn't have to deal with the nagging darkness that enveloped her.

"Just go ahead and get another glass of wine," Stephen said. "That's your answer."

Lizzie felt angry, embarrassed, and out of control. Normally, there were three ways to de-escalate the tensions between her and Stephen. The first line of defense was always Eddie, who would take the diplomatic approach. He would pull her aside and ask the right questions to help Lizzie identify the underlying issue of her frustration. Eddie would also deflect and get Stephen to talk about himself and his interests. The second line was Carol. She would distract with a joke or an offer of food or steer the conversation to the kids. Carol was so transparent with her intentions that Lizzie and Stephen understood their fallacy and shifted to a more suitable discussion. And when neither Eddie, Carol, nor any other member of the family was successful in stopping the squabble, Kevin's booming Voice of God would come into play. With their father still unconscious in the bed in the middle of the living room, there was only Carol to provide the last-ditch effort to keep the peace.

"That's enough," Carol said. Her eyes were like fire as she looked at Lizzie and Stephen. Carol skipped past deflection and diplomacy and took Kevin's spot as final enforcer. "I will not have you two arguing like this in front of your father. You need to quit this shit *right now.*"

In all of her forty-nine years, Lizzie had only heard her mom swear five times, and she had specific memories of each of them. Carol thought curse words were undisciplined and showed a lack of vocabulary. But there was clear intent and purpose, and the entire room looked at Carol. She had everyone's attention.

Heidi stood up. "Hey, Bart, Andrea, let's go take a walk."

The teens hadn't moved so fast in ages, and the three of them got up and walked out the front door.

* * *

All through the top of the inning, Brett obsessed over the error. Not even Dustin Reese's home run, as it sailed over Berman's head with a trajectory toward the BART station, distracted him. Brett didn't even look back. All he thought about was the error.

You didn't deserve that weak-ass hit anyway. That was your best chance at getting .400, and you're not getting it back.

He descended the steps into the dugout. Garza was on the bottom step, leaning against the rail, looking at his stats, trying to think up a way to return Shakely to reality.

"Garza, I'm going to look at some film," Brett said. "I'll keep watch."

Garza nodded but was more concerned with how Joe Schmitke was going to get on base this inning. They needed that run back.

Brett had to hustle up the tunnel to get to the clubhouse before turning left into the video room, with its bank of televisions and other equipment to help players find anything to give them an edge. But he wasn't looking for an advantage with Shakely, he needed to see the play.

"Show me the error," Brett said to Tom Philips, the video attendant.

It began with Shakely looking down to Tomlin for the sign. Tomlin flashed the deuce for the curveball. Shakely cracked a knuckle, then went into his windup. A slight grin came across Brett's face before rearing back and swinging. Shakely's curve had a little more bite than Brett had expected, which caused the dribbler.

"C'mon," Brett said.

"I know. He had to get on his old-ass horse to make that play," Philips said. "But here's where I think the scorer decided the error."

Philips paused the tape and hit frame-by-frame.

"See, Shakely regrips and throws. When he does, it comes out weird and it goes to the bullpen."

"Fuckin' A," Brett says. "That regrip is going to cost my ass .400. Fuck."

"You probably have at least one more at bat."

But Brett, you're not sure if you're going to get a hit then either? That was your best shot. Even a tipped pitch couldn't help you.

"Where's the iPads with Shakley's starts? I need to watch him some more."

What happened to see ball, hit ball? Didn't you have a thing about overthinking it? Am I getting in your head, Brett?

Philips handed Brett the tablet. Brett never watched tape during the game, but this time it was different. He needed an edge. He never hit Shakely well, but it was going to change. He was going to get this hit.

Behind Brett, Jason walked by.

"Oh, hey, Brett," Jason said. "You got screwed on that error. Fuck that."

"I know," Brett said, eyes still focused on the tablet. "What are you going to do? Some overweight asshole deciding my history."

"Right," Jason said. He fished something out of his back pocket. "Hey, I was going to put this in your locker. Rich, the head usher, got this down to me. Apparently, Fred, you know the usher near you? The one retiring? He wanted to give you this note and urged you to read it. He said it's from a fan, and it's important."

Jason held the crumpled envelope in his hand. Brett eyed it with suspicion.

"I don't read fan mail, particularly shit given to me during the game." Brett focused back on the iPad.

"Do you want me to just put it in your locker?"

"Sure, go for it."

Brett dismissed Jason with a flip of the hand. He was focused on Shakely's arm angle and why that asshole had found the fountain of youth today, of all days.

CHAPTER 21

Top of the Sixth

	1	2	3	4	5	6	7	8	9	R	H	E
SEA	0	0	0	0	1					1	3	1
OAK	0	0	0	0	0					0	0	0

[Dan Muir] More than halfway through our game in Oakland, and Brett Austen is still looking for that hit to send him into the history books.

[Tyson Porter] The crowd is still buzzing after that controversial error in the fourth inning. They still think Austen should be over .400.

[Dan Muir] During our interview earlier today, Dana Peck talked to Brett Austen about mounting pressure to get a hit throughout the day.

[Dana Peck in prepackaged interview] So, Brett, you've made your decision to play today. But what if you don't get a hit in that first at bat or the second. Now the pressure builds with each at bat. How will you approach those plate appearances?

[Brett Austen] As I have each time. Trust myself. Trust my swing. Trust what got me here. It's when I start to lose that trust in myself that things start to go bad. Fortunately, that hasn't happened for me so far this season, and I don't expect that to happen today either. If I keep my process, everything will be fine.

[Dana Peck] So what's the difference for you between .400 and .398?

[Brett Austen] Good question. For one, it's a historic number. And who doesn't want their name mentioned with Ted Williams, Ty Cobb, and Rogers Hornsby? Beyond that, it's an accomplishment. When you run a marathon, do you stop at twenty-six miles? Or do you run that extra point-two? It means something, even though it doesn't mean anything. When I hit .400, it's etched in my career, and it's uncorruptible. There's no doubting my accomplishment.

[Dana Peck] Will you be fine if you don't get .400?

[Brett Austen looks to the side, then back to Dana Peck] It won't matter. I'll get that hit today.

[Dan Muir, live] Brett Austen isn't lacking confidence.

[Tyson Porter] Brett Austen is a confident man. But that's how you gotta be if you're gonna be playing at this level.

Inside the tunnel, under the stadium, and behind home plate, "Mom" appeared on Dana's phone again. Dana sighed. She hated having this conversation. She was going to have to let her mom down and say she wasn't going to make it to Illinois tonight. She'd have to wait until after the postseason to make a visit. In the meantime, she would wire her money and support her until a better solution revealed itself.

"Hi, Mom," Dana said.

On the other end, she heard several voices before her mom cut through.

"I'm on the phone with my daughter. Yes, this is her. Can you please let me speak to her?" Kathleen's voice, which was distant, became clearer. "Dana, are you there?"

"Mom, yes. What's going on?"

"Well, I just had a little episode. They say it was a panic attack, but I thought it was a heart attack, like the one I had years ago."

"What?"

"You remember? I was watching the football game, and I felt a tightness in my chest and could hardly breathe?"

"Yes, Mom, I remember. I got the call right before I was going on air."

Dana's mind raced to five years prior when her mom was admitted with a minor heart arrythmia, serious enough for her to call an ambulance. Fifteen minutes before taking her spot behind the SportsCenter desk, Dana had received the call from the hospital letting her know Kathleen was stable and doing okay.

"That's right. I remember watching you on TV in the hospital. Even though they had me drugged up pretty good, I remember watching you with such pride. I told the nurses all about it."

Dana was sure that the doctors currently had her on something else. She needed her mom to refocus.

"So, it wasn't a heart attack?"

"No, just your typical panic attack. But they did find one of my arteries was ninety percent blocked, and they want to put in a stent tomorrow."

"Tomorrow? Can anyone be there with you?"

"I've got Sheri, but are you coming home?"

Dana closed her eyes. Whether it was the drugs or the moment, Kathleen's voice quivered with hope and need. There was nothing she could do that would help her mom. Even if she could get a flight out tonight, by the time Dana arrived, Kathleen would be in surgery or recovery. But with that question, Dana heard fear and uncertainty and Kathleen needed support, like the kind she had given Dana her entire life. This was the moment. The choice was her career or her mom. For years, the choice was clear, and she chose career every time. Now? She fudged.

"I'll try. But Mom, I gotta get going. Game's still going on."

"Oh, that's right. I'll be here."

Dana ended the call and leaned her head against the wall with a large exhale. She thought about the logistics of dropping everything and flying to the Midwest. First, she'd need to call her boss Jared Casey in New York and let him know she was unavailable for the wild card series. He wouldn't be pleased that he'd have to find someone with a day's notice to fill in. Then there was booking a red-eye flight to Illinois. If she was lucky, she might be at the hospital just in time for her mom to be rolled into surgery. The alternative was to have her mom go into surgery with her only daughter choosing a game over her.

Her phone buzzed again with Jen Small, her agent. Shit. Another crossroads coming down the pike at a hundred miles per hour.

"Jen, what's up?"

"Sorry to call, I know you're working, but Sasser just announced on air he's retiring from play-by-play. So, of course, my first call was to Stan Love, the director of TV ops. Well, I told him you were interested and would love the opportunity to try out for whatever opening they have."

Dana was shocked it had moved so fast. Just this morning, it was only a rumor, and already her agent had made contact? Dana felt lucky she had Small in her corner.

"And what did Stan say?"

"Well, here's the best part. He confirmed what we already knew." Jen's words came fast and excitedly. "While they're not officially interviewing yet—I mean, they have five months, and you're going to love your agent after this—but, just like I said, Stan is going to be in LA tomorrow, so I've set up that coffee for tomorrow morning. I know you love me, but I have a husband. So, sorry, I'm honored, and you're really good looking, but I can't leave him for you."

Dana's head spun at the stream of consciousness pouring out over the phone. She smiled at Jen's confidence and ability to make things happen. But at the same time, Dana's heart sank, and her stomach twisted.

"Umm, Dana, where are the whoops and the cheers for your badass agent?" Small said. "I didn't expect silence."

"Sorry, Jen. This is fantastic news, and I'm so thankful you've found this opportunity for me."

"So why do I think you're going to destroy me right now?"

"It's not that. It's just that I got some news about my mom. She got scammed and lost a lot of money. And she just went into the hospital with a panic attack. I think I'm going to have to call Jared and tell him I need to fly to Illinois tonight to see her and might miss the Wild Card."

"Oh crap. How bad is it? I mean, is it so bad you can't wait until after tomorrow?"

"She's getting a stent. And she lost a *lot* of money."

"Oh. That's not good. Well, I wasn't going to say this, but they're also bringing in Taylor Murray."

"Oh shit," Dana said.

Taylor Murray was an equally talented and competent play-by-play announcer, who was calling minor-league baseball in Savannah, Georgia. She was also attractive and probably didn't have a mom in crisis.

"Yeah, that's why we really need you to get talking to Stan as soon as possible."

"I don't know," Dana said. "I was just about to call Jared to tell him about the situation and beg him for a few days off, then catch a late flight. I don't know what the right thing to do is, because if I get to Kansas City, then I'll have a little more stability, and Mom can stay with me. As of right now, I'm on the road even more. I just..." Dana's voice broke. It was all just so overwhelming. What was the right thing to do right now? What was the right thing to do to set her up so she could be with her mom and support her long term?

"It's going to be okay," Jen said. She knew Dana's story. "We'll make this work. Maybe the coffee's out, but he'd have to be a real jerk not to be understanding. We have some time, but you'll want to be one of the first people he meets with, particularly with your profile, your talent, and everything you offer to the job."

"I really want this job, especially now."

"I know. We'll get it sorted, and you and your mom can set up a happy home in Kansas City, okay?"

"Thanks, Jen."

Dana said goodbye and ended the call. She continued to look at her phone. She hoped this was the right decision. If she flew home to her mom, she'd not only be stepping out of the Wild Card gig but also this important coffee. No chance to position herself to realize her dream as a play-by-play announcer.

Clarkson popped his head into the tunnel. "Hey, Palmetto wants us ready for a standup in the next inning. Is everything okay?"

Not even close, Dana thought.

* * *

As long as they all stuck to baseball, the conversation between Will, Paul, and Amanda flowed naturally. They talked shifts, positioning, sabermetrics, pitch counts, exit velocity, and all matters of the game with the analysis of ESPN commentators. It was when the conversation strayed from the game that things got cringy. There was the moment when Paul had forgot he'd interviewed Amanda for a profile on her high school softball team last spring. Or when Will had asked a bland question about Amanda's classes. In every case, awkward silence descended. Thankfully, baseball was their continued savior to steer the conversation back to safe ground.

"I guess Garza's seen enough," Paul said.

The infielders surrounded pitcher Ruben Terranova as the A's manager made the slow walk from the dugout to the mound. Terranova dropped his head. He wasn't happy.

"Wow, he's only given up the home run," Amanda said. "That's a little harsh."

"I think he saw something in that walk to Cooper," Paul said. "He was missing the frame his catcher was putting out there."

"He wasn't even close to the plate," Will said. "Looks like they're bringing in Keeler."

From a couple rows back, Will heard the whispers of "Paul Buckley." Great, more distractions and selfies. Amanda looked at Will, amused. Paul gripped his seat a little tighter.

"Hey, Paul Buckley, what's the catch of the day?"

Paul turned back, smiled, and waved. "Try the salmon."

Will turned back too. About three rows up was a group of eight, all older than him, in their early twenties. Even in his little experience of drunks, he knew these people were toasted. The guy, who looked like he was ready for the club with his oversized sunglasses, big hair, and a V-neck, was amused Paul Buckley had acknowledged him.

"Fuckin' A, it's Paul goddamn Buckley," he said.

Paul turned back around, his jaw clenched, like he knew what was coming next and knew he had made a mistake. He was normally calm and cool with whatever came his way. Amanda's look of amusement turned perplexed. Will was confused and looked back at Paul. Why was he so concerned that a few drunks had recognized him?

"I'm sorry. I screwed up. Don't turn around. Just watch the game," Paul said. "Frat bros are the worst. I was one of them. It gets worse if you acknowledge them, like I just did."

"Hey, Paul Buckley, I don't like salmon. What other fish do you recommend?"

There were laughs from the guy's buddies.

Will tried to focus on the game. Keeler continued his warmup pitches. The break in the game made each small taunt reverberate through their section.

"How about sushi? A little Tiger roll?"

More giggles from behind them.

"Maybe some tuna? A little bluefin? Chicken of the Sea."

Will glanced over at Amanda, who also stared forward. Talk about uncomfortable. Will didn't know what to do. Paul's mouth was tight, his eyes narrow, brow furrowed. He wasn't going to turn around and tell this guy to shut up? Will was surprised. No one else was speaking up either. Everyone kept staring forward.

"You gotta any sole, Paul Buckley?" The guy laughed at his own joke.

"Eric, can you just stop? You're so annoying sometimes," a girl said.

"Just asking if Paul Buckley has any sole."

"Dude, just let him be," said another guy.

"Shut up, Robbie," Eric said. "Besides, Terranova's got the hook."

Paul kept looking forward. Will thought about calling toward the retiring usher in front of them for help or turning around and asking those guys to shut up. Paul always stuck up for him-self, but here he was just ignoring the situation.

"Paul, why don't you tell that guy to shut up?" Will finally said.

"Will, it's not worth it, believe me, and it's a no-win situation for us," Paul said. "Acknowledgement is encouragement. And then the cell phones come out, it's on social media, and all of a sudden, I'm the bad guy for speaking up."

"But—"

"Just let it go." Paul's voice was clipped.

"I hear crab season is near," Eric said in the background.

CHAPTER 22

Bottom of the Sixth

	1	2	3	4	5	6	7	8	9	R	H	E
SEA	0	0	0	0	1	0				1	3	1
OAK	0	0	0	0	0					0	0	0

[Dan Muir] The story in Oakland at the beginning of the day was all about Brett Austen and whether or not he'd get to .400, but Clint Shakely has flipped the narrative. Heading into the bottom of the sixth inning, Shakely has not allowed a hit and struck out five on only forty-eight pitches.

[Tyson Porter] Yeah, Dan, we're now heading into the part of the game where Brett Austen's hit doesn't seem inevitable, and with the way Shakely's pitching, may now be considered improbable.

[Dan Muir] As we mentioned, Shakely was acquired from the Mets at the trade deadline to bolster Seattle's rotation for a postseason run, despite his, shall we say, "abrasive personality." In the end, does this help or hurt the Mariners in the playoffs?

[Tyson Porter] He has helped already. Kenny Roberts, who was supposed to start today, will now be rested and prepared to start Game 2 of the Wild Card. Shakely's work today also gives the Mariners' bullpen a break before the playoffs. About his personality, the playoffs have a way of bringing teams together and forgiving trespasses. They'll put up with him if he delivers, like he has been today.

"One more lemonade for the road, Fred?" Derek asked.

"You finally gonna comp me?"

"Nah, guy, I pay for that. That's what straight commission means."

Derek and Fred had a version of this conversation almost every game. Derek would come down to the rail, turn, hold up his wares, and start hawking lemonade, beer, pretzels. Derek would reach Fred in the aisle and ask if he wanted what he was selling. Fred always shook his head but asked for a freebie. Derek would then continue his way up the steps, selling to the fans.

Derek lingered. Who knew if this was the last time he'd see the old man?

"I still remember you asking me about being a hawker all those years ago," Derek said. He was still in his late twenties and picking up any shift available, when visions of community college, getting a degree, and living a normal life were still possible. Meanwhile, Fred was a retired fifty-year-old and bored out of his mind.

"Worked out pretty well."

"I thought you were nuts wanting to just stand around all day."

"Oh no, my fifty-year-old knees wouldn't have been able to handle these stairs very well, let alone my seventy-year-old knees."

"I feel ya. I'm starting to feel it in my forties."

"You going to scale these steps forever?"

"I'm working on things but gotta get through today, right?" Derek thought for a moment. Today was a day of transition for Fred and possibly for himself. "We're gonna miss you, Fred. It's been a pleasure to see you every day. Good luck in Sacramento."

"Thanks, Derek. I'll be around. Maybe you can comp a fan a lemonade when I come back."

"Fat chance," Derek said and began moving back up the stands. He patted Fred on the shoulder. "See ya."

Derek moved up the steps. He'd miss Fred. He had worked with ushers who were authoritarians. He also worked with ushers who were passive and let everything slide. The best ushers were like Fred—understanding, empathetic, fan-focused, and eager to help.

Meanwhile, what was Derek's endgame? If it wasn't hawking, was it the food truck? He needed this commission gig, and he was good at it. But he was starting to feel the constant wear on his body, and he needed more income. Jasmine was only going to need more as she got older, and if Pam's threats were true, then he needed to earn more cash to keep up with child support. But first, he needed this score. He needed all of his bets to work out. He needed to hit his second parlay and the Austen bet. Then he'd be golden. Then he could work the food truck, maybe leverage that into something else. He could get everything in order, and if he got enough, he could even ask for joint custody. Yes, he was going to do it. He was finally going to make something more of himself. Just have to get through today.

"Hey, lemonade guy," a voice called ahead of him.

Derek looked up to the group that included the Club Maui kid. One of the girls in the group waved a hand. "We need a couple lemonades over here."

"Sure thing." Derek strode up the steps to their area. "How many you need?"

"Any of those hard lemonades?" one of the guys who looked straight out of *Jersey Shore* said.

"Nope, I don't sell those."

"I don't need any more alcohol," said the girl next to him. "I'll have a cherry lemonade."

"Karina, it's your last chance before alcohol sales stop next inning," the guy in the tight black T-shirt said.

"I just said I don't need more alcohol. I'll have one," the girl named Karina said.

"I'll have the other," another girl down the row said.

"What about you, Robbie?" the tight T-shirt guy asked.

Robbie, the guy from Club Maui, was slouched in his seat, his hat pulled down over his eyes like he was passed out. He jolted up. He was dozing, likely the result of too much alcohol.

"Hey, guy, you may need some water more than anything," Derek said. He handed the two lemonades down the line and took the payment.

"I need a beer," Robbie said and stood up, nudged passed Derek like he was a swinging door, and moved up the steps to the beer stand in the concourse.

"You better watch out for your boy," Derek said to the guy who had summoned him over.

"Whatever. Robbie's a champ. He can handle himself."

"We'll watch after him," Karina said, smiling but concerned. "He's having a tough day."

"Karina, this guy don't care."

Karina rolled her eyes. Derek looked at her.

"Just make sure he doesn't get sick or else you'll be kicked out, okay? I'm outta here."

Derek walked up. He hated being the voice of reason.

* * *

For an inning, Lizzie, Carol, Stephen, and Leticia didn't speak. Yet, there was no silence. Beyond the machines and the television. The pounding from the wine, along with the regret, blame, sadness, and frustration bounced around Lizzie's head. She replayed her entire day—heck, her entire life—while mindlessly watching the TV.

Lizzie's internal monologue and debate hadn't changed. She thought about Stephen's inadequacies almost every day. She thought about how he took advantage of their parents, how he was coddled, the one who partied in the house with no consequences, at least not the kind she had to endure. He often got drunk at family gatherings, and they just explained it away: *Oh, he was going through a tough time* or *He was just having a good time.* Yes, Stephen was the child who could do no wrong.

Lizzie played out all of the conversations in her head. The ones she wanted to say. The ones she would say if Stephen was out of line one little bit. The ones she would say if her mom apologized for Stephen one more time. And if Leticia said something, oh, she was ready for it too. She had them all in her mind, like arrows in a quiver, ready to pull out and fire if any transgression should occur.

Another part of her knew this was ridiculous. Fueled by the wine, she knew she was spiraling into irrational thought. *This is happening because your dad is unconscious and dying, and your husband is outside and your brother is an ass*, she reminded herself. Taken one at a time, everything was manageable. Bringing them all together was just too much. Perhaps she was the one who should have taken a walk. But friggin' Eddie was outside in his stupid-ass truck. Augh. Was there any place where she could have space to think?

"I think you should call Robbie," Carol said. "You should give him an update about what's going on?"

"Why? It's not going to change anything," Stephen said. "It's not like he's going to get back in time. And he'll be too drunk to get here."

Carol gave a look to Lizzie. "But he should know, regardless," Carol said. "Call him."

Stephen looked at Carol and Lizzie. Leticia also nodded.

"Fine," he said and brought up Robbie on his phone and called. Whether it was privacy or annoyance, Stephen turned away.

"No answer," Stephen said.

"Leave a voicemail," Carol said.

"I'll text him," Stephen said. "Easier to get a hold of him that way. I'll tell him I have an update on Dad and for him to give me a call ASAP. I don't want to give him news over text."

"Good idea," Lizzie said.

"Thanks," Stephen said. "Look at that. I got an acknowledge-ment from my big sister."

"Hey, look, I just think we all should have been here, that's all."

"Well, you know that he didn't just think that this was an opportunity to get drunk with his friends, right? Robbie ex-plained that this was the way he remembered his grandpa, and this was the way he wanted to celebrate him today."

"But don't you want him here with you?"

"I want him where he wants to be and that honors Dad. If that's at the game, he's an adult, and he makes those choices."

Lizzie looked at her father, his eyes still closed and light breaths fogging up the breathing mask. She hated to admit it, but Kevin would want to have Robbie at the game. That was their thing. That's what grandfather and grandson would discuss endlessly during holiday gatherings. Lizzie admired that closeness and was a bit jealous of their bond.

"Okay," Lizzie said.

"Okay, what?" Stephen said.

Lizzie breathed deeply and bit her lip. She gritted her teeth. She hated what she had to say. "I'm sorry," she said, her pride punctured but putting up a fight. "I'm sorry I jumped all over you about Robbie. I guess this is about a little more than him."

"Yeah, I think we've got some other reasons why we're on edge," Stephen said, looking over at their father. "I'm sorry too."

"Thank goodness," Carol said. "You two."

There wasn't going to be a dramatic hug. It wasn't their style. Besides, the door opened, the teens came in, and the moment was over. They were followed by Heidi...and closely thereafter by Eddie.

"Dad was just sitting out there, and I wanted him here," Heidi said. "I know it may be uncomfortable, but he's a part of the family."

Lizzie looked at Stephen, Carol, even Leticia. For a moment, Lizzie didn't know what to say or do. But then she watched Carol cross the room and hug Eddie like she had countless times over the course of their marriage.

"Good to see you, Eddie," Carol said. "It's getting close."

Eddie's eyes were swollen, and his cheeks were red. He had been crying. Eddie walked over to Kevin's bed across from Lizzie. He looked at Kevin, then Lizzie. Lizzie offered a hand. Lizzie knew Eddie wasn't a part of her life, but at least for today, he was a part of this family.

"And Shakely freezes Berman on a curveball for the strikeout, leaving Brett Austen in the on-deck circle," Dan Muir said on the TV. "The A's have no answers for Shakely, and at the end of six, it stays 1-0 in favor of the Mariners on the Baseball Broadcast Network."

CHAPTER 23

Top of the Seventh

```
            1 2 3 4 5 6 7 8 9   R  H  E
    SEA     0 0 0 0 1 0         1  3  1
    OAK     0 0 0 0 0 0         0  0  0
```

[Tyson Porter] I'd be so pissed to be in the A's dugout right now. To allow Shakely to get this close to a goddamn no–

[Dan Muir] And… um… we're on. Welcome back to the top of the seventh. Another pitching change. Hiroto Saiki, the Japanese right-hander, comes into the game, replacing Keeler. Saiki, in his second season with the A's, after playing for the Yomiuri Giants in Japan for several years, is now called upon to keep this a 1-0 game.

[Tyson Porter] Um, yeah. Uh, when the A's brought him into the league last year, they were hoping to make him the closer and end games for them. But he just hasn't developed that killer mindset that feeds off that pressure. He's been a pretty good middle reliever, though, and the A's need him to keep it a one-run game.

"I wonder if Saiki will catch some of that sushi I've been wanting. What do you think, Buckley?"

Initial amusement from the crowd had turned, but Eric continued his intermittent heckling, now tinged with racism. Still, Paul didn't turn around again, nor did he capture the attention of the old usher to get them to stop. Will and Amanda sat staring forward, happy the game could offer a distraction from the onslaught coming from behind.

"Maybe he can catch some eel. Hey, Buckley, you never told us your favorite fish. Like, when you go to the Wharf, what do you get? I think you're lame and just get salmon or clam chowder."

Amanda looked at Paul, then Will.

"Thanks so much for letting me hang out with you guys. I should probably get back to my parents' seats," Amanda said.

"Probably a good idea," Paul said.

"You don't have to go," Will said. He didn't want the glow of her presence to dim, especially because of this guy.

"Nah, I should," she said. "I need to hang out with my family."

Now, it was Will's turn to suppress his anger—anger at Eric and his buddies for their heckling; anger at Paul for not standing up to these idiots; even anger at Amanda for bailing.

"At least, let me walk with you back to your section," Will said, trying to be chivalrous. "I mean, I want to get an ice cream sandwich anyway."

"Such a gentleman." She winked.

Paul gave a little smile.

Will let Amanda go up first. As they walked up the steps, Will glared at Eric, who didn't give him a second look while laughing and giggling with his friends. Will wanted to tell him to knock it off but wondered if that would make it tougher for Paul. Eric's girlfriend sat next to him, her fingers splayed over her face in embarrassment. The man in the A's tank top, whom Will recognized as the guy who had wanted to talk to Austen before the game, also wasn't amused. When they got to the concourse, Amanda turned and raised her eyebrow.

"So, that was awkward," she said.

"Yeah, sorry. That was pretty annoying, right?"

"I guess almost famous isn't always great," she said. She leaned in, like she was letting him in on a secret. "I can hang a little longer. I just wanted to get away from that asshole."

Will was more than happy to oblige. Any extra time with Amanda, and he was in heaven. Maybe a walk the long way around the stadium would give him the chance to make that final impression? Maybe he could even be bold and ask her to homecoming?

They turned left toward the right-field bleachers and emerged from the cold shadows of the stadium into the late-afternoon sun. While Will shielded his eyes, Amanda pulled down her cap. He copied her, then followed her to the corner lookout beyond the foul pole and leaned against the railing.

"You know, Paul's not a bad guy." Amanda turned toward Will. He was intimidated and knew if he turned too, he'd wilt. His only strength lay in watching the game in front of him

"Well, I don't know what it's like to lose a parent or have a new stepparent, but—and don't be pissed—but I think you should give Paul a break."

"Um, okay?" Will kept looking forward.

"I think he's trying. I bet he asked your mom to stay home to be alone with you. He really wants to be a part of your life, and that's a gift, you know? I mean, like, we both know people at school who don't have a dad or stepdad. Or they do, and those guys don't give a crap about them."

"Yeah, he wants to be noticed, and I'm just a prop," Will said. "That heckler was over the top, but Paul's been taking selfies all day."

"Sometimes, giving everybody a little something is easier. I mean, it's not the same, but sometimes I just want to quit TikTok and Instagram because it becomes about living up to some ideal. I'm constantly chasing likes and follows and being this, I don't know, image or something. It's so exhausting."

"What, to be popular?"

"I know. It's fucked up. I wish people just led their own lives and not mine. Like, I bring it on myself, but still, people should be able to see through it, you know?"

"I don't believe that."

She gave him a look, as if to say, *Don't bullshit me.* "Well, you found out I was coming to the game because you saw my pic on Instagram, right?"

"Yeah."

"And you thought this was a chance to get to know me better."

Will shifted his feet. Was he that transparent? He nodded.

"It's okay. I've had fun, but Paul's just trying to keep everyone happy, and I guess sometimes people get the short end of the stick."

"But it's not the same. Whenever he's around, I get lost in this whole Paul Buckley thing. Like, just now. We can't enjoy a game, because he's Paul Buckley, and some assholes think it's funny to heckle him."

"Have you talked to him about it?"

"He wouldn't get it."

"I think he would."

They stood in silence for a minute. It was too awkward, but Will was done talking about Paul.

"They gotta take out Saiki," Will said.

"I know. He's been awful against lefties this year, especially ones who pull the ball. That's Bishop, and look, he's one for two today. But Saiki has good velo on his fastball. I say he tricks him with a couple breaking balls, then comes with a high fastball to strike him out."

Will wasn't sure what he was feeling—love, admiration, understanding, surprise. He'd had these debates with Paul several times, but he was impressed.

"What? Don't get all weird," Amanda said. "And don't be the typical guy who thinks he knows more about sports."

"I was just saying that you're wrong. Bishop's a high-ball hitter. You've gotta keep throwing low to him to get a ground ball. Good try, though."

Amanda bumped her hip against Will's. He bumped it right back, a smile plastered on his face.

* * *

You've only got one more shot, Brett. That's it.

Brett was always thinking about hitting, even when he wasn't at the plate. He wasn't exactly sure on the math. Going one-for-three would get him exactly .400. One-for-four would fall short. So, his next at bat was it. Either he reached everlasting glory or an asterisk to the storied game. Shakely was effective. He had extra movement on his pitches today. Even with the tip-off, the curve was breaking exceptionally well. Lay off the high fastball and don't chase any bad pitches out of the strike zone. Find his pitch and will the ball into the outfield. He had done it all year.

Brett was on autopilot, still in the game on instinct but not focused on the play in front of him. Saiki threw a high fastball to Bishop.

Crack.

You weren't paying attention. Now you're really going to let the team down.

Brett turned to his right and sprinted toward the wall. Bishop's ball was high and moving. Because of the warm fall sun, the ball was carrying. Brett continued back toward the right-field wall. Brett hated wearing sunglasses, but he wished he had some now as he lost the ball in the sky for a moment. He picked it up again. It was catchable. He blocked out every sound but his breathing. His feet hit the clay of the warning track. By instinct, he put his arm out, ready to leap and climb the wall in order to catch the ball. Out of the corner of his eye, he saw the green vinyl. The ball was coming down fast now. He had to time his leap. He jumped off his left foot, his right foot up so his spikes could dig into the vinyl-covered wall and propel him higher into the air. His right hand felt the top of the wall and grabbed hold. His left hand raised the mitt high into the air to meet the ball. He lost sight of it again, but felt the ball slam into the webbing of his glove, carrying his left arm over the wall. He brought it back.

Brett felt the ball in his glove. He released his right hand from the top of the wall, but instead of sliding down the wall to the ground and celebrating his defensive play, his right spike stuck and tugged on the wall, disrupting his balance. He curled the glove into his body and reached out with his right hand to brace for a fall.

When Brett landed, he felt a surge of pain in his shoulder. It was almost unbearable, but relief came when the ball remained nestled in the webbing of his glove. He raised his left arm, and the sounds of the crowd flooded into his ears. It was almost enough to mask the sharp pain he felt in his right shoulder.

Almost.

* * *

From their spot in the far right-field corner, their view of the field and the catch was minimal. Instead, their eyes were focused on the video scoreboard while listening to the crowd. Will thought the perfect spot to watch that play was where they had just left.

When the crowd roared and raised their hands in triumph, Will and Amanda leapt with excitement. They gave each other high fives, then hugs. For a moment, Will lost all thought. This was his chance. Just like in the movies, he was going to take her in his arms and kiss her, and they'd walk through the halls of the school hand in hand. It felt so right.

He leaned in and closed his eyes. This was it.

Instead of her lips, he felt her arms push him away.

"Will, what the hell are you doing?"

The look of jubilation he saw on Amanda's face a moment before had vanished. Instead, Amanda's forehead crinkled, and her mouth was open in shock. Will scrambled for words.

"I got caught in the moment, I guess?" He tried to play it cool, but who was he kidding? He didn't have any coolness in him. His skinny arms and bushy hair were a constant reminder he was out of his element. "I thought the moment was right."

"Well, it wasn't," she said. She turned back to the field. People continued to dance and jump around.

Will was humiliated. The confidence he had felt just ten seconds ago had crashed and burned into a heaping pile of shit. He knew better. He wasn't in her league and never would be. He felt like he was going to cry, but letting his emotions take over would make it even worse. He leaned his sharp elbows on the rail and cupped his face in his hands.

He could hear little else but the continued white noise of cheers.

"Look, I know you like me. I've known it forever, but I just don't feel that way about you. I think you're a great guy, and I hope we can be friends."

Will nodded. He was the supreme ruler of the friend zone. He couldn't have felt worse.

"I'm serious," she said. "I know we've got different things going on at school, but I really liked hanging out with you today;

well, except for the heckling assholes and you trying to kiss me. But, really, you're a good guy. And I like you, just not in that way. But you know, maybe we can hang out sometime?"

Will forced a smile. A pity party was no consolation prize. But Paul was right. He shouldn't have set his expectations so high. Didn't he say to just enjoy her company and have a good time, and if she wanted more, she'd let him know? Well, she did. She was extremely clear she didn't want more.

"Sure, yeah, sometime."

Amanda's phone buzzed, and she pulled it out of her back pocket. She rolled her eyes and looked at Will.

"That was my mom. They want me back at the seats. I should go."

Will nodded. His consolation prize for rejection was people heckling Paul.

"But hey, let's take a picture together. I'll post it, and maybe now you'll be seen."

With the field as the backdrop, Amanda held the phone so she and Will could be in the frame. Will tried to look cool, but he knew his image needed more help than being around Amanda for a single game. She was just like Paul. It was effortless for them to direct the sun to shine on them or anyone else they saw fit. And they were doing everyone a favor by allowing them to be a part of their world.

"Oh, good shot, you look cute," she said. "Cool, I'll post it. Okay, I better get back. I'm serious. I had fun with you. I'm glad we reconnected. We should hang out at school sometime."

Will nodded, but he knew it wasn't true. They'd go back to their groups. Maybe she'd nod in the halls or steal a quick greeting in passing, but to hang out with each other was as likely as Brett Austen dedicating his .400 hit to Will.

Will watched Amanda walk away and toward her parents seats. In a crowd of forty-three thousand, he was alone.

* * *

Brett jogged back to the dugout, keeping his right arm close to him. Each step caused his shoulder to throb. At second base, Berman caught up.

"Oh yeah! What a catch."

"Yeah, but my shoulder fucking kills."

"Do you need help?"

"No." The crowd gave him an adrenaline boost that helped mask the pain. Besides, he didn't need to give Garza any excuses to take him out. Brett needed this at bat. "I can't let on I'm hurt."

Brett, you're really up Shit Creek now. Can you even swing a bat?

"You need that hit," Berman said. "Knock Shakely off that damn pedestal."

"No doubt."

Brett jogged in and gave high fives with his gloved hand, not wanting to put any extra strain on his right shoulder, which was killing him. He avoided Garza.

"I need to take a whiz," Brett said and walked into the tunnel and to the side bathroom. He would be last out of the dugout, and he wouldn't get many practice swings.

Brett stepped into the bathroom and closed the door. The pain was nearly unbearable. His shoulder wasn't dislocated, but it certainly didn't feel right. Ever since his dad had pushed him down a flight of stairs for going 0-for-5 in a high school game and dislocated his shoulder, it'd get stiff whenever he landed on it. Usually, he took a couple days off to get back to normal. He didn't have that luxury today.

Brett knew he should call the trainer and loosen it properly. But he also knew Shakely would see his weakness. Instead, Brett grabbed ahold of the industrial shelving bolted into the wall, set his feet, bent his knees, then pushed away from the wall to make it loose. He grunted in a burst of agony before the ongoing pain became tolerable. He ran the faucet and put his hands through the cold water and over his face. When he exited, hitting coach Ed Cardinale stood outside the door. Ed's eyes told Brett he knew what had happened.

CHAPTER 24

Seventh Inning Stretch

[Dan Muir] We're in the seventh-inning stretch, but the A's fans don't need "Take Me Out to the Ballgame" to prompt them to get up on their feet. Listen to this crowd.

Take me out to the ballgame

Take me out to the crowd

Buy me some peanuts and cracker jacks

I don't care if I ever get back

For it's root, root, root for the A's

If they don't win, it's a shame

For it's one, two, three strikes you're out

At the old ballgame!

[Tyson Porter] This is just what the A's needed to get this crowd back into the game. Shakely had put them to sleep silencing the A's' bats, but they've just received a shot of espresso, courtesy of Brett Austen. And guess who's up to lead off the bottom of the inning?

Derek smiled when the replay of Austen landing on his shoulder appeared in the commissary.

"That's gotta hurt," Roy said.

Derek was checking out his last tray of inventory. He was back on pace, though he wished he was out in the crowd for the stretch. Mike, the peanut guy, was behind him. His timing must be off too. He typically wanted to be out for the seventh-inning stretch since the song was essentially about him.

"Roy says you've got big money on this game," Mike said.

"A bunch of games," James said, his grumpiness never diminishing.

"Bears still down, but only by three, Cardinals in the lead, and it doesn't look good for the Dolphins," Derek said. "I've got a dime and a half on those games."

"A what?" Mike asked. Mike didn't gamble. He hated it. He didn't even like fantasy football.

"Fifteen hundred," Derek said.

"Damn, that's a lot of dough," Mike said.

"But I'm already up," Derek said.

"That only cuts your debt," James said. He was pushing the lemonades onto the counter for Derek to place in the tray. "You can't win if you're always trying play from behind."

Roy leaned in close and said, "You're in good shape, right? I mean, I vouched for you to Verne."

"You're golden, guy. After today, I'm free and clear and leaving that behind and going legit. Trust me."

Derek smiled, but the Dolphins game wasn't looking good against the 49ers. San Francisco was up by ten and on the two-yard line finishing up the third quarter. Derek watched the

Niners quarterback drop back, roll to his right, then turn to his left and throw to the running back in the backfield. From offscreen, a Miami defensive back jumped the route, stepped in front of the running back, intercepted the pass, and ran toward the opposite endzone.

"Oh shit," Roy said. "He's going to take it to the house. Wow, that changes things."

Derek wasn't as nonchalant. He raised his fists in the air. He was still in it. Debt free and dance classes were still within his grasp.

* * *

Dana looked at Clarkson when Austen's grunt reverberated through the bathroom door next to the tunnel to the A's dugout. They didn't have to communicate more than with their eyebrows. Austen's catch had come at a cost, and now her upcoming standup report had more value.

Clarkson called over the trainer, Chuck Miller. Miller's nickname was "Dr. Fit," not only because of his ripped physique, accentuated by his tight polo shirts, neck veins, and superhero chin, but he also had a PhD in Kinesiology from Stanford. He was overqualified to be the A's' trainer, but his profile as Dr. Fit had launched a website, book, videos, and a speaking tour.

When Clarkson flagged him down, Miller jogged over, his powerful jaw chomping on a wad of gum.

"What's up?" Miller asked.

"What happened to Austen?" Clarkson nodded over to Austen, who was climbing the steps to the batting circle. As

Austen swung the bat to warm up, his jaw clenched, willing his pain to remain inside him.

"What's there to tell?" Miller said. "The guy hit the wall hard, made the catch, is back up to bat, and ready to help us win this game."

"Did you treat him?" Clarkson asked. Dana was standing behind him with French nearby.

"No, he just needed some time to put that amazing play behind him and get ready for this at bat. He's very tough and wants to finish out the game."

Dana knew Miller was being evasive. He knew more but wasn't going to give any more information unless under penalty of perjury.

"So, as far as you know, nothing's wrong?" Dana asked.

"Nope," Miller said. He put up his hands and backed away. Likely, Austen had refused treatment, so technically he was right. Still, Dana watched Austen squint and his thick jaw bear down. He was in obvious pain. She looked at Shakely, who sneered, his mouth curled into a devilish grin after seeing Austen's tentative swings. He smelled blood, and he was going to take advantage.

"I heard your exchange with Miller," Palmetto said. "Give me what you got coming out of the break. Coming to you in thirty seconds."

Dana didn't have any note cards or cues from Clarkson to get her through. She'd be giving her report on the fly. Part of the job, she thought, even the play-by-play gig.

Shakely gave his final warm-up pitch, a screamer that thwopped into the catcher's mitt.

"Coming out of the break in five, four, three, two..."

CHAPTER 25

Bottom of the Seventh

	1	2	3	4	5	6	7	8	9	R	H	E
SEA	0	0	0	0	1	0	0			1	4	1
OAK	0	0	0	0	0	0				0	0	0

[Dan Muir] Well, if Brett Austen needed a shot of adrenaline for his next at bat, he certainly has it. The question is if Austen injured himself making that catch. For more, let's go to Dana Peck near the A's' dugout. Dana?

[Dana Peck] The Mariners still lead the A's one to nothing in the bottom of the seventh. The crowd is still buzzing after that spectacular play by Brett Austen, climbing the wall to save a home run; however, it looks like his cleat stuck, causing him to fall on his right shoulder. Coming into the dugout, he was in obvious pain. I've talked to the trainers, and they told me that they provided no treatment to Austen, and he's ready to take another crack at the plate to get to .400. Guys?

[Dan Muir] Thanks, Dana. Austen has no time to even think about that play as he steps into the box as the leadoff hitter.

[Tyson Porter] The crowd is certainly appreciative of that catch and willing him to get that hit in likely his final at bat of the season. He can't be feeling too good right now. He landed hard on that shoulder. But, as Dana said, the trainers didn't give him any treatment. So, either he's fine and ready to hit, or he's going to grit out this at bat.

[Dan Muir] The A's have one of the best in the business, Chuck Miller, otherwise known as Dr. Fit.

[Tyson Porter] Have you looked at Dr. Fit's website? I talked to him earlier today. You might want to sign up.

[Dan Muir] Hey there, I do my best. It sounds like you did a lot of work on the field today.

[Tyson Porter] Just my due diligence, Dan. Needed to know how Austen was going to approach the game.

[Dan Muir] Well, he's got to get a hit here.

Brett, if you don't get a hit here, kiss history goodbye. And you can't even swing the bat.

Brett shook off the demon. He had to get back to the basics. He needed more focus on Shakely's pitch selection, arm slot, and spin of the ball to get his bat on it. The question was whether his swing was still fast enough to make contact.

Brett hadn't given Garza the chance to talk to him. After leaving the restroom, he grabbed his helmet and bat and took practice swings. With each one, his shoulder burned.

"Now batting, number five, Brett Austen," the stadium announcer said.

The beats blasted over the loudspeakers again. The crowd whipped up to a frenzy.

This is it. If you don't get a hit, you're finished.

As he walked the distance from the on-deck circle to the plate, Brett tapped the barrel of the bat against his helmet. He needed to knock that demon away.

Brett looked at Shakely, who at first sneered back at him, before chuckling and shaking his head, just like he did when he'd humiliated Brett in that first game in Stockton.

As Brett slowly walked to the batter's box, his blood began to get hot. He wanted to wipe that grin off Clint Shakely's face. Maybe a line drive off Shakely's forehead would do the trick.

Getting that confidence back? How's that shoulder feeling?

Since the catch, his shoulder had felt better, but not much. His swings helped loosen it up, but it would take more than that for him to pull the bat through the zone. Brett still felt he was going to get a hit. After the catch, it was destiny. He leaned into that feeling.

Brett stepped back into the box.

"If he wasn't my guy, I might be rooting for you, hoss," Tomlin said from the crouch. "But love him or hate him..."

"Hate him."

"Well, he's got a thing going himself."

"Sorry I'm going to ruin his day."

"We'll see."

Brett dug in and got into his routine, causing a fire to shoot through his shoulder. His eyes narrowed, trying to play it off as he squinted in concentration. He just hoped neither Shakely nor Tomlin caught on. He got into his stance. Forget the pain. See ball, hit ball.

Shakely's first pitch was a fastball down the middle. A perfect pitch to pull and drive down the line. But Brett's shoulder tenderness slowed his bat enough that he fouled it to the right-field seats.

0-1

Brett scrunched his nose, hoping to mask his agony in outward frustration. Man, that was the pitch. He wasn't sure he'd get it again. Brett shook his head. Okay. He'd seen the fastball a few times. He'd seen the curve and the tip-off. He was behind that fastball, so the best play was to wait for the off-speed stuff and hope for the best. He was sure if Shakely threw two more fastballs, he would likely strikeout.

Brett stepped back in.

"He's got the good shit today, don't he?" Tomlin said.

"He does," Brett said.

"Told you it was going to be hard."

"Indeed," Brett said, and he swung the bat around again. The shoulder was still hurting, but at least he knew it, was friends with it, and could perhaps coax it into being a little forgiving for one good swing.

Shakely's next pitch was a slider that looked outside the moment it left his hand.

1-1

Cracked knuckles and a curveball in the dirt.

2-1

Shakely slammed his mitt on his thigh before calling for the ball. He grabbed it out of the air, then talked to himself. When he turned around to take the mound again, he narrowed his eyes and spit in Brett's direction as though it was intended for him.

Why was Shakely afraid of throwing the fastball again? Brett was so thankful for it but surprised. Brett stepped in. Another cracked knuckle. There was that tell again. Brett was ready and let out a little smile. If it was anywhere close, he was swinging away, getting his hit, spit back at Shakely, then tell Garza to pull him.

The ball left Shakely's hand, but the trajectory was off for a curve. Instead, it pushed toward Brett, coming down toward his thigh. Brett jumped back to get out of the way, but the ball caught the top of his knee. Brett went down in a heap. That was going to leave some burst blood vessels tomorrow. Brett looked over at Shakely, who smiled at him.

"Bastard did it on purpose," Brett said. He started toward Shakely, who strutted toward Brett. Tomlin got in front of Austen and pushed him back.

"Hey, Brett," Tomlin said. "Hey! Calm down. He didn't mean it. I called for the curve, and it got away."

"Sure as hell, that fucker did that on purpose. Hey, Shakely, Fuck you. Don't come at me again, man."

"What are you going to do? I embarrassed you in the minors. I'm going to embarrass you now in your final at bat. The way I'm pitching, I'll see you in the bottom of the ninth, buddy."

The umpire finally pushed forward and looked at Shakely.

"I'm warning both of you. I don't care what you have going in this game, I'm not afraid to toss either of you. So, watch it, or you're done."

Brett listened. Davidson had already given his warning. It was within his right to toss either or both of them right now. But there was too much at stake. They were lucky. Shakely also understood and looked away from Brett. The good news: Brett was back on base with a chance to help get the A's back in the game, and a hit-by-pitch didn't count as an at bat. The bad thing: Now his shoulder hurt, his knee hurt, and he still didn't have his hit.

"Knee?" Miller, who came out to check on him, asked. Brett was walking around gingerly now that he was focused on the pain rather than the guy who had made it happen.

"Yeah." Brett tried not to show too much. He wasn't going to be lifted. He had a limp, but the pain was more surface-related. Just a bad bruise tomorrow. No ligament or knee damage. After a couple more steps, he jogged to first base with the crowd clapping, then cheering again for him. Even Tomlin had to be impressed.

* * *

"Did you get Amanda back to her folks?" Paul asked Will. Will nodded.

"Sorry if those assholes drove her off."

Will nodded. He had learned she wasn't into him and that he would never occupy the space of Amanda Wright and Paul Buckley. He was always going to be relegated to being one of the supporting characters to their stories.

"You okay?" Paul asked. "How did everything turn out?"

"She totally rejected me," Will said, his chin nearly resting on his bony chest.

"Oh, Will," Paul said. "I'm so sor—"

"Looks like *little* Paul Buckley lost his catch," Eric said. "Not enough bait on that tiny line." Eric laughed at his own joke, though there wasn't as much laughter from the others.

"Okay, that's it," Paul said. He stood up and walked up toward Eric and his friends.

Will turned and looked back.

All eyes, and a few phones, were on Paul. He stood in the aisle, one hand on his hip, another pointing, and his eyes staring at Eric. His tan face hued purple.

"Listen, you come at me, fine. I'll take it. But you don't come after my kid. Then we got a problem, all right?"

"Hey, man, chill out. We're having fun here," Eric said.

"No. *We* aren't having fun." Paul gestured to the entire section, then pointed at Eric. "*You* are being an ass."

"Eric, just let it go, okay, baby?" his girlfriend implored.

"Yeah, dude," the friend with the bright-green A's tank top said. His eyes were halfway closed.

The old retiring usher walked up to them. "Everything okay here?"

Paul looked at Eric and raised his eyebrows. Eric's anger was just under the surface. But he nodded.

"Everything's fine," Eric said.

"All right then. Mr. Buckley, please return to your seat."

"Certainly. Apologies for that." Paul's normal affable demeanor returned. He patted the usher on the shoulder "It's your last day. I don't want to make it hard for you."

"Of course not, sir," the usher said.

When the usher left, Paul turned to Will. "Sorry about that."

Will didn't know how to feel. Paul went full papa bear, and Will had never seen Paul act that way. Will felt proud that Paul had acted like he suspected his own father would. But he also referred to Will as "his kid" and, once again, Will was unsure where he fit in his future stepdad's story.

"I guess, before today, I didn't see the bad side of you being well-known," Will said.

"It's been a part of my life since I started in this business. I'm used to it by now."

"How about Mom? Is she used to it?"

"I suppose. She understands it's part of what I do."

"But what if she didn't want that?"

"Want what, the attention? Don't worry. It's all on me, so she's not concerned."

Will wasn't worried about getting unnecessary attention. He always thought any future stepdad would have to shift his identity to be a part of Will's family. He never dreamed he'd be absorbed in the world of Paul Buckley.

CHAPTER 26

Top of the Eighth

	1	2	3	4	5	6	7	8	9	R	H	E
SEA	0	0	0	0	1	0	0			1	4	1
OAK	0	0	0	0	0	0	0			0	0	0

[Dan Muir] With Seattle clinging to a 1-0 lead, Manager Frank Garza is going to stick with Hiroto Saiki to face Wilson Tomlin. Last time up, Tomlin led off the top of the sixth with a single and was stranded on third base, one of the times the Mariners have had the opportunity to add an insurance run.

[Tyson Porter] When you're trying to chase down a final play-off spot, you've got to push those runs across. Your pitcher, Clint Shakely, is doing his job, frustrating the Oakland hitters, but the Seattle batters have to step up and get those runs in. You can't let this pitching performance go to waste.

[Dan Muir] As we watch Austen jog to his spot in right field, he has a noticeable limp.

[Tyson Porter] Austen may leave this game on a stretcher.

Fred was concerned. When he looked up, Robbie was already on the second beer he bought in the last half inning. He'd seen it too many times. For some, the seventh-inning shut off of alcohol was a beacon to pound one or two more before having to go home. And Fred had watched Robbie go from moderately buzzed before the game to at least six more beers that he could count.

I hope you're watching that boy, Fred. He looks like he's in pain.

Robbie's friends weren't helping either. Fred had already admonished Eric three times, and he was sure Paul Buckley was going to clock him on the last one. It was getting so bad, Fred thought he might have to call security to haul Eric out. But hopefully, an encouraging word might be the difference. Fred needed to talk to Robbie anyway to inform him that the note was delivered to Austen's locker. That bit of good news was bound to bring Robbie out of the funk. Fred didn't want to deal with a passed-out Robbie, which would bring more attention and security hassles.

Fred strode up the steps to Robbie and stared into Robbie's blank eyes, his eyelids half closed. One beer was almost gone already.

"Hey, Robbie, good news. Your note got delivered," Fred said. "It's on Austen's chair."

Robbie's eyes perked up. "Really? That's fuckin' awesome. Thanks." His voice was slow and slurring.

"You're welcome," Fred said.

"What's happening?" Eric was now shirtless, the black T-shirt tied around his head.

What a buffoon, Fred thought.

"Fred got Robbie's note delivered," Karina said.

"So, the usher isn't a total dick, good job."

"Shut up, Eric," Karina said. "God, you're such a jerk sometimes."

"But you like it when I jerk for you."

"Gross. You're an asshole. I'm taking a walk." Karina stood up, stepped over Robbie, and placed her hand on Fred's arm. "That was nice what you did for Robbie."

Fred smiled and said softly, "You deserve better."

Karina smiled back and walked up the steps.

Eric shook his head and watched her go.

"Oh geez, Karina. I was just joking. God, she can be such a bitch."

Fred knew better than to get involved. The handful of times he had inserted himself into couple squabbles never worked out well. The customer was always right. Calling out personal bad behavior that didn't affect other fans was a recipe for disaster. But there was something about the way this Eric treated Karina that he wanted to set the guy straight. And maybe, because this was his last game, Fred felt a strong urge to confront him.

Instead, he turned toward the field to descend the steps.

"Man, if she wasn't such a great fuck, I'd dump her ass. She's such a pain."

Fred turned. Maybe a final warning would steer Robbie to the right place.

"Can you just settle down?" An older man a few rows down and to the left had turned and was pointing at Eric.

"Shut up, boomer," Eric retorted.

Now, things were escalating and about two seconds from getting out of control.

Every year, Fred called for security about twice a season to request expulsion but hadn't made a call this year. For one, he didn't have the energy as he coped with Marjorie's illness. For another, Fred didn't like to kick out fans. The game experience depended on fans being vocal. It wasn't a library, after all. Still, the stadium was a microutilitarian society, and Fred's job was to look to the overall fan experience. Now the line had been crossed.

Fred looked up and placed his wrists together above his head. Don, the usher at the top of the section, acknowledged the signal and nodded.

"Sir, I'm sorry, but I'm going to need you to have a discussion with security," Fred said.

"What the fuck, man?" Eric said. "Just because this old fuck got upset?"

Fred stared down the other fan, expecting a reaction. He didn't need this to blow up anymore. The man got the message. Fred wasn't messing around. He returned his focus to Eric.

"Sir, you've been disrupting the other guests around you all game. It's time."

It was telling his friends didn't object and come to his defense. Two members of the A's security force walked down the steps. Jay and Quentin, in their black "A's security" uniforms, always showed tremendous restraint because they had a quiet power and intimidation that worked on most people. One look at their physiques, and most people knew it was better to submit than fight.

Fred stepped to the side, then pointed to Eric.

"Sir," Jay said.

"You gotta be shitting me," Eric said. He crossed his arms like a petulant child. "Nope. I'm not going."

"Sir, can you come with us for a bit?" Jay said.

"Dude, just go with them. Promise to be better and all that shit," Robbie said. He was struggling to keep his eyes open.

"Fuck off, Robbie," Eric said.

"Sir," Jay said. "It's a lot easier if you come up with us and we have a conversation."

"What if I want to stay here?"

"Sir, you're taking away from other guest experience. If you refuse, we'll remove you from the stadium."

"Oh, dude, they're going to kick your ass out," Robbie said, slurring.

Robbie stood up and moved into the aisle to let in Jay and Quentin. Eric stared forward and ignored the encroaching security force. It was the first time Eric had watched the game in silence.

"Sir?" Jay asked.

"Fuck you," Eric answered. "I'm not going."

"Sir, please. Let's make it easy on everyone," Jay said. His voice communicated ease and affability, but he stood ready for anything.

Eric turned, stood, and tried to rush Jay, pushing his head into Jay's sternum and wrapping his head around his waist. Jay's stance allowed him to shift his weight to the side, causing Eric to miss a clean shot and shoot past him into Quentin's arms, who held him up while Jay quickly put Eric's hands behind his back with a zip tie.

Fred shook his head and exhaled.

The fans, including Robbie and his friends, clapped.

Out of the corner of his eye, Fred saw Paul Buckley turn and grin.

"Fuck you guys," Eric said in a final attempt to assert himself.

As Eric was led up the steps, Fred turned back to the field. He wouldn't miss this part of the job. In fact, he was hit with relief. He'd never have to deal with disruptive fans again. He loved his neighborhood, but these moments always left him not wanting to come back. He didn't have to worry about that anymore, and he didn't mind. Barring something crazy, this was it.

* * *

Derek spotted a family ripe for some lemonade sales. Without much deduction, Derek knew they were together. The two kids, one son around ten, and the daughter, about twelve, were the direct composites of the adults next to them, complete with pink, puffy faces. Without a coat of sunscreen applied earlier that day, they looked like a family of lobsters. Derek lifted one of the sweatiest lemonades in his carrier.

"Lemonade. Ice-cold, refreshing lemonade. The kind that makes even the hottest days that much more pleasant."

The boy tugged on his father's arm, pleading for the drink. The father put up a weak protest. Derek quickly pulled up the steps and sold the family his final four drinks, then pushed his way down to the upper concourse. The Jumbotron showed the latest NFL scores. Bears were still in it. The Cardinals were winning, and the Dolphins were back to life. Plus, his prop bet with Carlos would give him enough for a little breathing room. When that curveball had connected with Austen's knee, he almost shot his arms up in triumph. An out would have been better, of course. That would guarantee he wouldn't get to .400 for the year. But with a bruised knee to go with an ailing shoulder, Austen was sure not to get a hit now.

Derek felt his flip phone buzz with a text from Carlos.

Carlos: *How does it feel to be rooting for someone else's pain?*

Derek didn't respond. Why poke the bear? Carlos reveled in this torture. He liked to prime the pump a bit, just to make it more than about the money and playing the numbers. He liked to make the bets personal; engaging his bettors and needling them to respond, which somehow enticed players to keep playing with him. Derek wasn't going to take the bait. He shook his head. This little extra spending money wasn't worth the antagonizing from a two-bit banger like Carlos.

Derek felt an uneasy churn in his stomach, and it wasn't due to watching this overweight family stuff their faces with enough sweets to trigger an automatic diabetic diagnosis. It was the first time he wondered if he had fucked himself over.

CHAPTER 27

Bottom of the Eighth

	1	2	3	4	5	6	7	8	9	R	H	E
SEA	0	0	0	0	1	0	0	0		1	4	1
OAK	0	0	0	0	0	0	0			0	0	0

[Dan Muir] The A's have only six more outs to pull out a win in the final game of the season, and as we look at the scoreboard, we're not just looking at Austen's place in the lineup but also the A's score line. Zero runs and zero hits. Tyson, maybe this historic day won't be for Brett Austen but instead Clint Shakely.

[Tyson Porter] As I looked into the dugout while the Mariners were at bat, Shakely was like an island—nobody sitting around him or talking to him, not wanting to jinx a potential capstone to his career.

[Dan Muir] Partner, did you ever think you'd be getting out of bed this morning and watching this kind of drama?

[Tyson Porter] Not since my playing days on the road in some strange neighborhood.

Lizzie hadn't left her father's side in six innings, and those glasses of wine and water were now sitting in her bladder. As she excused herself, she glanced over to Heidi, who sat on the couch next to her father. Eddie had screwed up their marriage, but at least he hadn't screwed up his relationship with his daughter. Lizzie thought that was more about Heidi's heart and less about Eddie's ability to charm her. Heidi was the best of them, and Lizzie couldn't have been prouder.

The halls were adorned with constant reminders of Lizzie's dad. There were photos of her parents when they were kids, transplanted from their childhood homes after their own parents had passed. There were wedding photos; Carol and Kevin, Stephen and Leticia, and a space where her and Eddie's photo had been. The nail hole had yet to be painted over.

Then there were the Sears family photos with her bad eighties perm with high bangs and enough hair spray to destroy the ozone, and there was the unfortunate old-time photo of the four of them in Nevada City. Complete with bandanas, shotguns, and bags of cash, her dad and Stephen dressed as outlaws, she and her mom portraying Vaudeville starlets. The guest bathroom showed all of her childhood trips to Dillon Beach, the Monterey Aquarium, and the Santa Cruz Boardwalk. With every picture, a flood of memories overwhelmed her tear ducts. Her daddy was in the other room, closer to death than life, his body a shell of what she saw in these photos. Soon, his face would be just a memory, preserved on photo paper. Lizzie knew it was only a matter of time. Every moment now was precious. She washed up and came back to the room.

Eddie caught her in the hallway. His face portrayed anguish, sorrow, and loneliness. He reached out for her hand to hold and some sort of comfort they could share. She didn't take it.

"Hey, I just want to say, thank you for letting me be here. I know this is a hard time for you, and—"

"Heidi wanted you here," Lizzie said. She didn't want any allusions to explicit permission. Eddie was here because it was easier. "She made it clear she needed you and wanted you to be here, and Mom was fine with it. I wasn't going to be the one to make a fuss, especially not right now. I'd rather you be here and in a corner, than outside and part of some drama. That's the last thing we need on top of everything else."

Eddie was stunned. For once, his charms and vulnerability weren't going to work on her.

"Well, still, thanks. I know how much your dad means to you—well, to all of us—and I'm thankful to be here. He meant a lot to me too."

"I know, Eddie. I know after your dad died, my dad decided to take you under his wing, but you broke his heart when you broke mine."

Eddie nodded and looked to the ceiling. "Yeah, I'm sorry. I can't undo what I've done. But you and your family are what's important, even if it's too late to salvage anything."

"Well, you're here for our daughter and my mother, so that's something."

"Thanks." Eddie moved in for a hug.

Lizzie jerked back. The thought of his touch was revolting. "Nope."

Eddie shirked away, putting his hands up. Lizzie turned and walked past him back into the living room. As she entered, Stephen was on his phone. Carol and Leticia were crowded around Stephen, hoping to hear what was being said on the other end.

"Robbie finally called back," Carol said.

"Yeah, we think it's happening soon," Stephen said into the phone. "I don't know if you can make it back here, but..."

All eyes were on Stephen trying to decipher what Robbie was saying.

"Well, sober up, and try to make it out... Right, we're all here. It looks like a good game." Stephen's look went from annoyed to concerned. "Robbie, you gave him a note? What did it say?... Why don't you want to tell me?... Well, I think you've done all you can do to get his attention." Stephen whispered to the family, "He gave an usher a note to give to Brett Austen," before shaking his head. He went back to talking to Robbie. "I'm sure players get so much fan mail. I mean, I don't know... It's not that big of a deal if he doesn't get it. I'm just saying. Don't worry about it. Just get home as soon as you can, okay?"

Stephen looked back at Leticia and rolled his eyes, shaking his head. Lizzie put out her hands wondering what Robbie was talking about.

"Be safe, sober up, and we'll talk soon."

Lizzie looked across the room, all eyes on Stephen.

"Promise me you'll get home... Robbie? Robbie?"

Stephen hung up and stared at his phone. He typed out a text message.

"What's going on?" Leticia said. "What's Robbie doing?"

"I don't know. He was drunk, that's for sure. He talked about doing something for grandpa, something about getting Brett Austen's attention."

"What does that mean?" Lizzie asked.

"You know Robbie. He's always going after the dramatic."

"Wonder where he got that from," Lizzie said, but bit her lip. This wasn't the time to take a cheap shot. "Sorry, that was inappropriate."

"Well, he joked about sneaking into the locker room. I told him that was the last thing we wanted him to do. I told him to get here as soon as he can, but unless he gets a ride, he's not going to be here for a while."

Lizzie shook her head. "Yeah, we don't want him doing anything stupid."

* * *

Dana looked at her screen and at Jared's contact. This could keep her from the dream job she's coveted her entire life, but there was nothing left to do. Looking around, she wished she was calling in a more discreet location than the lower concourse, but with Palmetto putting her on no-hitter watch, she had no choice. She brought up Jared's contact and pushed *Call*.

"Hey, Dana, looks like you've got a great game there," Jared said. "Drama, great performances. Shakely's pitching his ass off."

"Yeah, it's been crazy," Dana said. She looked at her feet. Things were going to change with the next few words. "Hey, look, something's come up with my mom."

"All right. Is she okay?"

Dana knew Jared's heart was in the right place, but putting her boss in a position to scramble would certainly test his empathy and compassion.

"Not really. She was a victim of a scam and lost most of her retirement. And she's been hospitalized after a panic attack."

"Oh wow," Jared said, though he sounded relieved, which wasn't the reaction she was hoping for. "She lost everything? That would cause me to panic, for sure."

"She's got some artery blockage, and she's getting a stent put in tomorrow. So, um, I was hoping to get to Illinois tonight and see her, which would mean I wouldn't be in LA tomorrow or for the Wild Card Series."

Dana braced herself for the reaction.

"Oh," Jared said. He paused. "Well, we've got you slated to be sideline."

"Yeah, I know, but I really need to get to her. I'm sure you can find someone. I mean, it's LA. We have studios there. It's like calling in sick."

"Dana, c'mon, it's not like other jobs where you can easily call in sick. You've got to be close to your deathbed. You remember Claire Woodson two years ago on FOX. She had food poisoning and carried around a bucket for the entire game."

"Well, that was dumb, and I seem to recall John Gray being able to take leave on a moment's notice."

"He was about to have a kid, and we knew it was coming. The Wild Card Series begins Tuesday. You know that once you give someone else a chance, sometimes your own chance goes away. Don't be a Wally Pipp."

This analogy had become a cliché. Pipp, the starting New York Yankee first baseman in 1925, had asked to be taken out of a game because of a severe headache. Lou Gehrig came in and went on to play in 2,130 straight games. Meanwhile, Pipp was gone by the end of the season. It wasn't the first time she'd heard it. The anecdote was always used as a veiled threat that she was replaceable. This was it. Dana needed to make a stand and make a sacrifice for her mother.

"Jared, I have to be there for my mom," Dana said. She found confidence in her voice. She remembered what that usher had said about priorities. "I'm sorry. She needs me to be there. I'm all she's got. If you find someone who can possibly replace me, go for it. But I know I'm an asset to this network."

"So, then why are you putting out feelers to Kansas City?"

Dana scrunched her eyes.

"Yeah, it seems like it's the worst secret. You know Jen Small has reached out about your contract. This doesn't look good."

Dana's anger bubbled up. One thing wasn't about the other. She wasn't trying to get leverage for a new contract. Her mother needed her. The one family member who gave Dana everything and received nothing in return because Dana had been so focused on this career. Through all of her adult life, Dana had put the job first. That meant missed holidays, abandoned trips to Bloomington, quick phone calls, missed weeks of catch-up conversations. Dana's priorities crystallized before her, and no form of intimidation was going to stop her now.

"Jared, my mom needs me. That's the reality. You do what you need to do for the Wild Card Series, but don't try to conflate this with my contract or Kansas City. That's repulsive if you think that my mom's pain is a negotiating tactic."

"I didn't say that."

"Well, it sure as hell came off that way. I'm truly sorry that I sprung this on you. That's not fair, but it's reality. I promise to be in touch regularly and to be ready for the division series."

There was silence on the other line. Dana looked over at the men's-bathroom exit. She was distracted by a young man in a bright-green A's tank top with bright-gold trim. Water was dripping off his face, like he had just dunked his head in the sink. His eyes were red and puffy.

Jared broke the silence. "All right, I get it. Just keep me updated, and I hope everything turns out okay for you. I'll find a replacement for Tuesday."

"Thanks, Jared." Dana continued looking at the young man, who stared back at her. His eyes showed determination, fear, sadness, and just a little bit of crazy. He was also clearly drunk, which made that combination even more dangerous. That stare made Dana uncomfortable, and she stepped back and turned away from him.

"You'd better get back to the field," Jared said. "Shakely just struck out the side and is now three outs away from a no-no. What a game."

Dana looked up at the monitor. Shakely walked off the mound staring at the ground, his thoughts focused and primed and ready to create history, instead of being a footnote to it.

She ended the call and looked back for the young man. He was gone.

Clarkson and French came up to her. Clarkson was texting on his phone. She put her earpiece back in.

"Palmetto wants us to go down to the Mariners' dugout," Clarkson said. "He wants us in the photo well so that Shakely is in the background as you deliver a standup."

"Shakely's not going to like that," Dana said. "But, well, if this is my final game, might as well go big."

"What?"

"I talked to Jared. He talked a good game, but I wouldn't be surprised if I'm phased out."

"Don't be like that," Clarkson said. "I'm sure it'll be fine."

"Let's get going, people," Palmetto yelled. "I need you at the Mariners' dugout—now."

CHAPTER 28

Top of the Ninth

	1	2	3	4	5	6	7	8	9	R	H	E
SEA	0	0	0	0	1	0	0	0		1	4	1
OAK	0	0	0	0	0	0	0	0		0	0	0

[Dan Muir] Can you feel the tension? We're heading into the last inning of this final game of the regular season, and the crowd hasn't sat down since the seventh-inning stretch. We thought this game would only be about Brett Austen and his quest for .400, with the Mariners being just a footnote, trying to win and gain homefield advantage for the Wild Card Series on Tuesday. But out of nowhere, Seattle's veteran starter Clint Shakely has found his form of 2015 and is one inning away from throwing a no-hitter. Next to the Mariners' dugout is Dana Peck. How is it down there?

[Dana Peck, with the Mariners dugout behind her] Clint Shakely is pitching the game of his life tonight, an efficient, dominant performance. He's just three outs away from tossing a season-ending no-hitter. But he'll have to get through Brett Austen one more time to do it.

[Clint Shakely, coming into the frame] Get the fuck out of here, bitch. Can't you see we're trying to win a fucking game here?

[Dana Peck, turning back] Hey, I'm just doing my job.

[Clint Shakely] You don't belong here. Leave my dugout.

[Dana Peck, back to camera] Clint Shakely, as intense as ever. Back to you.

Brett ran to his spot in left field. He kept his head down. Unlike any other time this season, he was unsure of what he was going to do the next time he was up.

Despite Brett's best efforts, the demon occupied all his thoughts.

So, finally having doubts? Took you long enough. And now you're going to let down all these fans, not to mention everyone across the country. After today, what club is going to make you their savior? I mean, it's clear you've lost your mojo. How can you sign a big contract if you know that you're a piece of shit and not worthy of it? You could retire, you know. You could "leave on top," but you'd know the reality. You peaked yesterday. You should have listened to the league, to your manager, hell, even that asshole PR guy. You'd be taking a well-deserved day off, sitting in the dugout, laughing and giggling, not caring how Shakely's doing. And later tonight, you'd be getting laid, maybe with two girls, and you'd be a legend.

But nope, you had to be a stubborn ass. You said, "no fear" is what got you here. See ball, hit ball, and all that shit. Even when you knew that pompous Clint fucking Shakely was on the mound. How's that working out for you? It didn't work for you that time in Stockton, and it hasn't worked since.

You were so excited that day. Your father was coming to see your pro debut. But you forgot how professional baseball parks sell beer when high schools don't. By the time you came onto the field, your father was gone, and I, your drunk daddy, had taken his place. Your father was the one who taught you how to hit. I was the one who threw you down the stairs and dislocated your shoulder. Your father helped you plot your career. I almost destroyed it. Your father was so proud of your success. I hated your failure. And I could see regret all over your face when I came up to you before that first at bat in Stockton. You knew what would happen when your doubts were all laid out. I was so up in your head. Your hands practically squeezed that bat into sawdust.

When you struck out so badly against Shakely, I saw how weak you were, and I was disgusted. I hadn't taught you anything at all. This wasn't the boy I'd driven to tears night after night of drinking a case of Bud and throwing pitches at you. I did that to make you tough, boy, and here you were, striking out like a little pussy. I was embarrassed of you when I left, driving your fancy bonus car to the bar, slamming a few more drinks, the hard stuff, before totaling that brand-new Mustang GT into a tree. You were relieved. I was out of your life for good.

But I'm so fucking glad you've left a small space in your head for me to come back from the dead just to say my piece, particularly when Shakely's pitching. Sometimes, I'm a little upset you don't let me in more often, but here I am on your big day and in the biggest inning of your career. Are you going to pansy out again? Probably. You can't handle the pressure, boy. Never been able, and now everybody's going to know.

* * *

Fred looked at the scoreboard. Unless this game went into extra innings, this would be his last. Fred had to lean back against the right-field railing to catch a breath. Part of him wanted to take in this moment and appreciate everything he had seen and experienced over the years. Another part of him knew that if he really took that moment, he might break down in a fit of tears.

Hold it together, dear.

"It comes down to this. Isn't this great?" Even Winnie was on her feet, and Fred was worried she was going to throw out her hips dancing to the crowd noise.

"Well, did you know this might be only my fourth no-hitter?" Fred asked.

"You're not going to see it, Fred. We know Brett's going to come through."

"I certainly hope so," Fred said.

"Don't hope. Believe," Winnie said. "We've seen enough games to know weird things go on in this place. The sun is super bright. The winds swirl. Even the seagulls play a part. It just takes our will and devotion, and all will be okay."

"I'm there with you. I want to leave on a high note."

"This isn't high enough for you?"

A crack of the bat ended their conversation. Fred looked up, instincts taking over. He watched the eyes of the fans and followed the ball toward his neighborhood. The trajectory went a little to the right, and he began to make his way toward the area he thought it might fall. As the ball began its descent, some guests ducked. Some shirked. Some spilt beers. Some came into the aisles. Finally, he watched Paul Buckley reach up in the aisle with his bare hand and miss. The ball careened off the concrete at an awkward sixty-degree angle and hit one of the fans avoiding the ball, squarely in the jaw. The fan, a woman in her midforties, went down, held up by someone who might be her husband. There was a clamor for the ball, and as soon as a fan came up with it and people returned to their seats, he saw the woman slumped in her seat, her eyes shut. Fred closed in.

"Grace?" the man asked. The woman's eyes were closed as her body rested on the seat. The man was holding her, her head resting on his shoulder. To Fred, she looked unconscious. "Grace, wake up."

Fred held up his hands and looked over at Denny. He crossed his arms in a *T*, then pointed to the woman, signaling an immediate need for paramedics. With his signals, Fred knew help was on the way, and he just needed to keep everyone calm for a few minutes.

"Grace, wake up," the man said again. Panic began to set in. He caressed her cheek, then lightly shook her chin, then a little more. "Grace. Grace."

"It's going to be okay. I've called the paramedics, and they're going to be here soon."

The man looked at Fred with mixed annoyance, anger, fear, and concern. Fred recognized this hopelessness in the man's eyes. Four months ago, Fred had sat by Majorie's bedside and watched her final smile turn into a blank stare. Fred had never felt so helpless. She was gone, even before the doctors and hospital staff had unsuccessfully tried to resuscitate her and eventually declared her dead. And now he was moving on from their life together, to a new home, a new town, and a new life that didn't include her. Sure, there was John, Carla, and the boys. But today was it. He was leaving his neighborhood and all of his baseball family.

Suddenly, Fred felt alone.

Fred, you know you're not alone. I'm always here with you. Tomorrow, you'll move on to Sacramento, and I'll be there with you. I'll be there as you play with the boys. You'll meet new people, and I'll still be with you. You're not leaving me in Oakland. I'm coming with you. Know that, Fred. Believe it so you can take care of these nice people.

Grace's eyes fluttered open. She blinked a couple times, though her eyes remained distant. Fred looked at the man, who clutched her to his chest and kissed her head. Fred caught a glimpse of the paramedics maneuvering down the stands toward them.

"Oh, Grace," the man said.

"What happened?" Grace said. She sat up and looked around.

The fans around her began to clap. Meanwhile, paramedics arrived.

"Jason, what happened?"

"You were hit by a foul ball," Jason said.

"The paramedics are here, and they're going to help you," Fred added.

On cue, two fit twenty-something young men took over Fred's space in the aisle, squatting next to Grace. One was tall with reddish-blond hair. His mustache wasn't at all attractive, but Fred figured he had it to show he was old enough to buy beer or be a paramedic. His partner was short, and his uniform strained to contain his physique. He would fit in like any of the players on the field if they all walked together in a group.

"Hello, ma'am. My name is Manny," the stocky one said. "This is Elliott. We're here to help you today. Is it okay if we check up on you?"

Grace nodded.

* * *

Will thought for sure Paul would catch the foul. It was coming right to their seats. But because of Will's stupid crush on Amanda, Paul didn't have his mitt, and whether it was because he didn't want to injure his hand or he had misjudged the ball flight, his miss had partly caused the scene in front of them.

"Thank God she's okay," Paul said, taking a big breath and blowing the air out before wiping his brow. "That's a relief."

Paul's attention had been on the woman and her husband from the moment she had slumped over. Several times, he had put a hand to his mouth and run his hands through his hair, willing her to return to consciousness. When her eyes flickered open, he released an incredible sigh.

"Maybe we should have brought our gloves," Will said. Now that it looked like she was going to be okay, he wanted to add some levity.

Paul didn't say the actual words, "I told you so," but his eyes said everything.

Will looked back to the field. Schmitke caught a pop-up, prompting Garza to come to the mound for another pitching change.

"Looks like he's bringing in Mauro," Will said.

* * *

Derek hated foul balls. They distracted fans from buying lemonade. Fans sometimes tried to run through Derek to get to the ball, and on more than a few occasions, he had been hit by one. Derek was focused on his final six lemonades. He needed every one of those commissions. He made his turn around the concrete pillar to Section 105 and toward the Mariners' dugout. He was one step away from running into that reporter again.

She stopped and put her hand out, her eyes filled with fear.

"Oh my God," she said. She looked like she might say something snarky, but instead her shock turned into a smile.

"Less lemonade this time," Derek said.

"Good thing," she said. "I don't have any spare shirts."

"Neither do I. We'd just have to get naked." Derek smiled.

She just closed her eyes, stepped back, and let him pass.

It took Derek a moment to realize it, but he watched a fan take the steps down two at a time toward the wall. He was wobbly but fast. Derek instantly recognized him. Club Maui.

"Oh shit," Derek said.

* * *

Dana heard the vendor, turned, and followed his eyes toward the field. Dana was stunned and put her hand to her mouth.

Wasn't that the guy with the scary eyes who had just come out of the bathroom?

* * *

Fred's attention was back on Manny, who was applying an icepack to Grace's head. He felt a whoosh of air pass by him. He looked to his left. Robbie bolted down the steps toward the wall where the foul netting ended. Fred turned and started after Robbie. His old legs weren't exactly cooperating with his brain, but he was moving fast for a seventy-five-year-old. He waved his arms to attract the attention of the on-field security guards, who were looking at relief pitcher Don Mauro running to the mound.

"He's rushing the field. Hey! He's rushing the field."

Robbie had picked the perfect time. Everyone was distracted by Grace and the reliever coming in from the opposite bullpen. When Robbie hopped against the wall and dropped onto the field, Kurt, one of the on-field security personnel, was facing away from the stands and watching the bullpen. Robbie was behind him. A wave of fear and dread swept over Fred. On his last day? Come on. He had dealt with fans rushing the field for the last twenty years. Mostly, they were drunks who wanted the attention. But Robbie wasn't running for attention. No, Robbie had a purpose. Oh God, what if Fred had totally misread Robbie's intentions and that note was some kind of threat or assassination creed?

Fred swung his legs around the stands to get on the field. Unfortunately, the drop was about eight feet, and he landed and felt his old legs buckle. When he looked up, Robbie was about thirty feet from Austen and closing.

* * *

This is a good game, Lizzie thought. *Just what Dad would want.*

"In this one-run game, Garza wants his closer, Gary Mauro, in the game," said Porter on the TV.

Dan Muir interrupted him. "Well, hold on. It appears that a fan has rushed the field and is running toward Austen. Oh, this is a scary scene."

"Wait, is that Robbie?" Heidi said, pointing to the TV. "Hey, I think that's Robbie."

Everyone looked up and stared at the TV, but the shot had already cut to the batter. In order to discourage fans running onto the field, the networks always cut away from the disruption.

"Rewind," Eddie said. "See if we can catch it."

Heidi found the remote on the coffee table and hit rewind for a few seconds. It was unmistakable. Even in high definition, Robbie's green tank top showed like a blur as it came from the right side of the screen and onto the field. It was definitely Robbie.

"Oh shit," Carol said.

* * *

"Oh shit!" Will pointed toward the field and watched a guy scoot over the right-field fence, land on the ground, and run toward Austen in left field.

"Oh man, this isn't good," Paul said.

* * *

Brett's eyes were focused on the bullpen and reliever Gary Mauro.

Garza's got to keep this to a one-run lead. He still believes in you. How stupid. We both know you're not going to come through. You better hope Berman gets a leadoff hit. Wouldn't it be poetic if Shakely's no-hitter is reliant on your failure? What the fuck? Who the fuck is that?

The demon left his head. In his place came the reality of a kid in a green tank top running toward him. Brett needed a moment to process the reality of a fan on the field. He had seen plenty over the years, but they always avoided him. But this one was heading straight for him. Adrenaline flooded his chest. Security was several steps behind this guy. Brett was going to have to defend himself. He widened his stance and faced the sprinting fan.

Mauro was one of the first to notice and stepped off the mound, directing everyone's attention to Brett and the approaching fan. Out of the corner of Brett's eye, Berman turned and ran toward him, but Brett knew he was on his own for the first charge. Brett stepped back to a defensive stance. Brett was confident he'd take down an approaching drunk. Years of professional baseball, going to bars after games, and facing drunks whose careers stalled in high school or Little League provided many opportunities to lay out some asshole. Austen thought to be a matador and sidestep the guy, or at least withstand a glancing blow, then push him to the ground and let security do their job. Brett's adrenaline was pumping, and the pain in his shoulder and knee was pushed back in his consciousness.

"C'mon, you drunk bastard," Brett said to himself.

The fan was now less than ten feet away. Brett was ready. He threw down his mitt and got ready for what would happen next. But whether it was the stress of the day or the tension of the moment, he felt the muscles in his lower back tighten. A wave of pain shot through his spine. But instead of lowering his shoulder, the fan slowed, then stopped in front of him.

"Mr. Austen?" The fan was out of breath. "I met you in Stockton. My grandpa's dying."

* * *

Fred's body wasn't cooperating. He stood at the base of the wall where he had landed. His legs refused to move. He was lucky that he hadn't injured himself more.

In chasing after Robbie, Fred had broken all sorts of security protocols. He was supposed to stay on the rail and look up and make sure no one else breached the wall. That was his job, to show authority and dissuade any others from crossing the line. He had done it dozens of times in his career. But during his last game, he had forgotten all of it to chase after a boy he hardly knew. Why did Robbie have such a pull on him? Maybe it was what he remembered of Robbie's grandfather Kevin. Or he recognized the hurt in Robbie's eyes, similar to his own pain this last year. Or Robbie reminded him of Donovan and Walker and the relationship he hoped to have with them after retirement. Or he didn't want anything tragic to happen during his final game.

Fred thought the worst when Robbie ran out to Austen, but when Robbie just stopped and started talking, Fred watched Austen's posture change from defensive to perplexed, then acknowledgement. What was it about Robbie's grandfather, and what was so important that he was willing to risk everything?

The conversation was brief. Kurt, an off-duty Fremont cop, and Jackson, a bouncer, surrounded Robbie and closed in. Thankfully, they didn't have to resort to tackling Robbie. He didn't resist, and security secured him.

Fred knew he should go to the gate on the fence and back to his station, but he had to know why. If this was the last time he'd ever see Robbie, he had to understand. He shuffled his pained knees to the gate along the right-field wall where security led Robbie on its way to the Coliseum jail where they'd process him.

"What were you thinking?" Fred asked. He tried to make sense of all this.

"I did it for my grandpa." Robbie's words were slurred.

"What?"

"There's hardly any time left."

* * *

Dana, Clarkson, and French waited for the fan and security at the outer gate. This wasn't for broadcast. They weren't even going to turn on the camera. They were the Baseball Broadcast Network and weren't going to glorify fans rushing the field. But Dana needed to know what had happened, if only to report it on camera. Why had the fan stopped in front of Austen and talked to him? And was Austen okay? He was seen holding his lower back and surrounded by the three members of the training staff. Austen only slightly grimaced while performing a series of stretches directed by the trainers. There was no hiding for Austen.

They waited for security to escort the fan up the private steps from the field to the concourse. When the door opened, Dana was ready.

"What's your name?" she asked.

"Ma'am, please get out of the way," the security guard—Kurt, according to the nameplate—said.

They were turning to go under the outfield stands to process the fan.

"Why did you stop to talk to Austen? What did you say?"

The fan looked down. "My grandpa."

"Was Austen hurt? He was holding his back."

"Ma'am," Kurt said.

"I just want to know why you ran out there and stopped? Not a lot of drunk fans rush the field only to stop and talk to a player. I saw you just before you went onto the field. Were you planning this all along?"

The fan turned his head. His eyes were just as puffy as when she had first seen him about five minutes ago. She expected the fan to be angry, defiant, or blissful for doing what some fans only dream of. She might even see him full of regret, realizing the stupidity of rushing the field and being banned from the stadium. But his eyes were full of sadness, and tears streamed down his face.

They got to the door that led to the security office under the outfield stands. Kurt opened the door for the other guards to lead in the fan. Kurt followed.

"Hey, Kurt," Dana said.

Kurt turned, surprised she knew his name, before remembering about the nameplate.

"What happens to the kid? Does he go to jail?"

"We'll scare him a bit, then he'll fill out some forms, acknowledging that he's banned from attending another A's game, then we'll lead him out of the stadium and let him go."

"That's it?"

"Yeah. He didn't harm anyone. But obviously, we're not going to tolerate fans rushing the field. I gotta go."

"Well, thanks. Do you know what he was talking about? His grandpa?"

Kurt shook his head. "He just kept saying, 'I did it, Grandpa. I told him.'"

* * *

Derek sold his final lemonades as security led the Club Maui guy off the field. It was like the fans needed something to calm their nervousness, and lemonade was the only way to go.

He bounded down the stairs to the concourse. Derek was overjoyed. There was no way Austen was making history now. His body was broken, his psyche was all over the place, and Shakely still had a no-hitter going.

"Things are looking good, Roy," Derek said with a broad smile.

"You're sick. Austen could have gotten hurt."

"Dude, you won't believe this, but I met that kid earlier today."

"Seriously?" James said.

"Oh yeah, he wasn't right either."

"Why didn't you say something?" Roy asked

"I can't predict the future. Besides, he just seemed sad, like most of the world."

"Jeez, dude," Roy said, dripping with disappointment.

"What? If I'd have known that he'd be going out on the field and freak Austen out, I would have bet more, okay?"

"How much do you really have on the line today?" Roy said. "Honestly."

"Well, I was down eight before the day, won six earlier. If Miami covers, I'm up four grand. Then I got another fifteen hundred on Austen not getting a hit."

"You made that bet?"

"I told you I had the feeling, but I had to go to Carlos to cover that one."

The look on Roy's face told Derek he had revealed too much.

"Carlos? Carlos Ramirez? Fuck, you're in with that guy?"

"Just this once. I had to lay down this bet, and Owen wouldn't let me because I was down too much."

"You have a problem," James said. "Seriously."

"Verne was right," Roy said. "I can't have you managing all that cash if you're working with Carlos."

"Hey, I'm good." Derek looked up at the TV. "See, Miami's driving. It's the two-minute warning. They get a field goal, and I cover, and it doesn't even matter what happens with Austen. But then I'm square, I've got Jasmine in dance tights, and I'm working your food truck. All good."

Roy turned and shook his head.

* * *

"What's going to happen to him?" Leticia said. "Is my boy going to be arrested and taken to jail?"

"He's going to need a lawyer," Stephen said.

They all turned to Eddie. "Eddie, can you?"

Eddie hadn't left his spot in the hallway. Lizzie was glad he'd kept himself out of the way. The Eddie of a year ago would have inserted himself into this situation a long time ago, but Lizzie's warnings had taken their toll. He wanted to disappear, but now he was being thrust into the drama. Eddie glanced over at Lizzie, who nodded.

"You know I'm more of a lobbyist than a lawyer. I mean, I have a license, but I haven't looked at this stuff since law school."

"But you can get him through this first part," Leticia said.

"Maybe, but first let's Google what might happen."

Now, all eyes were on Eddie, but they didn't crowd him. They looked at Lizzie to see if it was okay that he be involved. It was all so surreal. A year ago, she'd have thought the ex-husband googling legal advice about baseball-field trespassing while her dad lay in a hospice bed in the living room was spectacularly unrealistic. Yet, here they were. Lizzie just wanted this drama to be done and to refocus back on their father, still lying in his bed unconscious.

"Looks like since no harm was done, he's probably going to be ejected and banned from the stadium for life. Trespassing charges are fifty-fifty."

"Ouch. That would be pretty bad for Robbie. He loves the A's," Bart said.

A fog of uncertainty and anxiety settled into the living room. Everyone was lost in thought. They had questions without answers.

Lizzie sat down next to her father, holding his hand again. She wouldn't lose perspective. They were there for her dad, not to wait for what happened next with Robbie. She had to bite back her desires to scream out, "I told you so." Her better self won out. Rather, Lizzie felt Heidi's calm, sitting behind her, rubbing her shoulder and neck. How did she deserve this daughter of hers? Such a better outcome than what Stephen got with Robbie.

CHAPTER 29

Bottom of the Ninth

	1	2	3	4	5	6	7	8	9	R	H	E
SEA	0	0	0	0	1	0	0	0	0	1	4	1
OAK	0	0	0	0	0	0	0			0	0	0

[Dan Muir] Do you want the dramatic? Well, you've got it. Who says you need lots of scoring to make baseball exciting? We've had big catches, questionable calls, and fans rushing the field, and that's just Brett Austen. On the other side, we have Clint Shakely, who's delivering one of the best performances in his illustrious career and is three outs away from tossing his first no-hitter.

[Tyson Porter] Dan, this is the type of moment where you should be glued to your TV. This is what makes baseball great, the moments. Each at bat has led us to this last of the ninth inning. It's what we imagine as kids, and here we are.

[Dan Muir] What's it like in the dugouts right now?

[Tyson Porter] Take what we're feeling up here in the booth, and amp it up by a factor of a thousand. It's the feeling of the playoffs with the outcome hanging on every pitch. Man, thinking about being back down there is giving me goose bumps.

[Dan Muir] You're missing it down there, aren't you, partner?

[Tyson Porter] The game is a drug, and down there, it's the biggest hit you can take. Look at the coaches. Look at the players. It's the final game of the season. They pack up tomorrow, and that will be it for this team. But today, they're in it. They want it. And they want the chance to take it. I'm telling you, Dan, even coming to work up here, ain't nothing like being down there.

The demon in Brett's head, the voice of his father, took a break. That's what happens when some random fan jumps out of the stands just to talk. The adrenaline, produced by Brett's fight-or-flight instincts, continued to pump through him, even after the fan, Robbie, had been taken away. But what Robbie had said stayed with Brett and sent him sprinting toward the dugout and the clubhouse as the top of the ninth inning concluded.

The note.

Didn't Jason bring in a note a few innings ago?

"You doin' okay?" Garza said when Brett reached the dugout steps.

"Yeah, I just gotta check on something," Brett said, and he left the dugout and raced to the clubhouse. His back was still tight, and he felt a twinge of pain every time he went up a step.

"Brett, aren't you on deck?" Jason said when he entered. Jason was laying out towels for the showers.

"Yeah, but didn't you leave a note in my locker?"

"Oh, right. One of the usher supervisors gave it to me. Said it was a personal favor to that retiring old guy. It was kinda sketchy. The envelope was all bent and stuff. But it's at your locker. Are you sure you want to look at a piece of fan mail now?"

Brett ignored Jason and went to his chair where he saw the envelope. Jason was right. It looked like it had come out of somebody's pocket. It had some name scribbled out, then Brett Austen written below it. On TV, they were still in commercial. He had a few moments left. He ripped open the envelope. In it, he pulled out two Stockton Ports tickets, just like Robbie had said. He read the note and put his hand to his face. The writing said it all. The memory of his father's actions that day was emblazoned in his memory, but he had completely forgotten about the old man and the kid leading the rest of the sparse crowd in a standing ovation. And that unexpected moment of compassion had changed everything.

* * *

Stephen's phone buzzed. "It's Robbie." He answered it. "Robbie, are you okay? Oh, good. What happened?"

"Ask him about Stockton," Bart said.

Stephen waved Bart away and listened some more. From what Lizzie could determine from Stephen's side of the conversation, Robbie was fine. He was on his way out of the stadium, but he was never allowed to attend another game. Now, they were talking logistics about getting back to Sacramento. When Stephen hung up, he shook his head. His face was disgusted.

"I can't believe that kid," he said.

"What?" Carol asked.

"He needed to tell Brett Austen about this Stockton Ports game he went to with Grandpa when he was a kid."

"Why?" Lizzie said.

"But he's okay?" Leticia said.

"Yeah, he's fine. He's really drunk, though. What I gathered was Robbie and Dad saw Austen's first-ever game in Stockton, and he was sure Dad would want him to tell Austen about it. That somehow it would help Austen's hitting."

After a few moments, Bart chirped, "I don't get it."

Lizzie looked at her dad. The one person who could decipher the code was unconscious.

* * *

By the time Brett grabbed his helmet and bat, Berman was already loose. Shakely's warm-up pitches were still as sharp as in the first inning. Getting a hit was going to be tough, but now Brett focused on the pitcher in front of him, not the demon in his head. Robbie's note had shifted his whole perspective, and a sense of calm blanketed him. Now, if only the pain would go away.

Brett stood on deck next to Berman. Berman looked back, giddy with excitement, like the pressure was all off him.

"Well, this is it," Berman said. "Don't worry, I'll get the hit and get rid of that storyline."

"Oh yeah?" Brett said with his first authentic smile of the day.

"What's up with you? You got that Zen look going on again. Is that what you were doing in the clubhouse?'

"Something like that. Just needed a reminder why I play the game. Now we gotta get to Shakely. Who knew Shakely had it in him?"

"He's gotten some breaks, like that friggin' error."

"Yeah, but the goose egg is still up there. We gotta change it. Watch for when he cracks his knuckle on the mound. It's a tell he's going to throw a curve."

"No shit? You been holding out on us?"

"Not really. I wasn't sure, and I didn't want him to know until…"

"Until you got your hit. I got you. Hey, if I was in your shoes, I'd do the same thing."

Shakely glared at them. Brett smiled. Berman blew him a kiss. That really did it.

"We don't need to piss him off," Brett said.

"Being respectful hasn't worked," Berman said. "Time to get in his head a bit. Let him feel the pressure a little more. He's got a no-hitter going. He's got a one-run lead. He's got the top of the lineup. And he's got you looking to get that hit. Plus, this whole crowd wants him to fail. Let's add to it and see if he cracks."

Shakely threw his final warm-up pitch. On his follow-through he stared at Brett. Yeah, Shakely was ready for the next inning. He wasn't backing down from this challenge. The umpire waved Berman over.

"I'll try to get in his head," Berman said. "If it doesn't work, then don't copy me."

* * *

While the heckling had stopped, surrounding fans continued to approach Paul asking for autographs and selfies. Will just wanted to watch and enjoy the game without the distraction. Will checked his Instagram again. It was easier to hide his frustration looking down at a screen.

"Don't be looking at your phone. It's the bottom of the ninth. Isn't this entertaining enough for you?" Paul asked.

Will rolled his eyes. "And here we go."

"What?"

"Nothing."

"Oh, c'mon. It's something. It's always something. What is it?"

"Nothing." Will's patience was at its end.

"If I'm going to be around more, you gotta feel open to talk to me, like you used to. Just because I'm marrying your mom doesn't mean our relationship has to change much."

"But it does."

"Why?"

"Because you're not my dad."

"I know. But you know me. I've been around for most of your life."

"When you're around, I'm more invisible than ever. You're the star of this show, and I'm just Paul Buckley's stepson. I'm never going to be just Will Jenson."

"That doesn't mean anything. The people who matter care for you. I'm still the same guy who watched you grow up. I'm still the guy who's been around for you and your mom."

"You're also the guy who promised my dad that you'd look after us, not move in."

Will said it before he realized it was too far. He closed his eyes. Ever since Paul and his mom had sat him down and told him of their dating and plans to get married, Will felt this nagging resentment and betrayal on behalf of his dad. How could one of his dad's best friends move in on his wife? Out of the corner of his eye, Will watched Paul nod and twist his lips to the side. Paul was never at a loss for words, but he just stared ahead, nodding and thinking. Maybe this was how he interviewed people. Let his subjects fill the silence.

"I guess I feel like my dad's just been tossed aside. Maybe it would be different if they were divorced and there was a reason they chose to be apart. But, I mean, my dad didn't do anything wrong, but, you know, die."

* * *

Fred stood at his spot in the lower cross aisle wondering how he could have handled the situation differently. He'd mis-read Robbie from the moment Karina had waved to him before the game. Should he have not given him hope of getting a note to Austen? Should he have thrown out the whole group along with Eric? Should he not have been so preoccupied with the fan struck by the foul ball?

In twenty-two years, Fred had seen countless drunks rush the field, mostly on a dare or a bid to get noticed. But they had wanted to draw attention to themselves. They never used it as a chance to tell a player about their own problems. In another game, he might talk it over with Denny or Rich or even Marjorie to see how he could improve. But this year, he didn't care. He was done. Whether it was the emotion of his final day, making that stupid leap onto the field, the come-down following, or just being in his seventies, Fred was ready to watch this last moment, see everybody out of the stadium, then go home and get ready for the final stage of his life. Coming into today, Fred had worried that everything in this game would make him rethink retiring or that he would want to do something in Sacramento. But it had the opposite effect. He was ready and hoping this game wouldn't go into extra innings.

"Let's go A's!" Winnie's voice cut through the burgeoning white noise cranked up to maximize volume. Her fists were raised, willing her team to get this win. "C'mon, Berman. Get on base!"

* * *

Lizzie was exhausted. The emotions of the day were too much. If she had a moment to clear her mind, she may sleep for a week. Her dad was lying unconscious. All this stuff with Robbie. Her ex-husband in the room. The wine didn't help. Then there was this crazy game and the drama unfolding on TV.

This was the type of game her dad lived for. First off, there was a stellar pitching performance. Regardless of the team, Kevin admired how a pitcher dominated a game, and he would have been riveted by Shakely's performance. Then, there was Brett Austen, of course. He'd have cursed that Austen's hit was incorrectly ruled an error earlier in the game. He would have stood up and cheered for Austen's home-run-saving catch in the seventh and jumped up at Shakely's errant pitch that pegged Austen in the knee.

Now, in the bottom of the ninth, with everything at stake, Lizzie pictured her dad out of his chair, pacing back and forth, transfixed on every pitch. She clearly saw his big, brawny body rocking back and forth, arms folded, the fingers of his right hand playing with his lower lip. He would ask her mom for a beer from the fridge so he had something to do while the agonizing torture gripped every fiber of his gut and body. And then, with every pitch, take a quick inhale as the ball sailed from the tips of the pitcher's fingers to the plate, where he then released. Instead, Kevin was lying in bed in the last moments of his life, and he wouldn't be able to enjoy them.

Lizzie looked from the TV back to her father. Kevin was staring right at her. Was that a smile on his face too? She looked closer, and he winked.

"He's awake!" she said. "Dad's awake!"

* * *

Unless the game went into extra innings, the hawkers' job was done, and most were now watching the game from the edge of the stands or underneath the stadium in the commissary. Derek shifted his feet back and forth next to Roy. Even with his good cardiovascular health, Derek's heart was pounding

"And bottom of the ninth," Mike said. As usual, he had sold every one of his bags of peanuts. "Austen's last shot, though I don't know how he's gonna get a hit. Shakely's still got the stuff."

"Shakely's gotta get the first out," Roy said. "If Berman gets on, then I think Brett locks in."

"No way," Derek said. "His head's still all over the place."

"I'd say, wanna bet? But you'd probably take me up on it."

"So?"

"Man, James is right, you've got a problem," Roy said. "At first, I thought it was interesting, but this whole thing with you, Carlos, this fan, and you being happy for it, it just rubs wrong, man. It's kinda pathetic."

"Shut the fuck up, guy," Derek said.

Roy didn't have to say it. The food truck was off the table. *Fuck Roy*, Derek thought. He was amped. This was the rush he craved. The moment when it was all on the line. There was nothing left to make up for any gains or losses. He'd either be up and debt free or he'd be looking to borrow a thousand dollars the next day to pay off Carlos. Or he may have another fist to the face or another cast on his hand. God, he loved this feeling. He never felt so alive than when it was all on the line. It was better than sex. It was better than anything, and when they came through, they were the happiest moments of his life.

On one TV, he watched the Dolphins throw five-to-ten-yard passes as the Niners were in a prevent defense. They were going to come through, he was sure. On the other TV, Berman was up at the plate and antagonizing Shakely.

"C'mon, Berman, get on," Mike said.

Derek felt a cold sweat beginning to form on his forehead.

"Are you doing okay?" James whispered to Derek. "What happens if this all blows up?"

"Don't jinx it," Derek said. "I'll figure it out. I might lose some fingers. Or any chance to be with my daughter. Maybe everything. But that's not going to happen. We're on our way to freedom."

James put his hand on Derek's shoulder, patted him on the back, and left.

* * *

Still silence from Paul. Will stared ahead as they watched Berman walk to the plate.

* * *

Brett watched Berman's act from the on-deck circle. On his way to the plate, Berman flashed his perfect smile at Shakely, its intention to disrupt him. Shakely's eyes bore into Berman. Berman's grin widened.

Shakely stepped off the rubber and regained his composure. He used his right foot to pull more dirt out from the front of the rubber to gain greater leverage and a severe angle on his pitches. He concentrated his gaze at the catcher's signs. As he began his windup, Berman practically laughed at Shakely.

Shakely threw the ball, and the pitch came way inside on the left-handed batter, passing on the other side of Berman's back. Typically, a batter might get angry at the pitcher for that intentional intimidation. But Berman just laughed at Shakely. He shook his head and then looked over at Brett. Brett decided to play along and also giggled.

Shakely didn't take this well. He stepped off the mound and moved toward Berman.

"I'm going to wipe that smile off that face, asshole," Shakely said.

"Go ahead and try. I'll own you," Berman said back.

"Shut your mouth, motherfucker. I'm going to strike your ass out, followed by your boy back there, and you'll just be a footnote."

Berman laughed. "Man, your diss track needs some help."

"Fuck that. You know something about that, boy?"

"*Boy*?" Berman didn't take kindly to subversive racism and walked toward the mound. Brett took a few steps toward the mound too, just in case. Tomlin stood up and got between Berman and Shakely to settle the tensions. Berman raised his hands in surrender and gave Brett a wink. Mission accomplished. Shakely's adrenaline had to be over the edge.

Shakely returned to the mound. There was no chance he could recapture a calm rhythm now. He took two deep breaths, his shoulders reaching up toward his ears. Brett wondered if Berman's antics had worked or not. If it was nasty, then Shakely had channeled his anger into his pitching. If not, then Berman had done his job.

Shakely wound his lanky frame up, his long hair bouncing beneath the cap, lurched forward, and slung the ball toward home plate. The pitch was a slider, but it didn't break and pushed into Berman's hip. Berman took it. He would have been nearly justified to rush the mound and take on Shakely, but he just smiled at Brett, then looked at Shakely and yelled, "Tying run at first, winning run at the plate."

* * *

Will watched Berman antagonize Shakely at the plate, but his mind was on Paul. For an eternity, Paul focused forward. Then he turned toward Will, his eyes locking in.

"You need to know I love you like my own son. Yeah, I'm not your dad. I can't be half the man he was, but he was my best friend, and he informs me every step of the way. Believe me, sometimes I feel I've betrayed him by falling in love with his wife. But I just feel in my gut that he sees what we've all been through these last few years and understands what it took to bring us back. I can feel him right here in my heart, talking to me about how he'd do things, particularly with you. But I can never replace him. Ever. All I can do is the best I can to be there for you."

"Then why does it feel like he's an afterthought?" Will said. "It's like you and Mom are removing Dad from our lives. Do we have to forget he existed? I want to be reminded of him. It's all I have left."

Paul sighed.

"Your mom loved your dad very much, and even though I make her happy, I know I'm always going to be third in her heart. I'm fine with that, given who has the top two spots, and in order for her to move forward, she's gotta let him go. She just can't live within that memory of him anymore."

Will took that in. Paul wasn't trying to replace his dad. His mom had to move on with her life. And it was best that she was with someone Will trusted.

"Look, when we get back, let's all talk about how we can honor your dad and allow us all to move forward. And as for you getting lost in the persona of Paul Buckley, I'll work on that. I get that my personality sometimes sucks everything else out of the room. I'll do better, but you also let me know when you need to shine your own sun, okay?"

Will nodded. "I just don't want my mom and me to get lost in the shuffle of your life. I want my own story, and this wasn't how it was supposed to be."

"I'll give you a hint: there isn't a blueprint for life. There are just circumstances and choices. Some are good, some are bad, and some are the best you can make given the circumstances. You just hope that when the time comes, you make them. Your dad taught me that."

"I wish I would have known him more."

"I wish he got to know the man you're becoming."

Was that a tear rolling down Paul's cheek before he dabbed it? The lines in his face turned up when Berman took the final pitch and tossed his bat toward the A's dugout and trotted to first.

"Here we go!" Paul cheered.

They were done with this heart-to-heart.

"Let's go, Brett!" Will screamed.

* * *

They crowded around Kevin's bed, all staring at him and watching his eyes moving to each of them with acknowledgement. Kevin made a point of staring at each person for several seconds. Though he couldn't communicate with his voice, he was sharing his love with each of them. He locked eyes with Heidi, then Bart and Andrea. Kevin was initially puzzled when his eyes fell on Eddie, but a smile came across his face, and he gave a weak squeeze of Lizzie's hand. Then he looked at Stephen and Leticia over his shoulder, before settling on Lizzie and finally Carol. He took a long, deep breath, the biggest he'd taken in the last twenty-four hours. Then his eyes locked on the TV to watch

Brett Austen's at bat, and Lizzie felt her father's grip tighten, like he did whenever big moments took place in her life.

Lizzie was taken back to being walked to kindergarten for the first time. The hand over hers right now was the same as the one that had danced with her for the first time at the daddy-daughter dance at the community center, sometimes as a goof twirling her around, other times with tears in his eyes when some sappy country song about fathers and daughters came on. These were the hands that reassured her when she got behind the steering wheel for the first time and shook her hand when she was accepted to Cal Poly San Luis Obispo. It was also the hand that led her down the aisle to marry Eddie and the hands to which she gave her baby. These hands held her life and now she was holding his.

Lizzie didn't watch the TV. She didn't care about Brett Austen. She wanted to watch the eyes of her father.

* * *

When the opening staccato bass of "Lose Yourself" blasted over the speakers, Brett felt the swagger return. True, his knee ached, his shoulder was still sore. His back was tight. He was hurting. But the support and enthusiasm of forty-three thousand fans on their feet supported his strut.

Instead of his father's voice tormenting him, the memory of two solitary fans standing with him at his lowest point was his inspiration. Brett could let go of this expectation that this hit would exorcise his demon. This at bat wasn't about accolades, letting anyone down, or his legacy. The earlier at bats, the robbed error, the shoulder, the fan, the pitcher on the mound didn't matter. He only had to live in the moment, make the most of it, let it play out, and accept the results. How the rest of the world reacted was their problem.

Clint Shakely no longer had the face of his father, nor the attachment to the guilt of failure and the drunk-driving death of Travis Austen. Before him was just ordinary crafty lefthander Clint Shakely, who was pitching a great game, yes, but wasn't the cosmic force that had plagued him throughout his career.

Shakely was now rattled for the first time. Like a crowd standing around the shark tank at the aquarium, the fans were just waiting for Brett to feast. In a moment, the crowd became a muffled white noise. There was just him, the pitcher, his swing, and the ball. That was it. One at bat. That's all that mattered. His mind raced through all of his other at bats of the day. Every pitch. Every arm angle. The knuckle crack. See ball, hit ball. Understand weaknesses, look for his pitch, and make Shakely pay. The .400 average could go to hell. Right now, it was all about this moment. Brett dug his feet into their spots and stared at Shakely, knowing it was just the two of them in this battle.

First pitch. High and outside. Shakely wasn't going to let Brett off the hook. He didn't want to give up a hit. He didn't want to give up the no-hitter, and he didn't want to give up a run that led to a loss. No, Shakely also knew that he had to focus on Brett. Berman got on base, but Shakely was locked back in, despite Berman's efforts. It was Brett's duty alone to get the hit.

Shakely delivered another pitch. Slider on the outside corner. Strike one.

1-1

Brett thought Shakely would come inside with a fastball and sat on it; however, Shakely went with a sinker, and Brett swung and missed. But the ball got away from the catcher, and Berman raced to second to put himself in scoring position. Brett smiled. Now, a solid base hit scored Berman, tied the game, and put the team in position to win. He needed the hit.

1-2

Shakely might go with a curveball, Brett thought. *No, he'll want to put me away with a high fastball*. Brett needed to lay off the high heat, but if he caught up to one, he could get the hit and tie this game.

Shakely went into the stretch, checked Berman at second, and delivered. Indeed, a high fastball, but Brett's bat wasn't fast enough. Foul ball to the back fence.

Still 1-2.

Ach. He had guessed right and missed. That damn shoulder slowed his swing down just that much. Brett grabbed his bat in frustration. Okay, back to the drawing board. A slider, a sinker, a fastball in, and another changeup. Curveball. He wants to send a message. Shakely wants to put it on notice that this game is his no-hitter and not Brett's ascension to legend. He's going to want to make Brett look silly, like in Stockton, so he's going to spin the shit out of that ball and try to make it break from twelve to six o'clock.

Brett was ready. *Bring that weak-ass shit. Send that shit my way, and I'll tag it to fucking Sacramento.*

Sure enough, Shakely pressed his thumb toward his knuckle. Brett smiled and relaxed. He wasn't going to get away with it this time. Out of the stretch, Shakely hurled the pitch.

The ball looked like a goddamn watermelon.

See ball, hit ball.

When Brett made contact, it felt as smooth as a good lover. He swung through as though he was meant to do it. The sound was crisp and clean.

* * *

Twenty seconds left for the Dolphins. They were now in range for a thirty-five-yard field goal. Not guaranteed but pretty much a lock for today's field-goal kickers. The Dolphins and their kicker, Neil Faison, lined up on the field.

For Derek, it all came down to Faison's kick. If he made it, Derek could be free of the gambling debt, in good graces with Pam, pay for Jasmine's dance classes, and figure out something better than hawking food and paying gambling debts. He might even be able to convince Roy to put the food truck back on the table. If he lost... Well, Derek didn't care to think about the alternative.

"C'mon, Faison," Derek said to himself.

"C'mon, Brett," Roy said.

The Dolphins snapped the ball.

Shakely threw a curveball. Austen swung.

Faison kicked the ball.

The balls flew simultaneously. Both edged toward big yellow poles.

Derek stopped breathing.

One sailed inside, while one went wide left.

Derek sank to his knees, hands over his eyes.

* * *

Dana got a text from her mom.

Mom: *Wow, this is some game.*

Dana: *Yeah, it is. I booked my flight. Will be flying out late tonight. Hopefully, I'll be there by the time you go into surgery.*

Mom: *You will? But what about work?*

Dana: *Mom, it's just a game. I love you.*

Dana had spoken and typed *I love you* thousands of times to her mother. Most of the time, she meant it. But as she looked at those words in the blue bubble, she realized that until today, she hadn't lived what it meant. She understood that love meant sacrifice and acts of selflessness when someone you loved needed it the most. And while Dana had received that love from her mom her entire life, it was time to reciprocate it. Her career would now have to fit around a future where her mom was a priority, not the other way around.

As the three-dot bubble appeared on her screen, Dana watched Austen lock in. This was pretty much it. If he got a hit here, history was assured. If not, he had one hell of a season. She felt the buzz. She turned back to her phone.

Mom: *Love you too. I'm proud of you. Be careful. Safe Flight. Thank you.*

As Dana read the final words, she heard a loud crack, followed by a huge roar. But she didn't look up. She just reread the words from her mom.

* * *

Lizzie felt the faint squeeze tighten around her hand.

"Oh my God, that's going out," her brother said.

"If it's fair, it's gone!" Eddie said.

She turned her head to the game. The sound coming from the TV grew to just noise. Everyone in their house started cheering and jumping up and down. The feeling in the room was electric. Brett Austen had done it. And her father had seen it.

Lizzie turned back to her father to share the moment. She was sure his eyes would return to the life in which she had grown accustomed.

But the grip around her hand had grown slack. His eyes were closed. The monitors attached to him emitted a singular tone.

* * *

The moment the ball had left the bat, the dull, muffled sound in Brett's ears lifted its veil, and it was the most deafening sound he had ever heard. He followed the ball, but he knew where it was going. The ball's flight had purpose and intention, and its trajectory projected power. Brett raised his left arm in triumph. His right arm was still too tender to lift above his head, so he pointed toward the barbecue pavilion in left field.

When the ball finally made it into the jumping masses beyond left field, the decibels multiplied. Brett waved his arm around and glided around the bases. He screamed but didn't hear himself. He knew he had to be running or jogging but didn't feel his feet on the ground or even the motion of his legs. For this moment, there was no pain, no demon, no average, no game. He saw the ball, he hit it with precision, and it soared to where no Mariner could reach it.

When Brett rounded first, he smiled when Reese reached out a congratulatory hand. This was bigger than Brett, bigger than the game. There was only one person in this stadium who wasn't happy with the result. Brett looked back to the mound. Shakely's face still showed he was pissed, but he put his left hand to the bill of his cap and pulled on it. Brett nodded. He was still a dick, but even Shakely recognized the moment.

Like Reese, the rest of the Mariners' infield held out their hands to congratulate Brett before they made their way back to the dugout. As he rounded third, Brett looked at the fans still jumping up and down, the cell phones raised, the teammates waiting for him to arrive at home plate. He shook third-base coach Dennis Christiansen's hand, and as he moved toward home, he looked at his teammates.

He didn't pull off his helmet as some often did. He would need every bit of armor to withstand the celebratory slaps his aching body was going to receive. As he touched home, he felt the pounding of his teammates slapping him and congratulating him. It was a little painful, but he gladly endured. He wouldn't swing a bat for at least a month, maybe more. He certainly wouldn't do it in another game for five months.

Brett emerged from the scrum overwhelmed. The fans were on their feet cheering for him, like they had all season. A sudden wave of exhaustion came over him, but he knew the moment he gave into it and sat down, he'd never get up again. No, Brett had to keep pressing on. The fans deserved this hit. He knew this now. Without that drunk kid and his note, Brett wouldn't be standing here.

POSTGAME

Final

	1	2	3	4	5	6	7	8	9	R	H	E
SEA	0	0	0	0	1	0	0	0	0	1	4	1
OAK	0	0	0	0	0	0	0	0	2	2	1	0

[Dan Muir] In a game with so many twists and turns, this final at bat was one for the ages. Two players—one pitcher and one batter—facing each other for their own attempts at a moment. For one, it was a culmination of a career, reaching back one more time for magnificence. The other, the culmination of a season for the ages. In the end, it was Brett Austen who waited for his final at bat to display the dramatic, a two-run home run that pushed his average to exactly .400 and gave the A's a season to remember.

[Tyson Porter] In the end, two players put it all on the field. Clint Shakely wasn't ready to concede to Brett Austen. But Brett Austen wouldn't be denied. What a day.

[Dan Muir] Austen is taking a victory lap around the stadium, slapping hands with fans, waving, and thanking them for their support during this magical season.

Fred put his hands to his face, trying to pull his jaw off the ground. He turned to Winnie and gave her a big hug. He felt his cheeks go wet and his emotions overwhelm him. He knew this was unprofessional, but he didn't care. He had an hour left of the job to go.

"I'm going to miss you, Fred," Winnie said.

They broke their embrace, though they held each other's hands.

"The thought of not having you standing on that rail makes me sad."

"Well, as you saw today, I think the job has passed me by. Time for a younger person to take my spot."

"But you'll still come to games."

"Of course, just not eighty-one of them a season."

"Well, there's always the train that lets out just outside, and you're welcome to come take Jerry's seat any time."

Fred nodded. "I'll take you up on that offer next season. Let's keep in touch."

"We sure will. Take care, Fred. Jerry and I love you and Marjorie."

Winnie squeezed Fred's hands. They came in for another hug. He'd miss this. The crowd was too much for Winnie. She took her cane and started the trek up the steps. She knew this was the time to get out before the crush of fans left and crowded the BART bridge.

Fred still had a job to do. Security was in force on the field, but he still had to keep fans from crushing others against the rail. Fred looked around at his neighborhood for the last time. All twenty-two years of memories flooded across the seats as he panned the crowd. Fred smiled. This wasn't about today or Brett Austen. This was about moving on from one phase of life. This moment was the end of this part of his journey. Most people don't get to have such exclamation points to mark such times. Often, it's just a slow fade. This was a final gift, and his Marjorie was by his side, as she always was. As she always would be.

Oh, Fred. I'm so proud of you.

* * *

While others in the living room were focused on Austen's home run, Carol and Lizzie felt the life leave Kevin Rogers. When Lizzie looked over to her mother, Carol nodded, and they reached for each other. This was their moment, before anyone else knew. Carol said a silent prayer. Lizzie's tears expressed her pain. One by one, members of the family turned their attention away from the TV and understood. Heidi came around and held her mom from behind, followed by Eddie, giving strength to his daughter. Stephen and his family crouched around Carol as they all said goodbye to the patriarch of the family.

"Well, he went out the way he wanted to," Bart said.

"Maybe not the exact way he wanted to," Stephen said. "But he saw Austen hit."

"I just can't believe he was awake to watch the bottom of the ninth," Lizzie said.

"That's your father, making deals until the end," Eddie said.

They all laughed through their tears, the tension and anxiety releasing. They were entering grief, but they felt better knowing his pain had passed, and for one last moment, he had felt euphoric.

* * *

Derek sat on the floor against the wall of the commissary, his head in his hands. Roy and James were cleaning the kitchen. Roy couldn't even look at him, while James wanted to say something but didn't know what.

The pit in Derek's stomach was a dark, cavernous void. This wasn't the first time he had entered this emptiness. A chronic gambler always has more lows than highs. That was part of the draw. It even made the good times better. But this time, Derek felt a deeper despair. He understood there was no way out of this mess. Derek sank his face into his hands and wept.

This was more than just being in the hole to two bookies with no way to pay it back. This was more than just the inevitable violence he'd need to endure. He didn't see the bets, the bookies, the money. There was only Jasmine. He had bet his place in Jasmine's life and lost. Pam was right. Gambling was Derek's first love. He had prioritized it. He had nurtured it. He had been proud of it. Everything else didn't matter. He was here because of his choices, and he had to accept them and finally handle the consequences, the biggest being letting down Jasmine and Pam taking her away from him. He was broken.

James went to his backpack, then returned. His movements were slow but smooth, like the Marlboro man ten years after the end of his career. He offered Derek his right hand, and when Derek took it, he clasped his left hand over it. James leaned down, and Derek heard his back creak. James put his mouth to Derek's ear: "You're not alone."

James stepped back and let go of his hand. Derek felt James leave something in it. But before he could ask, James turned and walked away just as casually as he had approached.

Derek looked into his hand at a piece of paper wrapped around a business card. He unfolded the lined paper torn from a notepad. On it was a note that read, "I've been there. Next GA meeting is tomorrow at 7:00 a.m. at Fruitvale Congregational Church on International. I hope to see you there."

Inside the note was a red business card:

Stop and Think
Before You Make That Bet
Stop and Think
We can live a life without gambling.

It was followed by other advice to help pivot a gambler's mind toward more productive thoughts. On the bottom, James had put his name and phone number.

* * *

Dana had been around for the end of World Series, come-from-behind playoff wins, and other historically significant moments in baseball. She had seen crowds go crazy, but this was beyond anything she'd ever experienced. The crowds in Oakland always had the reputation of being more college football than pro baseball when the place was full. But this brought it to another level. She took a moment and looked around in awe. The crowd wasn't stopping. Fans were still on their feet, cheering, jumping, and celebrating a moment, a game, a season, and a player.

"Henderson will bring Austen over," Clarkson said. "I don't have to tell you. Lean into the history. Lean into the accomplishment. Bring out any emotion you can."

Dana nodded.

"So, are you going to LA?" Clarkson asked.

"No, I gotta be with my mom. She needs me."

"I can't believe you left Kansas City on the table," French said. "I mean..."

"It's a choice I needed to make for her."

"Yeah. Still, your dream job."

Dana shrugged. Just then, a text came through and buzzed in her hand. She glanced at it and smiled. "Well, there you go."

"What's that?" Clarkson asked.

"Just got a text from my agent. I have a Zoom with Kansas City tomorrow afternoon."

Henderson led Austen over to Dana, Clarkson, and French. Austen was still looking at the fans in the stands, his fingers running through his long, dark, stringy, sweaty hair. In all of the interviews, public appearances, and photos, Dana had never seen Brett Austen's authentic smile. But before her wasn't the grizzled veteran who had made history, this was a boy who just enjoyed the game.

[Dan Muir] As Brett Austen completes his loop around the field, let's go down to the field and Dana Peck.

[Dana Peck] Brett Austen, after one hundred and sixty-two games and hundreds of at bats, you've accomplished a feat no one has

---

seen since the great Ted Williams eighty years ago. What does that mean to you?

[Brett Austen] I just can't believe it. There are so many things that go into getting a hit, and it's getting harder and harder with the sabermetrics, the shifts, the strategy, the pitching. But, all season, it was always my strategy to focus on the pitch and make the most of it. Today was no different, and I got a good pitch to hit.

[Dana Peck] Tell me about that at bat. It was quite a battle with Clint Shakely today, even with the both of you exchanging words.

[Brett Austen] You know, Clint's a proud competitor. I haven't hit Shakely well throughout my career and today; I mean, he was almost unhittable. He had some great stuff. He threw a great curveball, but I saw it, recognized it, and put a good piece of wood on it. I was just trying to get a hit and drive home Berman. Turned out okay, I guess.

[Dana Peck] You had more than your fair share of adversity today. The hit-error controversy, landing on your shoulder following your catch, the hit-by-pitch, and the fan. How did you keep it all together?

[Brett Austen] I honestly don't know. And don't forget that Shakely pitched lights out. It was like the ghost of Teddy Ballgame wanted to make me earn it today, that's for sure.

[Dana Peck] In the top of the ninth inning, the fan rushed the field but then stopped in front of you. What did he say?

[Brett Austen] First off, fans shouldn't rush the field. It's danger-ous for all of us. But we should remember fans like Kevin Rogers, who was devoted to the A's and brought his family to the game every year. Today, he may be watching his last game, but early in my career, he gave me a lift when I needed it the most. He believed in me, not just as a player but as a person, and I almost forgot that.

But his grandson reminded me that sometimes you need a sign of support to show that you matter. When you lose yourself in your own expectations, you need a reminder to lose yourself in the moment instead. It's the fans who make the difference. You carried me through today. This is as much your achievement as mine.

[Austen waved to all the fans, and their cheers echoed through the stadium again.]

[Dana Peck] Finally, is this your last game in Oakland?

[Brett Austen] That's a question for another time. Nothing can take this away from the best fans in baseball. Thank you, Oakland.

Like the rest of the family, Lizzie stared at the television set, her mouth open.

"I can't believe it," Lizzie said. "Brett Austen just gave a shout out to dad and Robbie."

"Fuckin' A," Bart said.

"Bartholemew," Carol said.

"Sorry, Grandma," Bart said. "Just didn't expect that to happen."

"Right. I guess Robbie knew what he was doing," Stephen said. "Maybe it was all part of Dad's plan."

"Wouldn't surprise me." Carol chuckled. "He always had a plan."

Carol walked over to Kevin's lifeless body. As she stood next to him, she ran her hand across his arm. Lizzie stood next to her mom, and soon they were all gathered around him. Carol leaned down and kissed Kevin's forehead.

* * *

Will and Paul remained at their seats watching the postgame festivities. Regardless of his future relationship with Paul, and even with Amanda, he was sure that this would be a moment that would be imprinted in his brain for the rest of his life. After they listened to Dana Peck's interview with Austen on the scoreboard, they turned up the steps toward the concourse.

Along the way, two fans stepped into the aisle with them. One of them, a small man with white hair spilling out of his A's hat, kept stealing glances at Paul. Will recognized the awkward glances as finding the courage to say something. When they reached the concourse, the elderly man touched Paul's arm.

"Excuse me, Mr. Buckley," the man said, his wife in matching A's attire standing beside him. "Would you mind taking a picture with us? My son is a huge fan of yours."

Paul smiled, his instinct to take a picture with this cute couple. But a wave of concern passed his face, and he turned to look at Will. At first, Will didn't understand why Paul was hesitant. Paul turned to the old couple, his eyes showing concern and empathy.

"I'm sorry...," Paul began.

"This is the worst place to take a photo," Will chimed in. "Let's go back into the stands so you can get the field in the background. I'll even take the picture."

The couple's smile grew, and it was Paul's turn to be surprised. Will realized Paul was ready to turn down this sweet old couple for him, and while he didn't want that either, Paul was listening, and it was time to cut his stepdad a break.

[Dan Muir] Well, it's been a pleasure, Tyson. Another regular season in the books. Now, off to Los Angeles and the Wild Card Series.

[Tyson Porter] Always a great experience to work with you, Dan and Dana. I've learned so much from you all.

[Dan Muir] And with that, we leave Oakland with stories to tell our children and grandchildren. This will be one of the games that will be shared year after year; the indelible highlight of Brett Austen's home run to break up the no-hitter, win the game, and cement his memorable season. As for the other storylines; Will Brett Austen return to Oakland? Will he approach .400 again? Is this the last great Clint Shakely outing? Those will be discussed another day. For the fans, what stories will they tell? We're all fans who come from diverse backgrounds and experiences to be together to watch sport. We watch to escape, to marvel at physical achievement, to celebrate the success of our heroes. But we also watch so we can have a moment of communion with each other, a memory we can all share and reference despite what's going on outside that moment. Today, we share and celebrate a moment. For Tyson Porter, Dana Peck, and all of the staff and crew here at the Baseball Broadcast Network, thank you for watching.

ACKNOWLEDGEMENTS

Depending on how you look at it, *Lose Yourself* has been either a three-year journey or a two-decade quest.

To really start this story, we have to go back to my honeymoon in Maui in 1999. My wife and I were *Living La Vida Loca* (or at least according to Ricky Martin, playing on the radio every hour on the hour). I brought three books with me, including two baseball novels, *Shoeless Joe* (the basis for the movie Field Of Dreams) by WP Kinsella and *Man on Spikes* by Eliot Asimof. I loved the baseball novel and its use of the game to set a tone for exploring larger themes. Later that year, my wife and I went to see *For Love Of The Game* with Kevin Costner (based on the book by Michael Shaarma). As we drove home after the movie, my mind raced. I wanted to write a baseball novel. Twenty-five years later, here we are.

While *Friends in Low Places* was inspired by my own life, *Lose Yourself* presented new challenges, including research and interviews with people with knowledge and experience in the lives of my characters. My first thank you is to Dave Kaval, Curtis Wiggington, Nicole Morgan, Elisabeth Aydelotte, and the (for-now) Oakland A's organization. They were gracious and welcoming, providing me full access to personnel and the facility. The characters and the Coliseum come alive because of the time and hospitality they showed me. Regardless of the move to Las Vegas, the A's were a class act to me.

Thank you to Josh Suchon, who helped me 25 years ago as I launched my first uncompleted novel. He stuck by me and as we embarked on separate career paths, was gracious enough to answer my questions on broadcasting and the road to Major League play-by-play. Also thank you to Joseph Orosco, who provided insights into the day-of-game production elements that were so intrinsic to Dana Peck's day. I am not a gambler and needed the expertise of Kent Elola, who is a sports betting advisor, to give me the lowdown on the business of sports gambling. Thanks to Joel Harworth, a financial advisor, for his input on financial scams.

As many writers can attest, the first draft is like going to the store, while the revisions are cooking the meal. And like a top restaurant, I had talented people help me prepare this novel. First, I thank my wife, Kristen, who pushed through the early drafts and shared her honest thoughts. My good friend Dave Jans read an early draft and also accompanied me to a game for research (I swear). Selena Ingram provided excellent insights for cultural sensitivities. I also can't thank my writing group enough for their help along the way. One chapter at a time, Rich Ehisen, Erin Burrell, and AG Block, provided critical feedback that took the narrative past my own understanding of these characters. A writer can create the narrative. But a good editor makes it unrelenting. Thanks to my editor Jonathan Starke for his work in tuning the engine that drives the words.

Finally, thank you to the readers. As with *Friends in Low Places*, your support means the world to me. I hope you found this book entertaining and thoughtful. If you enjoyed, please leave a review.

Vince Wetzel

Vince is a husband, father, friend and a lifelong sports fan. He's worked as a sportswriter for three newspapers, interned for the Los Angeles Dodgers, and has spent countless hours watching athletes perform at the highest level. He's also been a youth soccer coach and draws inspiration from sports novels and movies.

Lose Yourself is Vince's follow up novel to *Friends In Low Places*, published in 2021.

How strong are the bonds of friendship?

In his debut novel, Vince Wetzel explores the evolution of lifelong friendships and how they withstand the strains of human failures.

Jim organized their annual guys trip to the lake. He picked the date. He booked the spot. He even chronicled every adventure over the past 20 years in a ragged notebook. Now, he is a box of ashes that his four closest friends will take up to the lake one last time. Over the course of their final weekend together, they will read Jim's journal through his eyes, reliving their shared laughter, life moments, revelations, and regret while coming to accept their grief.

Friends in Low Places is a funny, poignant, sometimes heart-breaking portrayal of male relationships and the support they provide as boys mature into men. **Friends in Low Places is available at most online retailers.**

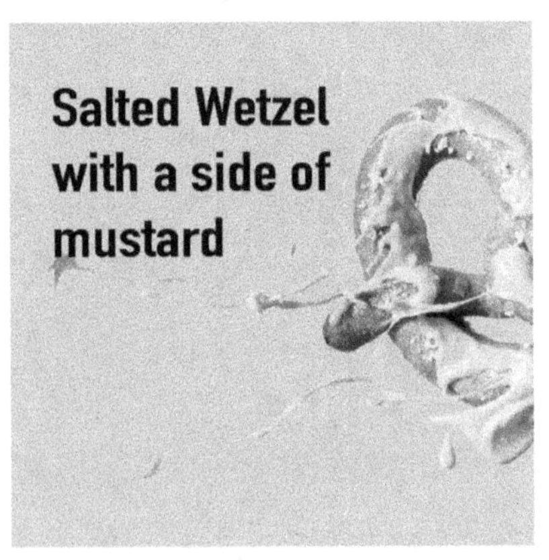

Salted Wetzel
with a side of
mustard